THE POET IN THE WORLD

Other Books by Denise Levertov

Poetry

The Double Image

Here and Now

Overland to the Islands

With Eyes at the Back of Our Heads

The Jacob's Ladder

O Taste and See

The Sorrow Dance

Relearning the Alphabet

To Stay Alive

Footprints

Translations

Guillevic/Selected Poems

Denise Levertov

The Poet in the World

A New Directions Book

ACKNOWLEDGMENTS

Grateful acknowledgment is made to the editors and publishers of books
and magazines in which some of the selections in this volume first
appeared: *American Report, The Anglican Theological Review, The
Antigonish Review, Caterpillar, Chicago Review, Field, The Michigan
Quarterly Review, Minnesota Review, The Nation, The New American
Poetry* (Donald M. Allen, ed.: New York, Grove Press), *New Directions
in Prose and Poetry 17* and *20, Stony Brook, things, Writers as Teachers,
Teachers as Writers* (Jonathan Baumbach, ed.: New York, Holt, Rinehart
and Winston). "H. D.: An Appreciation," "Some Notes on Organic Form,"
and "To Write Is to Listen" all were published originally in *Poetry*.

"Thaw" by Hayden Carruth (Copyright © 1969 by *Quarterly Review of
Literature*) is reprinted by permission of the author. The quotations from
"The Walls Do Not Fall" by H. D., from *Trilogy* (Copyright 1944 by Oxford
University Press; Copyright renewed 1972 by Norman Holmes Pearson)
and from William Carlos Williams's *Collected Earlier Poems* (Copyright
1938 by New Directions Publishing Corporation) and *Collected Later
Poems* (Copyright 1944, 1948, 1950 by William Carlos Williams) are
reprinted by permission of New Directions Publishing Corporation and
Laurence Pollinger Ltd. (London). Quotations from *The Book of
Nightmares* by Galway Kinnell (Copyright © 1971 by Galway Kinnell)
are reprinted by permission of the publisher, Houghton Mifflin Company.
"There Are No Gods" from *The Complete Poems of D. H. Lawrence,* edited
by Vivian de Sola Pinto and F. Warren Roberts (Copyright © 1964, 1971
by Angelo Ravagli and C. M. Weekley, Executors of the Estate of Frieda
Lawrence Ravagli), is reprinted by permission of The Viking Press, Inc.
and Laurence Pollinger Ltd. (London).

First published clothbound (ISBN: 0–8112–0492–8) and as New Directions
Paperbook 363 (ISBN: 0–8112–0493–6) in 1973.
Published simultaneously in Canada by McClelland & Stewart, Ltd.

Manufactured in the United States of America

New Directions Books are published by James Laughlin
by New Directions Publishing Corporation,
333 Sixth Avenue, New York 10014

Contents

For some years now, various friends, including my publisher, have been encouraging and even urging me to collect my scattered prose writings into a book. I have dawdled over this enterprise, partly because there always seemed to be so many other claims on my attention and partly because I was vague about what I would find these writings to consist of when I had gathered and reread them. With the exception of "Some Notes on Organic Form," which had been several times reprinted, I had only approximate recollections of much of the prose I had published or delivered as lectures—and I did not want to produce a potboiler.

What finally goaded me into taking stock of the material, and selecting from it what I wanted to preserve, was a growing sense that I was too often being asked—by students and by that proliferating phenomenon of the literary world, interviewers—for my views on subjects about which I thought it probable that, in some of these prose pieces, I had already expressed myself with some clarity. I began to tire of saying inadequately what I had already said better; and to hope that if I made these statements more accessible I could begin to count on the emergence of some fresher, more challenging questions, or that I could at least refer the questioners to the statements, as I could not when these were only to be found in back issues of obscure magazines. This would be for my convenience: but in regard to the more serious matter of students, I came at the same time to realize that often I had assumed they knew where I stood on this or that, simply because my own point of view was so familiar to me and I had written it, when in fact I had not discussed the point in question with them and they had never seen what I had written about it. That troubled me; for my desire has always been to share fully with my students whatever I know and believe. Here, then, was another, and less petty reason for putting this book together:

it would be a preliminary way for students to find out what ground of opinion I stood on, so that when our discussions took place they might do so from an understood point of departure. The section called "Work and Inspiration" is, in particular, what I would hope students of poetry may read; and of course, not only those I may meet, but those I never shall.

I speak of "opinion" because the prose of a poet is likely to be largely expository: to be the place where the didactic or polemical or theoretical parts of his or her life, which find scant place among the poems themselves, are expressed. But looking through my material, I found too a number of fictive or semifictive pieces—those included in the section called "Perhaps Fiction"—which are hard to place in any category but that uncertain one. Putting them alongside the essays on "Work and Inspiration" (with which, indeed, "A Note on the Work of the Imagination" might equally belong) I saw that a poet's prose, taken as a whole, is in some ways more self-revealing than poems; and for that very reason there would be a distinct dishonesty in the picture of the writer thus inevitably presented if it did not include also such prose as represented other than the meditative aspects of life: in my case, I mean, the whole area of political commitment. So much of that has entered my poems, it would be strange indeed if there were no place for it here; especially since I believe in the essential interrelatedness and mutual reinforcement of the meditative and the active. I selected as typical of the "activist" part of my life the items in the "Life at War" section, out of a mass of more or less repetitive and occasional pieces. Just as, in the preface to *To Stay Alive* (1970), I expressed the hope that the book might have some historical value (not instead of, but as well as aesthetic value, of course) in being "a record of one person's inner/outer experience in America in the '60's and the beginning of the '70's, an experience which is shared by so many and transcends the peculiar details of each life, though it can only be expressed

in and through such details," so by including these some-
what (but not entirely) topical statements here I hope to
show the reader something of that relation I feel exists,
and must exist, for the poet, between the inner and outer
life, and which may not be denied without imperiling both.

"The Untaught Teacher," being long, and the only item
on this subject I have included, forms its own section. Again,
such a collection would be incomplete without something
on teaching, an experience from which I have learned, and
continue to learn, so much, and which, though I don't think
it has influenced my poetry directly, has opened my life
in so many other ways: toward people, toward political and
social understanding.

For the last section, "Other Writers," I selected from
among reviews and introductions those which could be most
easily detached from their original context, and which
either, as in the case of "The Arena Where We Fight,"
said something I wanted to emphasize about poetry in
general, or, more frequently, paid tribute to some of the
poets who have been most influential for me, like William
Carlos Williams, or to my comrades, like Robert Duncan
or Robert Creeley. This section by no means represents
all my loves and loyalties—these are just some of the ones
I happen to have written about.

Finally, a word on the sources of quotations: I have had
in the past the bad habit of copying extracts into notebooks
without recording the exact source, only the author. Since
this book does not pretend to be a work of scholarship,
and since no one, least of all myself, has been available
to do minute research during its preparation, it has been
decided to note only those sources I happened to know.
Scholars will frown; but I have, after all, excellent prece-
dents! Look at Emerson, or at Hazlitt, for instance; hardly
a page but these great worthies cite the ancients (and others)
without a word as to chapter and verse . . . Are not exhaus-
tive notes of the pedantic kind somewhat a product of that
dubious aspect of 20th-century education which makes of

literature grist for the graduate-school mill rather than the common nourishment and conversation of a civilized people? But I am only half sincere in my excuses; for if I could have supplied all the contextual references, I would have done so. I must hope, then, that interested readers will themselves search them out; and meanwhile, I believe I can assure them that no missing note would give to any of my quotations, by providing a *contradictory* context, another meaning than that I have attributed to it within my own.

D.L.

SECTION I:
WORK AND INSPIRATION

I believe poets are instruments on which the power of poetry plays.

But they are also *makers*, craftsmen: it is given to the seer to see, but it is then his responsibility to communicate what he sees, that they who cannot see may see, since we are "members one of another."

I believe every space and comma is a living part of the poem and has its function, just as every muscle and pore of the body has its function. And the way the lines are broken is a functioning part essential to the poem's life.

I believe content determines form, and yet that content is discovered only *in* form. Like everything living, it is a mystery. The revelation of form itself can be a deep joy; yet I think form *as means* should never obtrude, whether from intention or carelessness, between the reader and the essential force of the poem, it must be so fused with that force.

I do not believe that a violent imitation of the horrors of our times is the concern of poetry. Horrors are taken for granted. Disorder is ordinary. People in general take more and more "in their stride"—hides grow thicker. I long for poems of an inner harmony in utter contrast to the chaos in which they exist. Insofar as poetry has a social function it is to awaken sleepers by other means than shock.

I think of Robert Duncan and Robert Creeley as the chief poets among my contemporaries.

This statement, written in 1959 for Donald M. Allen's anthology, *The New American Poetry,* has understandably given rise to misunderstandings, and I have long wanted an opportunity to correct it.

This testament is reprinted from *The New American Poetry, 1945–1960,* ed. Donald M. Allen (New York, Grove, 1960), pp. 411–12.

3

After reading those of my poems of recent years that concerned war and resistance, people have often asked me at what point I "changed my views about the scope of poetry," and so forth. I have not changed my views: but I failed to make clear what they were, especially in the paragraph which causes the misunderstanding, beginning, "I do not believe that a violent imitation," etc. Everyone has assumed—and I don't blame them, but admit the obscurity of the phrase—that I was talking about *content;* but in fact I was talking about form.

At the time I was reacting with irritation to the printing of some poets' work complete with spelling errors, e.g., Peter Orlovsky's "Frist Poem" [*sic*], to the eulogizing of Jack Kerouac's poems (his prose I dug, but thought—and still think—his poems inferior), and to the enthusiastic publication that was then taking place of anything any soon-to-be-forgotten imitator of Allen Ginsberg happened to scrawl on the back of the proverbial envelope. I have always strongly admired Allen's own poetry, and have often said so publicly and defended him fiercely against his detractors; but I didn't like the sloppy garbage that seemed in 1959 to be suddenly appearing everywhere in his wake. I don't know, retrospectively, that it was any worse than some of the *tidy* garbage I've seen since . . . At least it was sometimes funny and lively, which is more than one can say for the Midwestern Graduate School school. At any rate: I felt that the "vomit-it-all-out" concept of writing was totally alien to my belief in the poet as both "maker" and "instrument," and of poetry (not poets) as a *power,* something held in sacred trust.

Our period in history was (is) violent and filled with horrors, and I never for a moment considered it was "not poetic," not the concern of poetry, to speak of them—although at that time I had scarcely begun to do so myself. But the poems against which I was reacting were not dealing with these matters either: they simply seemed, in their formlessness, their lack of care for the language, for delving deep, for precision, to be imitating the chaos surrounding them. The best poems of recent years that are *about* that chaos were not—with the exception of *Howl*—yet written; I'm thinking, for instance, of Robert Duncan's *Passages*, Galway Kinnell's *Book of Nightmares*, some of the recent poems of Robert Bly, LeRoi Jones's poems of black rage; and all of these—including *Howl*—are intricately structured, not chaotic. The force is there, and the horror, but they are there precisely *because* these are works of art, not self-indulgent spittle-dribblings. They *have* the "inner harmony" that is a contrast to the confusion round about them.

The other misleading sentence in my 1959 statement says, "Insofar as poetry has a social function it is to awaken sleepers by other means than shock." Here again I was talking about form, not content. There are lines in poems of my own—for instance, a poem called "Life at War"—which have caused people to say to me, "That's a shocker!"; and they have also said that the poem served to awaken them in some degree from apathy. But this poem has at the same time a firm structure, I think. The kind of "shock" I was rejecting consisted, for instance, of the use of giant capital letters to scream like headlines in places where I felt a well-made poem would naturally carry the voice into due emphases without, except on very rare occasions, the use of outsize type faces. Also by shock I meant the *invention* of sadistic images (as if competitively!) when life already presented so many real instances of pain and cruelty. These are matters of craft and art, not restrictions on the suitability of subject matter.

Though I did not think it or write it with enough clarity, I was deploring shock as an end in itself, while espousing the act of "awakening sleepers" as a goal (not *the* goal) proper to poetry. Today I would stand by the concept, still, that poetry's social function is such an act; but rather than stopping to question whether it has a social function at all, I would take it as obvious that it has, while qualifying that

5

function as not being a primary goal. The poem has a social *effect* of some kind whether or not the poet wills that it have. It has kinetic force, it sets in motion (if it really is a poem, not something else masquerading as one) elements in the reader that otherwise would be stagnant. And that movement, that coming into play of the otherwise dormant or stagnant element, however small, cannot be without importance if one conceives of the human being as one in which all the parts are so related that none completely fulfills its function unless all are active.

Some Notes on Organic Form

For me, back of the idea of organic form is the concept that there is a form in all things (and in our experience) which the poet can discover and reveal. There are no doubt temperamental differences between poets who use prescribed forms and those who look for new ones—people who need a tight schedule to get anything done, and people who have to have a free hand—but the difference in their conception of "content" or "reality" is functionally more important. On the one hand is the idea that content, reality, experience, is essentially fluid and must be given form; on the other, this sense of seeking out inherent, though not immediately apparent, form. Gerard Manley Hopkins invented the word "inscape" to denote intrinsic form, the pattern of essential characteristics both in single objects and (what is more interesting) in objects in a state of relation to each other, and the word "instress" to denote the experiencing of the perception of inscape, the apperception of inscape. In thinking of the process of poetry as I know it, I extend the use of these words, which he seems to have used mainly in reference to sensory phenomena, to include intellectual and emotional experience as well; I would speak of the inscape of an experience (which might be composed of any and all of these elements, including the sensory) or of the inscape of a sequence or constellation of experiences.

A partial definition, then, of organic poetry might be that it is a method of apperception, i.e., of recognizing what we perceive, and is based on an intuition of an order, a form beyond forms, in which forms partake, and of which man's creative works are analogies, resemblances, natural allegories. Such poetry is exploratory.

First published in *Poetry*, Vol. 106, No. 6, September 1965; reprinted in *New Directions in Prose and Poetry 20* (New York, New Directions, 1968).

How does one go about such a poetry? I think it's like this: first there must be an experience, a sequence or constellation of perceptions of sufficient interest, felt by the poet intensely enough to demand of him their equivalence in words: he is *brought to speech.* Suppose there's the sight of the sky through a dusty window, birds and clouds and bits of paper flying through the sky, the sound of music from his radio, feelings of anger and love and amusement roused by a letter just received, the memory of some long-past thought or event associated with what's seen or heard or felt, and an idea, a concept, he has been pondering, each qualifying the other; together with what he knows about history; and what he has been dreaming—whether or not he remembers it—working in him. This is only a rough outline of a possible moment in a life. But the condition of being a poet is that periodically such a cross section, or constellation, of experiences (in which one or another element may predominate) demands, or wakes in him this demand: the poem. The beginning of the fulfillment of this demand is to contemplate, to meditate; words which connote a state in which the heat of feeling warms the intellect. To contemplate comes from *"templum,* temple, a place, a space for observation, marked out by the augur." It means, not simply to observe, to regard, but to do these things in the presence of a god. And to meditate is "to keep the mind in a state of contemplation"; its synonym is "to muse," and to muse comes from a word meaning "to stand with open mouth"—not so comical if we think of "inspiration"—to breathe in.

So—as the poet stands openmouthed in the temple of life, contemplating his experience, there come to him the first words of the poem: the words which are to be his way in to the poem, if there is to be a poem. The pressure of demand and the meditation on its elements culminate in a moment of vision, of crystallization, in which some inkling of the correspondence between those elements occurs; and it occurs as words. If he forces a beginning before this point, it won't work. These words sometimes remain the first, sometimes in the completed poem their eventual place may be elsewhere, or they may turn out to have been only forerunners, which fulfilled their function in bringing him to the words which are the actual beginning of the poem. It is faithful attention to the experience from the first moment of crystallization that allows those first or those forerunning words to rise to the surface: and with that same fidelity of attention the poet, from that moment of being let in to the possibility of the poem, must follow through, letting the experience lead him through the world of the poem, its unique inscape revealing itself as he goes.

During the writing of a poem the various elements of the poet's being are in communion with each other, and heightened. Ear and eye, intellect and passion, interrelate more subtly than at other times; and the "checking for accuracy," for precision of language, that must take place throughout the writing is not a matter of one element supervising the others but of intuitive interaction between all the elements involved.

In the same way, content and form are in a state of dynamic interaction; the understanding of whether an experience is a linear sequence or a constellation raying out from and into a central focus or axis, for instance, is discoverable only in the work, not before it .

Rhyme, chime, echo, reiteration: they not only serve to knit the elements of an experience but often are the very means, the sole means, by which the density of texture and the returning or circling of perception can be transmuted into language, apperceived. A may lead to E directly through B, C, and D: but if then there is the sharp remembrance or revisioning of A, this return must find its metric counterpart. It could do so by actual repetition of the words that spoke of A the first time (and if this return occurs more than once, one finds oneself with a refrain—not put there because one decided to write something with a refrain at the end of each stanza, but directly because of the demand of the

9

content). Or it may be that since the return to A is now conditioned by the journey through B, C, and D, its words will not be a simple repetition but a variation . . . Again, if B and D are of a complementary nature, then their thought- or feeling-rhyme may find its corresponding word-rhyme. Corresponding images are a kind of nonaural rhyme. It usually happens that within the whole, that is between the point of crystallization that marks the beginning or onset of a poem and the point at which the intensity of contemplation has ceased, there are distinct units of awareness; and it is—for me anyway—these that indicate the duration of stanzas. Sometimes these units are of such equal duration that one gets a whole poem of, say, three-line stanzas, a regularity of pattern that looks, but is not, predetermined.

When my son was eight or nine I watched him make a crayon drawing of a tournament. He was not interested in the forms as such, but was grappling with the need to speak in graphic terms, to say, "And a great crowd of people were watching the jousting knights." There was a need to show the tiers of seats, all those people sitting in them. And out of the need arose a formal design that was beautiful—composed of the rows of shoulders and heads. It is in very much the same way that there can arise, out of fidelity to instress, a design that is the form of the poem—both its total form, its length and pace and tone, and the form of its parts (e.g., the rhythmic relationships of syllables within the line, and of line to line; the sonic relationships of vowels and consonants; the recurrence of images, the play of associations, etc.). "Form follows function" (Louis Sullivan).

Frank Lloyd Wright in his autobiography wrote that the idea of organic architecture is that "the reality of the building lies in the space within it, to be lived in." And he quotes Coleridge: "Such as the life is, such is the form." (Emerson says in his essay "Poetry and Imagination," "Ask the fact for the form.") The *Oxford English Dictionary* quotes Huxley (Thomas, presumably) as stating that he used the word organic "almost as an equivalent for the word 'living.' "

In organic poetry the metric movement, the measure, is the direct expression of the movement of perception. And the sounds, acting together with the measure, are a kind of extended onomatopoeia—i.e., they imitate not the sounds of an experience (which may well be soundless, or to which sounds contribute only incidentally)—but the feeling of an experience, its emotional tone, its texture. The varying speed and gait of different strands of perception within an experience (I think of strands of seaweed moving within a wave) result in counterpointed measures.

Thinking about how organic poetry differs from free verse, I wrote that "most free verse is failed organic poetry, that is, organic poetry from which the attention of the writer had been switched off too soon, before the intrinsic form of the experience had been revealed." But Robert Duncan pointed out to me that there is a "free verse" of which this is not true, because it is written not with any desire to seek a form, indeed perhaps with the longing to avoid form (if that were possible) and to express inchoate emotion as purely as possible.[1] There is a contradiction here, however, because if, as I suppose, there is an inscape of emotion, of feeling, it is impossible to avoid presenting something of it if the rhythm or tone of the feeling is given voice in the poem. But perhaps the difference is this: that free verse isolates the "rightness" of each line or cadence—if it seems expressive, o.k., never mind the relation of it to the next; while in organic poetry the peculiar rhythms of the parts are in some degree modified, if necessary, in order to discover the rhythm of the whole.

But doesn't the character of the whole depend on, arise out of, the character of the parts? It does; but it is like

[1]See, for instance, some of the forgotten poets of the early 20's—also, some of Amy Lowell—Sandburg—John Gould Fletcher. Some Imagist poems were written in "free verse" in this sense, but by no means all.

painting from nature: suppose you absolutely imitate, on the palette, the separate colors of the various objects you are going to paint; yet when they are closely juxtaposed in the actual painting, you may have to lighten, darken, cloud, or sharpen each color in order to produce an effect equivalent to what you see in nature. Air, light, dust, shadow, and distance have to be taken into account.

Or one could put it this way: in organic poetry the form sense or "traffic sense," as Stefan Wolpe speaks of it, is ever present along with (yes, paradoxically) fidelity to the revelations of meditation. The form sense is a sort of Stanislavsky of the imagination: putting a chair two feet downstage there, thickening a knot of bystanders upstage left, getting this actor to raise his voice a little and that actress to enter more slowly; all in the interest of a total form he intuits. Or it is a sort of helicopter scout flying over the field of the poem, taking aerial photos and reporting on the state of the forest and its creatures—or over the sea to watch for the schools of herring and direct the fishing fleet toward them.

A manifestation of form sense is the sense the poet's ear has of some rhythmic norm peculiar to a particular poem, from which the individual lines depart and to which they return. I heard Henry Cowell tell that the drone in Indian music is known as the horizon note. Al Kresch, the painter, sent me a quotation from Emerson: "The health of the eye demands a horizon." This sense of the beat or pulse underlying the whole I think of as the horizon note of the poem. It interacts with the nuances or forces of feeling which determine emphasis on one word or another, and decides to a great extent what belongs to a given line. It relates the needs of that feeling-force which dominates the cadence to the needs of the surrounding parts and so to the whole.

Duncan also pointed to what is perhaps a variety of organic poetry: the poetry of linguistic impulse. It seems to me that the absorption in language itself, the awareness of the world of multiple meaning revealed in sound, word, syntax,

12

and the entering into this world in the poem, is as much an experience or constellation of perceptions as the instress of nonverbal sensuous and psychic events. What might make the poet of linguistic impetus appear to be on another tack entirely is that the demands of his realization may seem in opposition to truth as we think of it; that is, in terms of sensual logic. But the apparent distortion of experience in such a poem for the sake of verbal effects is actually a precise adherence to truth, since the experience itself was a verbal one.

Form is never more than a *revelation* of content.

"The law—one perception must immediately and directly lead to a further perception."[2] I've always taken this to mean, "no loading of the rifts with ore," because there are to be no rifts. Yet alongside this truth is another truth (that I've learned from Duncan more than from anyone else)—that there must be a place in the poem for rifts too —(never to be stuffed with imported ore). Great gaps between perception and perception which must be leapt across if they are to be crossed at all.

The X-factor, the magic, is when we come to those rifts and make those leaps. A religious devotion to the truth, to the splendor of the authentic, involves the writer in a process rewarding in itself; but when that devotion brings us to undreamed abysses and we find ourselves sailing slowly over them and landing on the other side—that's ecstasy.

[2]Edward Dahlberg, as quoted by Charles Olson in "Projective Verse," *Selected Writings* (New York, New Directions, 1966).

●There is a poetry that seeks to invent, for thought and feeling and perception not experienced as form, forms to contain them; or to make appropriate re-use of existing metric forms.

●There is a poetry that seeks, for thought and feeling and perception not experienced as form, a mode of expression that shall maintain that formlessness, avoiding the development of rhythmic and sonic patterns.

●There is a poetry that in thought and in feeling and in perception seeks the forms peculiar to these experiences.

The first of these three categories implies a view of synthesis of form and content as an event brought about by the exercise of the artist's power and cunning, but not as an organic event, i.e., this view does not look on forms as inherent in content. The third category, on the contrary, does imply a belief in the immanence of form in content and seeks to discover and reveal it.

The second category tends toward *flow*, not toward form at all. It frequently has *pattern,* as a flow of water has the pattern of its ripples, but pattern is not permitted to become fixed in eye or ear, for if it did it would be in danger of becoming form. This category is what we may truly call "free verse."

The poetry of the third category, which I have elsewhere called a poetry of "organic form," is also commonly referred to as free verse. In what way is the term correctly or incorrectly applied to it? It shares with the second category a freedom *from* pre-existing, re-usable metric molds. But thereafter it *uses* its freedom to different ends: where true "free verse" is concerned with the maintenance of its freedom from all bonds, "organic" poetry, having freed itself

1966—written at the request of a student.

14

from imposed forms, voluntarily places itself under other laws: the variable, unpredictable, but nonetheless strict laws of *inscape*, discovered by *instress*. Its discipline begins with the development of the utmost *attentiveness*—and in this relates more closely to the first, or "traditional," category (where the keenest possible sense of the aptness of a form to a content is essential) than to "free verse" which, in its abhorrence of confinement, rushes or meanders along without fine attention to details or to implications.

1) *Music and inscape:* What I call *listening to experience* (a function of Negative Capability) can lead to discovery of the music inherent in the material. Few poems we feel are musical became so, grew so, out of direct intention of the poet toward musicality.

Pasternak wrote:

> The music of the word ... does not consist of the euphony of vowels and consonants taken by themselves, but of the relationship between the meaning and the sound of the words.[1]

Wordsworth announced (who was it reported this? Hazlitt? De Quincey?—I first wrote it down so long ago, twenty-five years ago . . .[2]) that: "Language is not the *dress* but the *incarnation* of thoughts." This is true of the highest poetry (as of the best prose, the best speech)—that is, the most impassioned, charged, and precise; but there is much poetry, much highly praised poetry of today, that is discursive, conversational, explanatory, far from song. In the writing of such poetry there occurs a hiatus between thoughts and feelings and the words in which they are written down.

These notes first appeared in *Chicago Review*, Vol. 18, Nos. 3 & 4, 1966.

[1]From *I Remember* (New York, Pantheon, 1959), p. 62

[2]Wordsworth in fact said (in his third "Essay upon Epitaphs"), "If words be not an incarnation of the thought, but only a clothing for it, then surely will they prove an ill gift." De Quincey (in his essay on "Style") paraphrases him, speaking of "the dress of thoughts," and comments in agreement that "you can no more deal thus [i.e., separating thoughts from language] with poetic thought that you can [with] soul and body." Carlyle likewise (in *Sartor Resartus)* says, "Language is called the Garment of Thought: however, it should rather be, Language is the Flesh-Garment, the Body of Thought." My thanks to Ian Reid of Adelaide, Australia, for rediscovering these references for me. 1972.

The poet feels, thinks, and then searches for words in which to *clothe* his thoughts. That is language used as dress. Such poems are not deeply musical, though they may sometimes be superficially so. The *music* of poetry comes into being when thought and feeling remain unexpressed until they become Word, become Flesh (i.e., there is no *prior paraphrase*). The awareness of them remains vague—perhaps oppressive—perhaps *very* oppressive—yet the poet does not give way to "irritable searchings" but waits in passionate passivity (Negative Capability) until thought and feeling *crystallize* (remember to reread Stendhal on this word) in words which haven't been hunted down but which *arrive,* magically summoned by the need for them. *Cante Hondo.* It arises from depths, takes us with it into them.

Carlyle:

> A musical thought is one spoken by a mind that has penetrated into the inmost heart of the thing; detected the inmost mystery of it, namely, the melody that lies hidden in it; the inward harmony of coherence which is its soul, whereby it exists, and has a right to be, here in this world. All inmost things, we may say, are melodious, naturally utter themselves in song.[3]

This "melody that lies hidden in it" is no other than what Hopkins, using a visual (but extensible) term, calls inscape.

"I heard flowers that sounded, and saw notes that shone," said St. Martin. The *being* of things has inscape, has melody, which the poet picks up as one voice picks up, and sings, a song from another, and transmits, transposes it, into tones others can hear. And *in his doing so* lies the inscape and melody of the poet's *own* being.

2) *Note to a student:* What you have been showing me is a kind of poetry, the poetry of ideas (as one says *the*

---

[3]Carlyle, "Prospectus," *Sartor Resartus.*

17

poetry of motion). It does not discover itself in words, in sound patterns, in actual verbal textures; it is language-oriented only insofar as it is probably not possible to dissociate *philosophic thought* from language (though the physicist and mathematician and musician—and painter and architect—do think nonverbally). If you had an adequate language of symbols (in the sense of signs, referentials) at your disposal, you could define/express, these ideas in *it* as well (better) than you can in poems. *The material of a poem must need to be a poem,* not something else (an essay, a story, or whatever). "The material of a poem is only *that* material after the poem has been made," says T. S. Eliot (in his introduction to the *Selected Writings* of Paul Valéry)—which is perhaps the same thing inside out, as it were. Your notes are often more interesting than the poem itself, which then seems mere *shorthand notes for the notes.* You must get the material *into the poem,* making explanatory notes unnecessary. Or else, you must recognize that certain material does not really depend on language, not, that's to say, on the *full resources* of language (as those resources are manifested in poems)—but only on a kind of utilitarian recourse to language *faute de mieux,* as signs representing ideas; in which case you should be prepared to write prose, and learn to write a prose as transparent, as unobtrusive, as you can, a pure medium for the ideas. What I've been saying might be mistaken for a statement of belief that there are poetic and nonpoetic "subjects." No, I don't mean that. It is not the subject, ever, in itself; it is the way the individual responds, relates, to it. When I speak of the material "wanting to be" a poem or an essay or a story or whatever (or an equation), I mean the *total* material—i.e., the "subject" plus the perception of it. One has to learn to recognize the tendency, the pull, of this conjunction, this inscape.

3) *Rhyme: Rhythm:* Sometimes a mood will sing itself as hoo ho hum, hum hum ho, o, o, hum hum ho, strolling along briskly. Sometimes ah, la la lara, lara li di dum, lara

da la d*a*ra, dora di dee dum, in a minor key, stirring the soup wistfully. Pre-establishment of rhythm or rhyme pattern in advance of the actual words, the defined image. I remember realizing how what was right with that boy's poem at Dartmouth that time was the rhythm, though the words were wrong. Tried to tap it out as on a drum.

4) *On the Olson "manifesto":* (the HEAD, by way of the EAR, to the SYLLABLE; the HEART, by way of the BREATH, to the LINE). Head (intellect) and ear (sensuous instinct) lead to syllable, which has intrinsic meaning but has not rhythm. It is when heart (emotion, feeling) influence the operation of breath (process) that we are led to the line (the phrase, the rhythmic, emotive grouping of syllables). Of course a single word too, though, can be *tonally* charged with feeling—and as soon as we get a single word of two syllables, we have the emotive force of rhythm.

5) *Need:* Realization the other day of overemphasis on "need"—that is, danger of letting the poet's need seem identical with the nonartistic need for expression, fulfillable in speech or gesture or action. In the artist fundamental emotional need must always be supplemented by, accompanied by, the need to handle the material, play with it, explore its possibilities. (*Shit,* says the Freudian. So? If there's nothing else around for the infant artist to start with ... The impulse to explore, to handle, doesn't it *anticipate,* pre-exist, the material?) In writing of the form sense—traffic sense, that was what Stefan Wolpe called it!—up to now, I've only spoken of it technically—or rather, as of *after the event;* this could be taken as advocacy of "self-expression." I must begin to make clear its *dynamic* function. It is as primary as the other kind of need.

Line-breaks, Stanza-spaces, and the Inner Voice

In an interview with me in 1964, Walter Sutton asked me to talk at some length about a short poem of mine. I chose "The Tulips" from *The Jacob's Ladder:*

> Red tulips
> living into their death
> flushed with a wild blue
>
> tulips
> becoming wings
> ears of the wind
> jackrabbits rolling their eyes
>
> west wind
> shaking the loose pane
>
> some petals fall
> with that sound one
> listens for

First, there was the given fact of having received a bunch of red tulips, which I put in a vase on the window sill. In general I tend to throw out flowers when they begin to wither, because their beauty is partly in their *short* life, and I don't like to cling to them. I thought of that sentence of Rilke's about the unlived life of which one can die[1]; and, looking at these tulips, I thought of how they were continuing to be fully alive, right on into their last moments. They hadn't given up before the end. As red tulips die,

---

Published in *Minnesota Review*, No. 5, 1965, as "A Conversation with Denise Levertov." This article is an extract from that interview.

[1]This phrase occurs in *Letters to a Young Poet* (rev. ed., Norton, 1954), letter of August 12, 1904. Rilke speaks of "unlived, disdained, lost life, of which one can die."

some chemical change takes place which makes them turn blue, and this blue seems like the flush on the cheeks of someone with fever. I said "wild blue" because, as I looked at it, it seemed to be a shade of blue that suggested to me perhaps far-off parts of sky at sunset that seemed untamed, wild. There seem to be blues that are tame and blues that are daring. Well, these three lines constitute the first stanza . . . Then came a pause. A silence within myself when I didn't see or feel more, but was simply resting on this sequence that had already taken place. Then, as I looked, this process continued. You can think of it as going on throughout a day; but when cut flowers are in that state, things happen quite fast; you can almost see them move. The petals begin to turn back. As they turn back, they seem to me to be winglike. The flowers are almost going to take off on their winglike petals. Then "ears of the wind." They seem also like long ears, like jack rabbits' ears turned back and flowing in the wind, but also as if they were the wind's own ears listening to itself. The idea of their being jack rabbits' ears led me to the next line, which is the last line of this stanza, "jackrabbits rolling their eyes," because as they turn still further back they suggest, perhaps, ecstasy. Well, this was the second unit. Then another pause. The next stanza, "west wind / shaking the loose pane," is a sequence which is pure observation without all that complex of associations that entered into the others. The flowers were on the window sill, and the pane of glass was loose, and the wind blew and rattled the pane. This is background.

Is it part of the sound that comes in, as you mentioned earlier?

Yes, although it doesn't really get into the poem quite as sound. Then again a short pause, and then, "some petals fall / with that sound one / listens for." Now, the petals fall, not only because the flowers are dying and the petals have loosened themselves, in death, but also because perhaps that death was hastened by the blowing of the west wind, by external circumstances. And there is a little sound when a petal falls. Now why does the line end on "one"? Why isn't the next line "one listens for"? That is because into the sequence of events entered a pause in which was an unspoken question, "with that sound one," and suddenly I was stopped: "one what?" Oh, "one listens for." It's a sound like the breath of a human being who is dying; it stops, and one has been sitting by the bedside, and one didn't even know it, but one was in fact waiting for just that sound, and the sound is the equivalent of that silence. And one doesn't discover that one was waiting for it, was listening for it, until one comes to it. I think that's all.

I think the line also turns back with the "one." There is a kind of reflexive movement for me, as you read it, emphasizing the solitary nature of the sound. Now in your comments on this poem you have talked mostly about the meanings, the associations of the experience, and their relation to images.

Also, though, about their relation to rhythm, about where the lines are broken and where the silence is, about the rests.

Where the silences fall. Now, "variable foot" is a difficult term. Williams said that it involves not just the words or the phrases but also the spaces between them. Is that your meaning also? That a pause complementing a verbal unit is a part of the sequence of events?

Yes, and the line-end pause is a very important one; I regard it as equal to half a comma, but the pauses between stanzas come into it too, and they are much harder to evaluate, to measure. I think that what the idea of the variable foot, which is so difficult to understand, really depends on is a sense of a pulse, a pulse in behind the words, a pulse that is actually sort of tapped out by a drum in the poem. Yes, there's an implied beat, as in music; there is such a beat, and you can have in one bar just two notes, and in another bar ten notes, and yet the bar length is the same. I suppose that is what Williams was talking about, that you don't measure a foot in the old way by its syllables but by its beat.

Though not by what Pound called the rhythm of the metronome?

Well, there is a metronome in back, too.

Is it like the mechanical beat of the metronome or the necessarily variable beat of a pulse? Is it a constant beat? Or is it a beat that accelerates and slows?

Oh, it accelerates and slows, but it has a regularity, I would say. I'm thinking of *The Clock* symphony of Haydn. Well, there's where the pulse behind the bars is actually heard—p*um*-pum, p*um*-pum, and so on. But then, winding around that pum-pum, it's going *dee*-dee-*dee*-dum, and so forth. Well, I think perhaps in a poem you've got that melody, and not the metronomic pum-pum; but the pum-pum, pum-pum is implied.

When you think of the variable foot, then, you think of beats rather than of the spacing of phrases or of breath-spaced units of expression?

I've never fully gone along with Charles Olson's idea of the use of the breath. It seems to me that it doesn't work out in practice.

Of course, he thinks of this as one of the achievements of the modernist revolution—that Pound and Williams inaugurated the use of breath-spaced lines.

But I don't think they really are breath-spaced. There are a lot of poems where you actually have to draw a big breath to read the phrase as it's written. But so what? Why shouldn't one, if one is capable of drawing a deep breath? It's too easy to take this breath idea to mean literally that a poet's poems *ought* by some moral law to sound very much like what he sounds like when he's talking. But I think this is unfair and untrue, because in fact they may reflect his *inner* voice, and he may just not be a person able to express his inner voice in actual speech.

You think, then, that the rhythm of the inner voice controls the rhythm of the poem?

Absolutely, the rhythm of the inner voice. And I think that the breath idea is taken by a lot of young poets to mean the rhythm of the outer voice. They take that in conjunction with Williams's insistence upon the American idiom, and they produce poems which are purely documentary.

What do you mean by the inner voice?

What it means to me is that a poet, a verbal kind of person, is constantly talking to himself, inside of himself, constantly approximating and evaluating and trying to grasp his experience in words. And the "sound," inside his head, of that voice is not necessarily identical with his literal speaking voice, nor is his inner vocabulary identical with that which he uses in conversation. At their best sound and words are song, not speech. The written poem is then a record of that inner song.

Work and Inspiration: Inviting the Muse

Poems come into being in two ways. There are those which are—or used to be—spoken of as *inspired;* poems which seem to appear out of nowhere, complete or very nearly so; which are quickly written without conscious premeditation, taking the writer by surprise. These are often the best poems; at least, a large proportion of those that *I* have been "given" in this way are the poems I myself prefer and which readers, without knowledge of their history, have singled out for praise. Such poems often seem to have that aura of authority, of the incontrovertible, that air of being mysteriously lit from within their substance, which is exactly what a poet strives to attain in the poems that are hard to write. But though the inspired poem is something any poet naturally feels awed by and grateful for, nevertheless if one wrote only such poems one would have, as it were, no occupation; and so most writers, surely, are glad that some of their work requires the labor for which they are constitutionally fitted. For the artist—every kind of artist, and, I feel sure, not only the artist but everyone engaged in any kind of creative activity—is as enamored of the process of making as of the thing made.

There is nothing one can say directly concerning the coming into being of "given" or "inspired" poems, because there is no conscious process to be described. However, in considering what happens in writing poems which have a known history, I have come to feel convinced that they are not of a radically different order; it is simply that in the "given" poem *the same kind of work* has gone on below, or I would prefer to say beyond, the threshold of consciousness. The labor we call conscious is, if the poem is a good one, or rather if the poet knows how to work, not

From a talk given at the Radcliffe Institute for Independent Study. Later published in *Field*, Oberlin College (Ohio).

a matter of a use of the intellect divorced from other factors but of the intuitive interplay of various mental and physical factors, just as in unconscious precreative activity; it is *conscious* in that we are aware of it, but not in the sense of being deliberate and controlled by the rational will (though of course reason and will can and should play their modest part too).

The two manifestations of this underlyingly identical process can both occur in the composition of a single poem. Either sections of a poem emerge "right" the first time, while other sections require much revision; or, as I hope to demonstrate, many drafts and revisions can prepare the way for a poem which at the last leaps from the pen and requires little or no revision, but which is emphatically not simply a final draft and indeed bears practically no resemblance to the earlier "versions" which make it possible. In such a case conscious work has led to the unpredictable inspiration.

I have chosen to tell the history of three poems from *The Sorrow Dance*—"The Son," I and II, and "A Man"—as examples of what happens, of how the laboriously written poem evolves and how the labor can sometimes lead to the entire "given" poem. The choice of these particular poems was determined by my happening to have kept all the worksheets for them and also by the fact of their close connection with each other.

The first of the three to be written was the first "Son" poem. The earliest note for it says simply, "Nik as a presence, *Who he was.*" This was a reference to an unpublished poem written almost seventeen years before—in the spring of 1949, just before the birth of my son. I did not publish this poem, because I came to feel it was too wordy, just not good enough; but I shall quote it now as part of the story of these later poems:

> One is already here whose life
> bearing like seed its distant death, shall grow

26

through human pain, human joy, shall know
music and weeping, only because
the strange flower of your thighs
bloomed in my body. From our joy
begins a stranger's history. Who
is this rider in the dark? We lie
in candlelight; the child's quick unseen movements
jerk my belly under your hand. Who,
conceived in joy, in joy,
lies nine months alone in a walled silence?

Who is this rider in the dark
nine months the body's tyrant
nine months alone in a walled silence
our minds cannot fathom?
Who is it will come out of the dark,
whose cries demand our mercy, tyrant
no longer, but alone still, in a solitude
memory cannot reach?
Whose lips will suckle at these breasts,
thirsting, unafraid, for life?
Whose eyes will look out of that solitude?

The wise face of the unborn
ancient and innocent
must change to infant ignorance
before we see it, irrevocable third
looking into our lives; the child
must hunger, sleep, cry, gaze, long weeks
before it learns of laughter. Love can never
wish a life no darkness; but may love
be constant in the life our love has made.

My note saying "Who he was" referred to my memory of
this poem, but I had not actually read the poem in several
years, so it is to its general sense of questioning rather than
to the specific words of the poem that I was harking back.

27

Next on the same piece of paper is the note, "*M.'s fineness of face—the lines—the changes out of boy-and-young-manhood. A life.*" Out of these notes all three poems emerged.

The first draft of the first poem went like this:

> He-who-came-forth was
> it turned out
> a man.
>
> Through his childhood swiftly
> ran the current of
> pain, that men
>
> communicate or lie,
> the intelligence behind silence
> not always heard.

In hyphenating "He-who-came-forth," making these words into a name or title, I think I may have had American Indian names obscurely in mind, and with them the knowledge that in some cultures a true name is gained only after initiation; and that some Indians achieved identity only after the Big Dream which established their special relation to life. I may also have had sounding in me the echo of a poem of Robert Duncan's, in which he writes: "Wanderer-To-Come-To-The-Secret-Place-Where-Waits-The-Discovery-That-Moves-The-Heart," (from "The Performance We Wait For" in *The Opening of the Field*).

In the second draft the first stanza remained, as indeed it continued to do throughout, unchanged, but I seem to have felt a need to elaborate the image of the current running through childhood, the current of knowledge of the human condition, that men communicate or lie, or one could say, communicate or die (or as Auden put it, "We must love one another or die"), but that this communication, which at times has to fight its way through silence, is a hard, hard

28

task. But though my intention was to make this clearer, I only got so far as to elaborate on the brevity of childhood:

> Childhood is very short
> and shot through hastily with
> gleams of that current
>
> straining to its . . .

This was obviously impossible; the words themselves were straining; instead of waiting in that intense passivity, that passive intensity, that passionate patience which Keats named Negative Capability and which I believe to be a vital condition for the emergence of a true poem, I was straining to *find words;* the word had not found *me.* The word "straining," however, led me to my third try, where, again preceded by the unchanged first stanza,

> He-who-came-forth was
> it turned out
> a man,

I continued:

> living among us
> his childhood sifted, strained out
> to retain
>
> all it held of
> pain, energy, lassitude,
> the imagination of man

Here the last words were intended to lead into another attempt at giving a sense of that knowledge of the human condition, the seed in the child of adulthood, of manhood, which I had tried to speak of in the first draft. Again it was abandoned, with the continuing sense that the words were not the right words. The fourth draft begins to pick up a more concrete sense of the presence being talked of, *how* he lives among us:

> Moving among us from room to room of
> *the soul's dark cottage*
> in boots, in jeans, in a cloak of flame no-one
> seems to see—
>
> it is
> the imagination's garment, that human dress
> woven of fire and seagrasses—
>
> how swift the current was,
> 'childhood,' that carried him here—

In this version appear details that immediately asserted themselves to me as vivid and necessary and were retained—"in boots, in jeans, in a cloak of flame"—but also an allusion I later felt was extraneous, to "The soul's dark cottage," a quote from the seventeenth-century poet Edmund Waller's wonderful couplet which I have loved since childhood: "The soul's dark cottage, batter'd and decay'd,/Lets in new light through chinks which Time hath made." Also in this fourth draft the current, which in the beginning had been the current of pain running through childhood, becomes itself the current of childhood, and the brevity of childhood is expressed as the swiftness of that current. A variant of this draft says:

> How swiftly childhood's
> little river carried him here!

and pain—or knowledge of pain, knowledge of suffering—is spoken of in an image quickly abandoned as seeming sentimental:

30

an injured dragonfly
cupped in his large gentle hands

In retrospect, I don't think this documentary image is *in
itself* sentimental; but it has the effect of sentimentality
in this context because it is digressive and does not bring
the occasion alluded to directly enough into the poem, let-
ting it remain an allusion. Of equal importance in the
immediate decision to strike it out was the sonically awk-
ward juxtaposition of "injured" and "gentle." I tried the
substitution of "tender" for "gentle"—an injured dragonfly
cupped "tenderly"—but no, the whole thing was going off
on a tack much too soft and pretty for what I wanted.

At this point I tried to get back to the human knowledge:

Man, whose imagination is not
intuition, whose innocence
cannot brace itself for the event
but is gone
over the edge, spared
no twist of joy's knife, never
missing a trick of pain

I was disgusted here with what seemed to me a cheap
attempt to use these well-worn idioms; I felt it was gim-
micky.

In the fifth draft I went back to the river image:

How swiftly the little river of childhood
carried him here, a current doubling back
on its eddies only as the embroidery of a theme,
a life's introduction and allegro!

Already heavy with knowledge of
speech and silence,
human perhaps to the point of excess,
of genius—

31

to suffer and to imagine

This version was abandoned because the musical allusion was, once more, a digression, an irrelevancy. In my sixth draft I went back yet again to write out all I had so far that seemed solid and right: the first stanza, "He-who-came-forth," and the second, which now changed to:

Moves among us from room to room of our life

instead of "the soul's dark cottage," and from which the "cloak of flame" I had spoken of him wearing, along with boots and jeans, was now elaborated as:

This mantle, folded in him throughout
that time called childhood (which is
a little river, but swift)
flared out, one ordinary day,
to surround him—

—pulled out of his pocket along with
old candy wrappers
a cloak
whose fire feathers are
suffering, passion, knowledge of speech,
knowledge of silence . . .

Now here, with the becoming aware of those old candy wrappers, I believe I was on the right track, but I didn't know it, for in a seventh draft I went back partially to "the soul's dark cottage":

Little shafts of day
pierce the chinks in our dwelling.
He-who-came-forth
moves across them
trailing fire-feathers. Slowly.

32

In the eighth draft the flame enwrapping him becomes a *fine* flame, and those shafts of light coming through the chinks become first "the harsh light we live in" and then "common light." I was getting close to a resolution. This process had been going on for some days by this time, and in order not to confuse you too hopelessly I have omitted reference to a number of variant words in some drafts. The eighth, and as it proved, final version, took place, as it had to, in a state where without further effort the elements I now had on hand seemed to regroup themselves, and the concrete evidence of the thing finally *seen,* instead of strained after, entered the picture. In this final draft I got back to my established particulars and was led, from the candy wrappers, to see the curls of dust that gather in the corners of pockets, and to realize how treasures are transferred from one garment to another—and this cloak of flame was after all a treasure. Instead of any disquisition on the nature of the cloak of flame, I now felt I could depend on the context to imply this; that is, it is stated right away that He-who-came-forth has turned out to be a man, yet the jeans and boots and candy wrappers suggest youth; and though the cloak of flame is something he has had from the beginning, it is only now that it is unfurled. The fact that "no one seems to see it" is modified to "almost unseen in common light"—have you ever looked at a candle flame in hard morning light, almost invisible? I now had a poem that seemed complete in itself though reduced from my original intentions—or rather, my dim sense of its possible scope; and some of my sense of its being complete came from my recognition of its sonic structure, the way certain unifying sounds had entered it: the *m* of *man* leading directly to the *m* of *moves, flame* echoing in *lain,* and the *err* sounds of *wrappers, transferred, curl, unfurled,* which bind the center of the poem, actually unfurling in the *f*'s, open *a, s*'s, *t*'s, and *i*'s of the last two lines.

THE SON

i   *The Disclosure*

He-who-came-forth was
it turned out
a man—

Moves among us from room to room of our life
in boots, in jeans, in a cloak of flame
pulled out of his pocket along with
old candywrappers, where it had lain
transferred from pants to pants,
folded small as a curl of dust,
from the beginning—

unfurled now.

The fine flame
almost unseen in common light.

Yet, in trusting that the image of the cloak of flame would
pull its own weight though unqualified, unsupported, and
would imply its meaning as a human and personal potential
coming into play, I had cut too drastically from the poem
any sense of the capacity for suffering inherent in this poten-
tial. I was eventually to come to the second "Son" poem
by way of a realization of this lack. But meanwhile, some-
thing familiar but always exhilarating occurred; the wave
of energy which had built up during the writing of one
poem led me directly into another. The note about the lines
on a face and "A life," written on the same piece of paper
as "Who he was" but referring to a man in the middle of
life, was mnemonic for a complex of feelings I had long
been carrying.

My first try at this poem was dull and explanatory:

34

A man dreams and
interprets his dreams
A man makes
fictions, but he passes
from making fictions on into
knowledge, into
laughter and grief.

And in the margin I wrote, "The dreams of animals pass uninterpreted." This was just an attempt to warm up, a casting about for a clue. The second draft began by picking up from it:

A Man is what
imagines the world, imagines
what imagines the world.
He can weep
for not having wept,
he laughs
helplessly at what is not, it is
so funny.

But then this draft got involved in an irrelevant conceit:

Seven long years ago
they stole little Bridget—
thy soul, man! O,
what deep lines
are dug in thy cheeks
by all She has undergone,
and you standing
so still, you thought,
on the one spot those
seven minutes!

What had happened here was that certain troubles had occurred seven years before in the life of the man I was

35

writing about, and their repercussions had continued ever
since; this made me think both of the seven-year units of
biological growth and change of which I had read, and of
the mythological importance of the number seven. Seven
years and a day is often the period of trial in fairy tales;
Thomas the Rhymer found he had passed seven years in
Elfland when he thought it was but a day; and in the poem
by William Allingham, a nineteenth-century Irish poet,
which I had quoted, or rather misquoted, little Bridget
is stolen by the fairies for seven years. My conceit identified
her with the soul, and tried to convey the idea that the
soul's experiences, even those that remain unconscious,
mark the face with expressive lines, though the conscious-
ness may suppose that no change and development have
been taking place. Both the conscious and unconscious
living of the inner life, *living* it and not denying it, are
essential to human value and dignity; yet we undervalue
the inner life at times when the outer life of action and
achievement does not synchronize with it; so that the man
of whom I was writing had spoken of himself in anguish as
having been at a standstill for seven years, because his outer
life seemed baffled. The last lines of this draft:

> How fair the dark
> of thy deep look is,
> the beauty
> of thy being
> a man!

comment on the visible effects of inner experience, trying
to say that the endurance of suffering, the acceptance of
the trials of the soul, even though the life of action in the
external world seems at a standstill, is what gives a man
his human beauty.

Feeling that the introduction of legend seemed (though
in fact it happened naturally) too recherché, especially since
when Bridget returns to the world she cannot live there

but dies of sorrow at all that has changed during her absence,
my third draft of this poem tried to be more direct but was
only prosy:

> 'Living a life' is what gives
> the beauty of deep lines
> dug in your cheeks
>
> Not what you have done but
> what seven years and seven
> or seven again gather
> in your eyes, in the

And at that point the poem was put aside for a day or so;
I felt baffled and dejected. But in this period of rest, or
at least of inaction, the force of creative intuition had a
chance to take over. All the explicit elements I have men-
tioned retired into some quiet place in my mind; and what
emerged, complete save for a single word, was the poem
"A Man" as it now stands.

A MAN

> 'Living a life'—
> the beauty of deep lines
> dug in your cheeks.
>
> The years gather by sevens
> to fashion you. They are blind,
> but you are not blind.
>
> Their blows resound,
> they are deaf, those laboring
> daughters of the Fates,

but you are not deaf,
you pick out
your own song from the uproar

line by line,
and at last throw back
your head and sing it.

Instead of the alien presence of Little Bridget, instead of
abstract references to seven-year units, I was given a vision
of "the years" embodied as figures that I think are at once
more personal and more universal. The facts about them
revealed themselves as I envisioned them—their blindness,
their deafness, their brutal laboring persistence. In the third
stanza I first wrote them down as "craftsmen," but I looked
again and saw they were female figures, resembling the
fates, the norns, and also the muses;[1] and then I suddenly
knew that they were not the fates themselves but the years,
the daughters of the fates. When the vision is given one,
one has only to record. And with visions, as with dreams,
comes some knowledge of what it is one is seeing. If one
is a poet, then the envisioning, the listening, and the writing
of the word, are, for that while, fused. For me (and I hope
for the reader) this poem *bodies forth* the known material
that led to it. Its images could not have been willfully created
as mere illustrations of a point. But in mulling over what
I knew I felt and thought, I had stirred up levels of
imagination, of things I did not know I knew, which made
it possible for the poem to emerge in metaphor and find
its songlike structure.

There was a lapse of some weeks between these two
and the writing of the second "Son" poem. A friend's criti-
cism and my own rereading of "The Disclosure" made it
clear to me how insufficient it was, how I had not implied

[1] I may have had some unconscious recollection of the Days in Emerson's
poem of that title.

but withheld some of its proper content. I felt the remedy
to be a second part, a continuation, rather than a refashioning
of what I had already written. I found myself, while I pon-
dered the problem, contemplating a wood-block self-portrait
my son had made not long before. What I had before me
was not only the print but the actual block of wood with
its carved-out surface. Looking at it, I came to realize that
"The Disclosure" told only that the boy had begun to wear
his heirloom, manhood, and said nothing of his nature. This
particular boy-becoming-man moved me for special reasons,
after all; reasons which had nothing to do with his being
my son, except insofar as that meant I knew something about
him. What I was moved by was the capacity for suffering
that I had become aware of in him, the suffering for instance
of the painful silences of adolescent shyness in a rather
conscious and not merely frustrated way; and by the way
such experience was beginning to be made over in creative
acts. No doubt the writing of "A Man" had intensified this
realization for me. This time the first image, which again
remained the central image of the poem, although in this
case the words changed, was concerned with the wood-
block.

> Knives bring forth from the wood
> a man's face, the boy's face in his
> mind's eye, weeping.

This was immediately followed by some lines that were
discarded and never reappeared in subsequent drafts:

> His horseplay,
> his loud laughter—their vibrations
> still shake some nervous bell
> down under, hung in a fern tree—

The idea here was that his childhood was still so recent
that the vibrations of it had only reached Australia, and

39

still had enough force to swing a bell there. I am ignorant in scientific matters and perhaps had misunderstood something I had read about the movement of sound waves and their long life; and my abandonment of this image was a result not only of recognizing its digressiveness—its focusing attention on a side issue—but of my sense that perhaps it was in any case merely fanciful.

The next draft brought in the action of making the wood block:

> He hacks a slab of wood with
> fine knives and there comes into being
>
> a grim face, his vision of his own face
> down which from one eye
>
> rolls a tear—his own face
> in the manhood his childhood
>
> so swiftly has led to, as a
> small brook hastens
> into the destiny of a river.

As you see, I had returned to the river image that had been so persistent in the first poem and yet had been dropped from it in the end. But the rhythms of this draft were wrong. In successive drafts, which I will spare you, as the changes in them are small and confusing, the following revisions were made: "hacks" was excessive and became simply "cuts." "Fine" was omitted as an unnecessary qualification for "knives." The force of "hacks" goes into "violently," and the "fineness" of the knives into "precise," so that "violently precise" says both things together. "Grim" ("a grim face") became first "crisscrossed with lines of longing, of silences endured" and eventually "downstrokes / of silence endured." On the same principle of condensation, synthesis, concretion, "his vision of" becomes "visioned" and "hastens" becomes the more active, particular, visually

40

suggestive "rock-leaping." The more vivid and specific a term is, the more extensive its possibilities of reverberation in the responsive mind. This is the essential meaning of William Carlos Williams's dictum that the universal is found only in the local. However, in one of the discarded drafts it was mentioned that the boy as a child had liked to draw fantastic inventions on graph paper; this was changed to "poster paints," which he had, of course, also used at one time, because in this instance the unique particular seemed likely to be relatively distracting, while poster paints are a widely shared and associative medium that nearly everyone remembers using or has seen their children use. A clause saying that the man's face in the wood block was "incised as the boy's inward eye / presages" was cut out as redundant.

THE SON

ii   The Woodblock
He cuts into a slab of wood,
engrossed, violently precise.
Thus, yesterday, the day before yesterday,
engines of fantasy were evolved
in poster paints. Tonight
a face forms under the knife,

slashed with stern
crisscrosses of longing, downstrokes
of silence endured—
                              his visioned
own face!—
down which from one eye

rolls a tear.
                    His own face
drawn from the wood,

> deep in the manhood his childhood
> so swiftly led to, a small brook rock-leaping
> into the rapt, imperious, seagoing river.

The resolution of the image of the "little river of childhood" into the lines which end the finished poem came, once more, by way of a clearer, deeper *seeing* of the metaphor: once I knew and recorded the way the little river, the brook, leaps over its rocks as it nears a greater stream, I was given the vision of the great river's rapt and majestic presence.

To conclude, I wish to point out that the process I have described does not take place in a condition of alert self-observation. When I looked through my worksheets I *remembered* what I had been doing, what I thought I was after, in each case; but the state of writing, although intense, is dreamy and sensuous, not ratiocinative; and if I had thrown away the worksheets, I would not have been able to reconstruct the history of the poems.

Some time in 1960 I wrote "The Necessity," a poem which has remained, for me, a kind of testament, or a point of both moral and technical reference, but which has seemed obscure to some readers. Since I don't think its diction or its syntax really are obscure, it seems to me their difficulties with it must arise from their unawareness of the ground it stands on, or is rooted in; or to put it another way, the poem—any poem, but especially a poem having for the poet that character of testament—is fruit, flower, or twig of a tree, and is not to be fully comprehended without some knowledge of the tree's nature and structure, even though its claim to *be* a poem must depend on internal evidence alone. What I propose to do here is not to paraphrase or explicate "The Necessity," which I assume to be a poem, but to provide and explore some of the attitudes and realizations to which it is related.

I keep two kinds of notebooks: one is a kind of anthology of brief essential texts, the other a journal that includes meditations or ruminations on such texts. In drawing from these sources, as I propose to do here, I am not implying that all of them are literally antedecents, in my consciousness, of this particular poem. In fact, although most or all of the sources—the quotations I shall be making from other writers—were probably familiar to me by 1960, and in many instances long before, and had been copied out by then into my private anthology, the reflections on them written in my journals are of later date. I am therefore not speaking of simple sequence but of habitual preoccupations, which accrue and which periodically emerge in different forms.

This is the Hopwood Lecture for 1968, given at the University of Michigan and later published in *The Michigan Quarterly Review*, Vol. VII, No. 4, 1968.

One such preoccupation forms itself as a question. What is the task of the poet? What is the essential nature of his work? Are these not questions we too often fail to ask ourselves, as we blindly pursue some form of poetic activity? In the confusion of our relativistic age and our eroding, or at least rapidly changing, culture, the very phrase, "the task of the poet," may seem to have a nineteenth-century ring, both highfalutin and irrelevant. Our fear of the highfalutin is related to the salutary dislike of hypocrisy; but I believe we undercut ourselves, deprive ourselves of certain profound and necessary understandings, if we dismiss the question as irrelevant, and refuse, out of what is really only a kind of embarrassment, to consider as a task, and a lofty one, the engagement with language into which we are led by whatever talent we may have. And precisely this lack of an underlying conception of what the poet is doing accounts for the subject-seeking of some young poets —and maybe some old ones too—and for the emptiness, flippancy, or total subjectivity of a certain amount of writing that goes under the name of poetry.

Years ago, I copied out this statement by Ibsen in a letter.

> The task of the poet is to make clear to himself,
> and thereby to others, the temporal and eternal
> questions. . . .

In 1959 or 1960 I used these words as the subject of one of "Three Meditations." The three formed one poem, so that in referring to this one alone certain allusions are lost; but it makes a certain amount of sense on its own:

> Barbarians
> throng the straight roads of
> my empire, converging
> on black Rome.
> There is darkness in me.
> Silver sunrays

44

sternly, in tenuous joy
cut through its folds:
mountains
arise from cloud.
Who was it yelled, cracking
the glass of delight?
Who sent the child
sobbing to bed, and woke it
later to comfort it?
I, I, I, I.
I multitude, I tyrant,
I angel, I you, you
world, battlefield, stirring
with unheard litanies, sounds of piercing
green half-smothered by
strewn bones.

My emphasis was on asking oneself the questions, internalizing them, on coming to realize how much the apparently external problems have their parallels within us. (Parenthetically, I would suggest that man has to recognize not only that he tends to project his personal problems on the external world but also that he is a microcosm within which indeed the same problems, the same tyrannies, injustices, hopes, and mercies act and react and demand resolution.) This internalization still seems to me what is essential in Ibsen's dictum: what the poet is called on to clarify is not answers but the existence and nature of questions; and his likelihood of so clarifying them for others is made possible only through dialogue with himself. Inner colloquy as a means of communication with others was something I assumed in the poem but had not been at that time overtly concerned with, though in fact I had already translated a Toltec poem that includes the line, "The true artist / maintains dialogue with his heart."

What duality does *dialogue with himself, dialogue with his heart,* imply? "Every art needs two—one who makes

45

it, and one who needs it," Ernst Barlach, the German sculptor and playwright, is reported to have said. If this is taken to mean *someone out there* who needs it—an audience—the working artist is in immediate danger of externalizing his activity, of distorting his vision to accommodate it to what he knows, or supposes he knows, his audience requires, or to what he thinks it ought to hear. Writing to a student in 1965, I put it this way:

> . . . you will find yourself not saying all you have to say—you will limit yourself according to your sense of his, or her, or their, capacity. In order to do *all that one can* in any given instance (and nothing less than all is good enough, though the artist, not being of a complacent nature, will never feel sure he *has* done all) one must develop objectivity: at some stage in the writing of a poem you must dismiss from your mind all special knowledge (of what you were *intending* to say, of private allusions, etc.) and read it with the innocence you bring to a poem by someone unknown to you. If you satisfy yourself as *reader* (not just as "self-expressive" writer) you have a reasonable expectation of reaching others too.

This "reader within one" is identical with Barlach's "one who needs" the work of art. To become aware of him safeguards the artist both from the superficialities resulting from overadaptation to the external, and from miasmic subjectivities. My reference above to "self-expression" is closely related to what I believe Ibsen must have meant by "to make clear to himself." A self-expressive act is one which makes the doer feel liberated, "clear" in the act itself. A scream, a shout, a leaping into the air, a clapping of hands—or an effusion of words associated for their writer at that moment with an emotion—all these are self-expressive. They satisfy their performer momentarily. But they are not art. And the poet's "making clear," which Ibsen was talking about, *is* art: it goes beyond (though it includes) the self-expressive verbal effusion, as it goes beyond the ephemeral gesture; it is a construct of words that *remains* clear even after the writer has ceased to be aware of the associations that initially impelled it. This kind of "making clear" engages both the subjective and objective in him. The difference is between the satisfaction of exercising the power of utterance as such, of *saying*, of the clarity of action; and of the autonomous clarity *of the thing said*, the enduring clarity of the right words. Cid Corman once said in a broadcast that poetry gives us "not experience thrown as a personal problem on others but experience as an order that will sing to others."

The poet—when he is writing—is a priest; the poem is a temple; epiphanies and communion take place within it. The communion is triple: between the maker and the needer within the poet; between the maker and the needers outside him—those who need but can't make their own poems (or who do make their own but need this one too); and between the human and the divine in both poet and reader. By divine I mean something beyond both the making and the needing elements, vast, irreducible, a spirit summoned by the exercise of needing and making. When the poet converses with this god he has summoned into manifestation, he reveals to others the possibility of their own dialogue with the god in themselves. Writing the poem is the poet's means of summoning the divine; the reader's may be through reading the poem, or through what the experience of the poem leads him to.

Rilke wrote in a letter: ". . . art does not ultimately tend to produce more artists. It does not mean to call anyone over to it; indeed, it has always been my guess that it is not concerned at all with any effect. But while its creations, having issued irresistibly from an inexhaustible source, stand there strangely quiet and surpassable among things, it may be that involuntarily they become somehow exemplary for *every* human activity by reason of their innate disinterestedness, freedom, and intensity. . . ."[1]

It is when making and needing have a single point of origin that this "disinterestedness" occurs. And only when it does occur are the "freedom and intensity" generated which "involuntarily become exemplary"—which do, that is, communicate to others outside the artist's self. That is the logic of Ibsen's word "thereby" ("to make clear to himself and *thereby* to others").

I'd like to take a closer look at this word *need*. The need I am talking about is specific (and it is the same, I think, that Rilke meant when in the famous first letter to the Young Poet he told him he should ask himself, *"Must* I write?"). This need is the need for a *poem;* when this fact is not recognized, other needs—such as an undifferentiated need for self-expression, which could just as well find satisfaction in a gesture or an action; or the need to reassure the ego by writing something that will impress others—are apt to be mistaken for specific poem-need. Talent will not save a poem written under these misapprehensions from being weak and ephemeral.

For years I understood the related testimony of Jean Hélion, the contemporary French painter, only as it concerned "integrity" and as an affirmation of the *existence* of an "other" within oneself, when he wrote in an English art magazine of the 1940s: "Art degenerates if not kept essentially the language of the mysterious being hidden in each man, behind his eyes. I act as if this hidden being got life only through the manipulation of plastic quantities, as if they were his only body, as if their growth were his only future. I identify him with his language. Instead of a description, an expression, or a comment, art becomes a realization with which the urge to live collaborates as a mason." But when I reconsidered this passage in relation to

---

[1]From a letter to Rudolf Bödlander. See *Letters of Rainer Maria Rilke,* Vol. II (New York, W. W. Norton, 1969), p. 294.

how the transition from the inner world, inner dialogue, of the artist, to communication with any external other, is effected, I came to realize that Hélion is also implying that it is through the sensuous substance of the art, and only through that, that the transition is made.

The act of realizing inner experience in material substance is in itself an action *toward others*, even when the conscious intention has not gone beyond the desire for self-expression. Just as the activity of the artist gives body and future to "the mysterious being hidden behind his eyes," so the very fact of concrete manifestation, of paint, of words, reaches over beyond the world of inner dialogue. When Hélion says that then art becomes a realization, he clearly means not "awareness" but quite literally "real-ization," making real, substantiation. Instead of description, expression, comment —all of which only refer to an absent subject—art becomes substance, entity.

Heidegger, interpreting Hölderlin,[2] says that to be human is to *be a conversation*—a strange and striking way of saying that communion is the very basis of human living, of *living humanly*. The poet develops the basic human need for dialogue in concretions that are audible to others; in listening, others are stimulated into awareness of their own needs and capacities, stirred into taking up their own dialogues, which are so often neglected (as are the poet's own, too often, when he is not actively *being* a poet). Yet this effect, or result, of his work, though he cannot but be aware of it, cannot be the *intention* of the poet, for such outward, effect-directed intention is self-defeating.

Man's vital need for communion, his humanity's being rooted in "conversation," is due to the fact that since living things, and parts of living things, atrophy if not exercised in their proper functions and since man does contain, among his living parts, the complementary dualities of Needer and

[2]Martin Heidegger's essay on "Hölderlin and the Essence of Poetry" is included in *Existence and Being* (Chicago, Regnery, 1950).

49

Maker, he must engage them if they are not to deteriorate. That is why Hélion speaks of "the urge to live collaborating as a mason" in the realization of art. The two beings are one being, mutually dependent. The life of both depends not merely on mutual recognition but on the manifestation of that recognition in substantial terms—whether as "plastic quantities" or as words (or in the means of whatever art is in question). The substance, the means, of an art, is an incarnation—not reference but phenomenon. A poem is an indivisibility of "spirit and matter" much more absolute than what most people seem to understand by "synthesis of form and content." That phrase is often taken to imply a process of will, craft, taste, and understanding, by which the form of a work may painstakingly be molded to a perfect expression of, or vehicle for, its content. But artists know this is *not* the case—or only as a recourse, a substitute in thin times for the real thing. It is without doubt the proper process for certain forms of writing—for exposition of ideas, for critical studies. But in the primary work of art it exists, at best, as a steppingstone to activity less laborious, less linked to effort and will. Just as the "other being" of Hélion's metaphor is *identified*, in process, with his language, which is his "only body, his only future," so *content*, which is the dialogue between him and the "maker," *becomes* form. Emerson says, ". . . insight which expresses itself by what is called Imagination *does not come by study*, but by the intellect being *where and what it sees*, by sharing the path or circuit of things through forms, and so making them translucid to others . . ." (my italics).[3] Goethe says, ". . . moralists think of the ulterior effect, about which the true artist troubles himself as little as Nature does when she makes a lion or a hummingbird."[4] And Heidegger, in "Hölderlin and the Essence of Poetry," writes: "Poetry looks like a

[3]From "Poetry," *Essays* (second series).
[4]Quoted by Thomas Mann in "Goethe and Tolstoy," *Essays of Thomas Mann* (New York, Vintage, 1957).

game and is not. A game does indeed bring men together, but in such a way that each forgets himself in the process. In poetry, on the other hand, man is reunited on the foundation of his existence. There he comes to rest; not indeed to the seeming rest of inactivity and emptiness of thought, but to that infinite state of rest in which all powers and relations are active."

"Disinterested intensity," of which Rilke wrote, then, is truly exemplary and affective intensity. What Charles Olson has called a man's "filling of his given space," what John Donne said of the presence of God in a straw—"God is a straw in a straw"—point toward that disinterest. The strawness of straw, the humanness of the human, is their divinity; in that intensity is the "divine spark" Hasidic lore tells us dwells in all created things. "Who then is man?" Heidegger asks. "He who must affirm what he is. To affirm means to declare; but at the same time it means: to give in the declaration a guarantee of what is declared. Man is *he* who he *is*, precisely in the affirmation of his own existence."

Olson's words about filling our given space occur in a passage that further parallels Heidegger:

> . . . a man, carved
> out of himself, so wrought he
> fills his given space, makes
> traceries sufficient to
> others' needs . . .
> here is
> social action, for the poet
> anyway, his
> politics, his
> needs . . .

Olson is saying, as Heidegger is saying, that it is *by* being what he is capable of being, *by* living his life so that his identity is "carved," is "wrought," *by* filling his given space, that a man, and in particular a poet as a representative of

51

an activity peculiarly human, *does* make "traceries sufficient to others' needs" (which is, in the most profound sense, a "social" or "political" action). Poems bear witness to the manness of man, which, like the strawness of straw, is an exiled spark. Only by the light and heat of these divine sparks can we see, can we feel, the extent of the human range. They bear witness to the *possibility* of "disinterest, freedom, and intensity."

"Therefore dive deep," wrote Edward Young—author of the once so popular, later despised, *Night Thoughts*—"dive deep into thy bosom; learn the depths, extent, bias, and full fort of thy mind; contract full intimacy with the stranger within thee; excite and cherish every spark of intellectual light and heat, however smothered under former negligence, or scattered through the dull, dark mass of common thoughts; and collecting them into a body, let thy genius rise (if genius thou hast) as the sun from chaos; and if I then should say, like an Indian, Worship it (though too bold) yet should I say little more than my second rule enjoins, *viz.*, Reverence thyself."[5]

What I have up to now been suggesting as the task of the poet may seem of an Emersonian idealism (though perhaps Emerson has been misread on this point) that refuses to look man's capacity for evil square in the eyes. Now as perhaps never before, when we are so acutely conscious of being ruled by evil men, and that in our time man's inhumanity to man has swollen to proportions of perhaps unexampled monstrosity, such a refusal would be no less than idiotic. Or I may seem to have been advocating a Nietzschean acceptance of man's power for evil, simply on the ground that it is among his possibilities. But Young's final injunction, in the passage just quoted, is what, for me, holds the clue to what must make the poet's humanity *humane*. "Reverence thyself" is necessarily an aspect of

---

[5]From Edward Young, *Conjectures on Original Composition* (1759).

Schweitzer's doctrine of Reverence for Life, the recognition of oneself as *life that wants to live* among other *forms of life that want to live.* This recognition is indissoluble, reciprocal, and dual. There can be no self-respect without respect for others, no love and reverence for others without love and reverence for oneself; and no recognition of others is possible without the imagination. The imagination of what it is to *be* those other forms of life that want to live is the only way to recognition; and it is that imaginative recognition that brings compassion to birth. Man's capacity for evil, then, is less a positive capacity, for all its horrendous activity, than a failure to develop man's most human function, the imagination, to its fullness, and consequently a failure to develop compassion.

But how is this relevant to the practice of the arts, and of poetry in particular? Reverence for life, if it is a necessary relationship to the world, must be so for all people, not only for poets. Yes; but it is the poet who has language in his care; the poet who more than others recognizes language also as a *form of life* and a common resource to be cherished and served as we should serve and cherish earth and its waters, animal and vegetable life, and each other. The would-be poet who looks on language merely as something to be used, as the bad farmer or the rapacious industrialist looks on the soil or on rivers merely as things to be used, will not discover a deep poetry; he will only, according to the degree of his skill, construct a counterfeit more or less acceptable—a subpoetry, at best efficiently representative of his thought or feeling—a reference, not an incarnation. And he will be contributing, even if not in any immediately apparent way, to the erosion of language, just as the irresponsible, irreverent farmer and industrialist erode the land and pollute the rivers. All of our common resources, tangible or intangible, need to be given to, not exclusively taken from. They require the care that arises from intellectual love—from an understanding of their perfections.

53

Moreover, the poet's love of language must, if language is to reward him with unlooked-for miracles, that is, with poetry, amount to a passion. The passion for the things of the world and the passion for naming them must be in him indistinguishable. I think that Wordsworth's intensity of feeling lay as much in his naming of the waterfall as in his physical apprehension of it, when he wrote:

> . . . The sounding cataract
> Haunted me like a passion. . . .

The poet's task is to hold in trust the knowledge that language, as Robert Duncan has declared, is not a set of counters to be manipulated, but a Power. And only in this knowledge does he arrive at music, at that quality of song within speech which is not the result of manipulations of euphonious parts but of an attention, at once to the organic relationships of experienced phenomena and to the latent harmony and counterpoint of language itself as it is identified with those phenomena. Writing poetry is a process of discovery, revealing *inherent* music, the music of correspondences, the music of inscape. It parallels what, in a person's life, is called individuation: the evolution of consciousness toward wholeness, not an isolation of intellectual awareness but an awareness involving the whole self, a *knowing* (as man and woman "know" one another), a touching, a "being in touch."

All the thinking I do about poetry leads me back, always, to Reverence for Life as the ground for poetic activity; because it seems the ground for Attention. This is not to put the cart before the horse: some sense of identity, at which we wonder; an innocent self-regard, which we see in infants and in the humblest forms of life; these come first, a center out of which Attention reaches. Without Attention—to the world outside us, to the voices within us—what poems could possibly come into existence? Attention is the exercise of Reverence for the "other forms of

54

life that want to live." The progression seems clear to me: from Reverence for Life to Attention to Life, from Attention to Life to a highly developed Seeing and Hearing, from Seeing and Hearing (faculties almost indistinguishable for the poet) to the Discovery and Revelation of Form, from Form to Song.

There are links in this chain of which I have not spoken, except to name them—the heightened Seeing and Hearing that result from Attention to any thing, their relation to the discovery and revelation of Form. To speak intelligibly of them would take more time and space than I have. But I hope that I have conveyed some idea of the true background of a poem, and have helped to define for others much that they have already intuited in and for their own labors, perhaps without knowing that they knew it:

THE NECESSITY

From love one takes
petal to *rock* and *blessèd*
away towards
descend,

one took thought
for frail tint and spectral
glisten, trusted
from way back that stillness,

one knew
that heart of fire, rose
at the core of gold glow,
could go down undiminished,

for love and
or in fear knowing

the risk, knowing
what one is touching, one does it,

each part
of speech a spark
awaiting redemption, each
a virtue, a power

in abeyance unless we
give it care
our need designs in us. Then
all we have led away returns to us.

*And indeed what are the heavens, the earth, nay, every
creature, but Hieroglyphics and Emblems of his glory?*
                                                    —Francis Quarles

*You cannot crack a myth as you can crack Minoan. In
hieroglyphic the meaning is embodied in the figure it-
self.*
                            —Elizabeth Sewell, in *The Orphic Voice*

*Deliberately to encode knowledge so as to hide it from
the vulgar is the task of cipher but never of myth or
poetry. . . . "This stands for that" . . . is cipher and not
myth.*
                                                            —Ibid.

"No ideas but in things" does not mean "No ideas."
Nor does it specify:
"No ideas but in everyday things
                modern things
                urban things." No! It means that:
poetry appears when meaning is embodied in the
figure.

Written for the magazine *things* (No. 1, Fall, 1964), in response to a
manifesto sent me by the editors, which said in part: "The title [of the
magazine] is from a line in W. C. Williams' *Paterson:* ' . . . no ideas
but in things.' It reflects our awareness that literature should be direct and
particular, grounded in the concrete events of contemporary life. It should
be literature of assertion rather than analysis, statement rather than
criticism. . . . The language . . . cannot be that of 'humanist'
literature. . . . Allusions to Actaeon do not speak to us of pain and ter-
ror. . . . We shall not . . . publish lyrics about Love, because each experi-
ence of love differs from every other experience. We will publish poems
which relate specific love experiences in the metaphor of the world we
recognize and live in. . . . The essays we publish will present human facts
not sociological generalizations."

Language is not the dress but the incarnation of thought.
—Wordsworth

Life is no less complex and mysterious than it has always been. That we dwell in enormous cities, and invent and use astonishing machinery, does not simplify it, but continually reveals the dissolution of limit after limit to physical possibility. Our still tentative awareness of the great gulfs of the unconscious, in constant transformation like the marvelous cloudscapes one sees from a jet plane, must surely lead to awe, not to supposed simplicity. Therefore if our poetry is to seek truth—and it must, for that is a condition of its viability, breath to its lungs—then it cannot confine itself to what you, the editors of *things*, in your prospectus, have called *direct statement*, but must allow for all the dazzle, shadow, bafflement, leaps of conjecture, prayers, and dream-substance of that quest.

"Allusions to Actaeon do not speak to us of pain and terror," you say. I know there have been many poems on mythological themes written by subject-seeking poets not seriously engaged with the life of art. Right. But if a poet within himself identifies with Actaeon; or has felt the hand of any god on his shoulder; or has himself been steeped in the cosmogony and mythological history of any place and time; then (if he *is* a poet) he can write of it so that his pain and terror, or delight, will be felt by the reader whether or not that reader's education has given him specific clues to the allusion. Or rather, yes, you are right, *allusions* tell one nothing: Actaeon (or any other personage of the imagination) must be present in the poem. It is that *presentness* that is the "direct statement" I *do* believe in; not the banishment of Actaeon. "*A poetry denies its end in any* descriptive *act, I mean any act which leaves the attention outside the poem*," Robert Creeley wrote in *To Define*. (And this—the attention being put or left outside of the work: given allusions, references, only, to things not present in the substance of the work—is not the same as

58

having the attention *led to awareness* of things that though not named, not visible, exist within the universe of the work.)

"We shall not publish lyrics about Love, because each experience of love differs from every other experience." But the idea of Love, the seeking to understand it, may be a passion in a man. Will you write off Dante, will you write off George Herbert? Will you write off Robert Duncan today, when he writes for instance,

> for I went down into the end of all things
> to bring up the spirit of Man before me
> to the beginnings of Love

or:

> The light that is Love
> rushes on toward passion. It verges upon Dark.
> Roses and blood flood the clouds.
> Solitary first riders advance into legend.

or:

> It is life
> that tenders   green shoots of
> hurt and healing

> we name Love.

"We shall look for innovation in the content and language of a poem, not in its form. There are no new forms: free verse is merely another vehicle available to capable craftsmen." This intention reveals a basic misunderstanding of the nature of form. Form exists only *in* the content and language. The visual shape of a poem is not its form but a result of the notation of its form. Oh, not to quibble, it is true that the set forms exist abstractly, too; sonnet, sestina,

59

etc., have their rules, and one can invent rules for new "forms" in this sense ad infinitum. But this is a rudimentary view. In fact—and not only in organic poetry and "free verse"—form is the total interactive functioning of content and language, including every contributing element. The form of a man is not that he has two legs, two arms, a head and body and no tail, but the sum of his anatomical, physiological, mental, textural, moral, motor, etc., structure. And the form of a poem comprises all the equivalent components you can think of.

"Form is never more than the extension of content." At the Vancouver poetry conference this summer ('63) I proposed to Robert Creeley, the originator of this now famous formula, that it should be changed to read: "Form is never more than the *revelation* of content."—(to which he agreed).

Against the editorial statement that "there are no new forms: free verse is merely another vehicle," etc., I pose my belief that the poet, not the poem, is a vehicle.

All poetry is experimental poetry.

—Wallace Stevens

Robert Duncan (in *The Day Book,* part of a work in progress centered in a study of the poetry of H.D.) has pointed out how the poets and critics of the school of Rational Imagination—and we still have them with us—have regarded words "not as powers but as counters." A misinterpretation of "No ideas but in things" can lead to a similar stance. But the poem leaves the room the moment the poet begins to use its fallen eyelashes, its nail-parings, its frozen tears, its drops of blood, and eventually its fingers and toes in his checker game. No sir.

"Ornament does not interest us." Here again you oversimplify. The "ornaments" in a harpsichord piece show how ornament can be functional. A lapel without a buttonhole, a buttonhole without a flower, are no more virtuous than those whose hole invites a flower, whose flower invites a smile.

We need a poetry not of *direct statement* but of *direct evocation:* a poetry of hieroglyphics, of embodiment, incarnation; in which the personages may be of myth or of Monday, no matter, if they are of the living imagination.

You asked for my "moral support," and how could I *not* give it to a magazine that takes its title from *Paterson*, and from a line that has always meant so much to me? You will know, I think, that it is given with genuine interest, just because, not in spite of, its being in the form of admonition.

I had never, until invited to take part in this conference, given much thought to what myth meant to me as a practicing poet, or to whether in fact elements one could call mythic appeared in my poetry at all. As soon, however, as I gave this question my attention, I began to find not only instances of mythological allusion but some traces, at least, of *a* myth running through all of my work from the very beginning. By *a* myth I mean the presence of what someone, speaking of the novel, has called "the plot behind the plot"—and I feel fairly certain that some such, perhaps unconscious, dominant or recurring theme is to be found, if one looks for it, in the works of all serious writers, however various their work and however many apparently radical changes the phases of their life's production seem to manifest. But though I took this for granted concerning other writers, I had till now been unself-conscious enough never to have considered what my own myth, in this sense, might be. It is a little frightening to be forced, by a question, into such self-scrutiny. One can't reject it: there is no going back: the experience is irreversible. You have played the part of the serpent, and offered me knowledge. Let us hope I can transform it into some degree of wisdom.

Myth can enter poetry as that dominant theme each writer has below the surface of the majority of his works; as allusion to, and incorporation of, specific known myths, the shared myths of his culture or borrowed from other accessible cultures; or by the invention of new fictions which (whether or not they pertain to that writer's dominant theme) attain mythic stature in the culture (perhaps because they turn

---

Written for a meeting, in Washington, D.C., 1967, of poets and theologians, convened to discuss parable, myth, and language under the sponsorship of the Church Society for College Work. Later published, under the title "A Personal Approach," in *The Anglican Review*, Vol.L, No. 3, 1968.

out to be new versions of archetypal stories). In my search through my own poems, then, for what is relevant to this symposium, I shall be looking for elements that were real to my imagination, whether in the form of culturally inherited myth or in the form of personal fiction; hoping to show what kind of myths enter one poet's work, and how.

It would be frivolous to mention my very first poem, dictated to my sister when I was five years old or less (and which I had in my possession until a few years ago, but can no longer find), were it not for the fact that its theme was a visit to fairyland. Though it was a rambling affair, full of by no means original descriptions of dinky persons arrayed in the most exquisite of delicate, shining raiment, offering sumptuous hospitality in buttercup-blossom dishes and dancing to grasshopper orchestras—pretty fancies drawn as much from the nursery paintings of Margaret Tarrant, I suppose, as from literary sources—it nevertheless dealt with a world very real to me and which I had, then and later, earnest hopes of really entering someday. And in an infantile way it introduced the theme of a journey that would lead one from one state of being to another that later I find defined in many poems as the sense of *life as a pilgrimage*.

Between that first poem, and those written between the ages of nineteen and twenty-two, which formed my first book (*The Double Image*, 1946), is a blank—there were many poems written but I cannot now find any of them. But for one who has not thought about myth I am astonished to find how full of mythic themes *The Double Image* is. The opening poem is called "Childhood's End." The specific mythological reference, to Syrinx, is merely incidental, though from this distance I rather admire the concept of her flying from Pan's "unimaginable sound," by which I presume I mean that, being destined to become "music's green channel," she was already sound-oriented and felt Pan's lustful approach as an assault by the thudding of his hooves, the panting of his breath, and the wild words she

63

intuited he would growl into her ear if he caught up with her, rather than experiencing her fear in visual or tactile images. However, Syrinx—though briefly vivid, and therefore not perhaps to be dismissed as *merely* allusion—is not truly germane to the theme of the poem, which concerns both the myth of expulsion from Eden and—again—the journey into another state or phase of being, the commencement of life's pilgrimage.

Many of these early poems, though they carry the theme of the life-pilgrimage in some degree, or contain some element of myth, are allegory or sometimes extended metaphor rather than being what I begin to see as authentically mythic poems. For example, a poem on Fear personifies fear as a traveling fool. He wanders, "seeking the music of life." The mythic theme is there, but the form is allegorical. By allegory I mean not only the deliberate encoding of meanings in fictive characters that Elizabeth Sewell calls *cipher*, but the *conscious personification of abstractions* as distinct from the *dynamic experiencing of archetypal characters or actions*. (Of course, it may be argued that primitive myth also personifies the abstract. But personally I cannot bring myself to believe that the gods originate in the mind of man and are merely his way of coping with natural forces or abstract ideas by giving them semihuman personalities and stories. When man describes the gods he certainly only approximates, and therefore distorts, the reality he intuits, but I fail to see the logic of assuming that therefore they do not exist.) Another poem, "To Death," probably the best in *The Double Image*, personifies Death as a Prince and Life as his bride. This poem seems to me an example of mythic elements used as metaphor, not myth.

"Return" is another example of metaphor in the sense I am trying to define. Such poems tell of one thing in terms of another, though not with the deliberation and systematic consistency characteristic of allegory; but their terms do not extend any compulsion upon the mind beyond their specific adequacy for the particular occasion. Metaphor, in this sense, is appropriate, merely, where myth is numinous.

"One There Was" is a kind of waking dream, a fantasy in which a vague St. Peter (not named) is placed both in the classical world (by the mention of Athene's owl) and the northern world of the future (where deer graze on amber afternoons and there is snow in the sky). His dream in the garden of Gethsemane, while the unmentioned Christ keeps vigil in agony, and even more his troubled but uncomprehending awakening, are not convincing because they are not clearly imagined and don't take account of any of the historical realities of the situation. Mythic allusion in poetry only becomes dynamic myth when the deep imagination, not the superficial fancy, is at work; and the imagination, while it may transform and shift, does not disregard historical reality capriciously.

The last stanzas of "Meditation and Voices" pick up—rather self-consciously—a strand of my journey-thread:

> Leave your dark autumn groves, the roads
> oppressed by drooping alder and repining cloud—
> lacklustre follies, harvests of reproach.
> Follow your sunrise shadow to the west!
>
> Each voice that comes to trouble you is your own:
> the hard, the hungry, lost or questioning.
> To find what land your lover travels, turn
> out to the waiting sea. You are alone.

And though "Ballad" was written as a love poem, it is another step along the same way, and even introduces the world "pilgrim." Here, in fact, remote in tone though it is, I recognize the influence of the hymn which, along with one of the versions of "Jerusalem the Golden," I loved best as a child and which my sister and I used to sing loudly to keep our spirits up as we tramped along Essex lanes at nightfall after a day's rambling from village to village, always getting home hours later than we had promised—Bunyan's "He who would valiant be." Among the books and tales that most early affected my imagination were *The Pilgrim's Progress*, and Hans Andersen's *The Snow Queen* and *The Bell*—both tales that present a definitely Christian sense of the nature of the life-pilgrimage—as well as the Charles Kingsley version of the Argonauts and the many fairy tales in the Andrew Lang collections typified by the one called, "The Water of Life," in which, passing through many trials and dangers, the protagonist "walked and walked and walked" until she finally came to the top of a great mountain and found the well or pool of living water. It seems to me that my strong desire, during my mid-childhood—at eight, nine, ten—to become a world traveler, discoverer, and explorer, was not unrelated to my yet earlier devotion to stories of this kind, later extending to a special interest in the *Bildungs Roman*, for instance *Wilhelm Meister* and Stifter's *Brigitte*. And the longing I had to step backward into time and become page or knight errant (or at the very least a girl disguised as a page!) was a part of the same constellation, represented the same bias. In the case of knight-errantry there was, again, some Christian tinge to my feeling, drawn both from the Arthurian legends and from "A Prayer of St. Richard," which I pinned upon my bedroom wall at a time when I belonged to something called, I believe, "The Church of England Children's League: Knights of St. Richard," or something along those lines. This romantic Christianity was something quite apart from the serious Christianity of my parents, and had nothing to do with being "good."

And finally there is "Autumn Journey," in which the Wanderer moves on from a seductive way station, resembling the old woman's garden where Gerda in *The Snow Queen* is beguiled for a time, toward "promises of treasure/over the hill, among the burning worlds"—and here, for this was

66

written in 1944, the burning worlds represent both the fall woods and the smoldering fires of W. W. II.

I have spent this much time on these early poems partly because I found there so many indications that myth as personal dominant or leitmotif not only long antedates the formation of anything that can be called an assured style, but antedates also the years of experience that would seem, in a poet's later work, to give rise to preoccupations and attitudes. In the work of a living poet the dominant personal myth may, in early or even in mature work, be only half formed; the poet himself does not yet know the whole story—if he did, he would stop writing. He is still in the midst of his pilgrimage, and often, finding himself on the wrong road, feels he must go right back to the beginning and start over. Yet from the first his bent, his cast of imagination, has declared itself. And the seemingly wrong roads are added, mile by mile, to the map of his journey.

Between the publication of *The Double Image* and my next book, *Here and Now* (1957), eleven years elapsed. I had married in 1947 and come to the U.S. in 1948. My son was born in 1949. The early '50s were for me transitional, and not very productive of poems; but I was reading a great deal and taking in at each breath the air of American life. William Carlos Williams became the most powerful influence on my poetry, and at that time, seeking as I was to engage my capacities as a poet with the crude substance of dailiness, as I had notably *not* done in the 1940s, I took as influence from Williams nothing of the profound mythic element we find (especially, but not only) in *Paterson*, but rather the sharp eye for the material world and the keen ear for the vernacular which characterize his earlier and shorter poems. My tendency was even to take at their face value some of his "antimystical" attitudes, and to adopt a kind of pragmatism not only inadequately representative of my own feeling but which Williams himself did not wholly or profoundly adhere to. What becomes of myth, then, in this book and in that which followed it, *Overland to the Islands* (1958)? "The Earthwoman and the Water-woman" or "Mrs. Cobweb," which are portraits of actual people in nonnaturalistic terms? No, these surely are meta-phor. "Homage" puts a beloved friend outside of time, speaking of him as magician and poet beaten upon by waves of suffering and joy but "undiminished," not worn down but continuing to sing, "dreaming wide awake with stone eyes," and to listen near the sea to "the crash and sighing, crash/and sighing dance of the words." The vision is of the artist's Orphic persistence, certainly; but I had no thought —perhaps even, at that time, no knowledge—of the con-tinuing song of Orpheus after he had been torn apart. If "Homage" has a mythic element, it lies in its implication of belief in poetry as a form of magiclike power, not confined within history and reaching beyond ordinary human limita-tions. Certainly it is, among my poems of this period, one of the least Williams-influenced in that line of influence derived from his most objective, antiromantic aspect. But it is rather *of the mythic world* than actually mythic in meaning, and this is partly due to its static quality. Little by little I'm trying to find out for myself what *are* the attributes of myth as a force in poetry; and I begin to see that what I would call truly mythic must *be* genuinely force-ful and that it therefore must partake in some degree of the dramatic. To reduce all myth to soul-journey or life-pilgrimage tales would obviously be too sweeping, and would blur the distinctions between myth and epic, as Joseph Campbell's idea of the monomyth has been accused of doing; yet it does seem to me that all myth has elements of drama, action, movement, forms of journeyings. Myth-related metaphor, on the other hand, is static; it shares with myth a deeper than merely descriptive meaning, but reveals only one instant, one fixed aspect, of such meaning.

I find my main theme again in the title poem of *Overland to the Islands:* "Let's go," it begins, "much as that dog goes/intently haphazard"; and ends, "there's nothing/the dog disdains on his way,/nevertheless he/keeps moving, changing pace and approach but/not direction—every step an/arrival." The last phrase, "every step an arrival," is quoted from Rilke, and here, unconsciously, I was evidently trying to unify for myself my sense of the pilgrim way with my new, American, objectivist-influenced, pragmatic, and sensuous longing for the Here and Now; a living-in-the-present that I would later find further incitement to in Thoreau's notebooks. An earlier poem included in this book does the same thing in another way. "The Instant" describes a childhood early morning in Wales, picking mushrooms with my mother on a dewy, misty mountainside, when suddenly the mist rolls back and:

> 'Look' she grips me, 'It is
> Eryri!
>   It's Snowdon, fifty
>   miles away!'—the voice
> a wave rising to Eryri,
>   falling.
>   Snowdon, home
> of eagles, resting place of
> Merlin, core of Wales.

Here the sensuous details of the hour and place, down to the scrags of sheep's wool caught in barbed wire, the cold firm feel of the fresh mushrooms, the sense of the square house behind us in which the other people are still asleep, are a here-and-now basis for the moment's glimpse not simply of a distant high mountain but of the world of Welsh legend. (Incidentally, though I am half Welsh and have enjoyed reading the *Mabinogion,* I have never felt close to this world nor been able to draw on it, perhaps because too many centuries of somber nonconformism intervened between the Wales of my mother's generation and that heritage, cutting the people off from their ancient heroes far more sharply than the Irish country people seem ever to have been from theirs. Yet in this instance it was the charged, legendary name Eryri, not the common "Snowdon," that did spring atavistically to her lips and deeply impressed me.)

"In Obedience," an elegy for my father, tells of doing a wild solitary dance among the fireflies in a New England garden one night while my father lay dying in London; a joyful dance that was yet a dance of love and mourning. It was only later that I learned that my father rose from his bed shortly before his death to dance the Hasidic dance of praise. In this I see the seeds of legend that could take on the dimensions of myth; might not some descendant of his and of mine say some day to a son or daughter, "We are of a line that dances in mourning and dances a joyful dance in the hour of death?" This poem quotes a letter from my mother, "After all, life/is a journey to this goal/from the outset," and follows it with the words from Bunyan that had most clearly remained with me from childhood. "And Mr. Despondency's daughter Muchafraid/went through the water singing"—(surely an epitome of the theme of pilgrimage)—bringing to my mind in this connection "Illustrious Ancestors," which carries the sense, shared by my late sister I believe, of having a definite and peculiar destiny which seemed signalized by our having had among our ancestors two men who, living at the same period (late 1700s, early 1800s) but in very different cultures, had preoccupations which gave them a basic kinship (had they known of one another and been able to cross the barriers of language and religious prejudice), a kinship that Olga and I felt must be recognized in heaven, or on earth would be somehow unified and redeemed in us. One of them was Schneour Zalman, the founder of Habad Hasidism; the other, Angel Jones of Mold, a Welsh tailor whose apprentices came to learn Biblical interpretations from him while cutting and stitching. The presence in the imagination of such figures and their relation to oneself is a kind of personal mythology, and can function as a source of confidence and as an inspiration for the artist; but I am unsure of whether, or how, it may acquire sufficient universality to affect others: perhaps by causing the reader to seek, and to recognize, parallels in his own background. For indeed, though these two do seem particularly remarkable, I have rarely met anyone who has not been able to find in back of himself some figure whose attributes could be regarded justly as stimulating or in some manner specially meaningful to him: but often, especially if an individual has had a particularly hard time emerging from the chrysalis of a perhaps drab or notably unsympathetic home environment, he will reject his antecedents out of hand unless something, as perhaps this poem might do, suggests to him that he may find unexpected support among the shades.

The story about Schneour Zalman's early rejection of the opportunity to learn the language of birds, and of his discovery in old age that this knowledge had been given him as a gift in any case, is recounted in Buber's *Tales of the Hasidim*. Mircea Eliade, in *Patterns in Comparative Religion,* says that becoming conversant with the language of animals, and particularly of birds, symbolizes access to the transcendent reality; and if the idea of pilgrimage is essentially that of passage from one spiritual state into another, then this poem also shares my unconscious dominant.

In "Scenes from the Life of the Peppertrees" some fragment of buried myth seems to appear, when the peppertrees, graceful, modest, even diffident, but with huge gnarled roots, first swallow up among their branches a robust cat who leaps confidently into them, and then walk over and tap on the bedroom window of an innocent sleeping man, an Adam unfallen, an Abel. The purpose of the trees in attempting to waken him is not revealed (by which I do not mean that I withheld information; I told all that I knew). What made me envision these trees, a species of which I am particularly fond, in this ambiguous role, I have no idea—unless it was the very fact of that contrast between their graceful general appearance and their massive, knotted roots. The poem ends with the question, "Will he wake?"

Much later, reading Tolkien's romances, I seemed to see in my peppertrees relatives of the *Ents*, tree-beings with manlike mobility. And in the course of writing this lecture, finding myself about to say, "The poet must have as vivid a relation to any myth as if he were a tree that had followed Orpheus," I embarked on a long poem spoken in the first person by such a tree. Curiously, I now notice that in a badly written early poem called "Listen" occurs the phrase "trees pulling away from earth." So that, though I am fully aware of the moisture-seeking, earth-gripping propensities of tree roots, it seems as if below the conscious level I have some rather persistent symbolism of trees as being, or wanting to be, or having once been, peripatetic, which in fact is alien and even somewhat repulsive to my conscious mind. Possibly the meaning of this recurrence of walking tree images is a symbolic representation of the concept that all creation strives to return to the primal oneness?

The title poem of *With Eyes at the Back of our Heads* seems to speak of one of those stages in the journey that are moments of vision presaging the secret that will bring the seeker to his goal, but which are quickly forgotten again, or hidden again from the imagination, just as the head of Snowdon, Eryri, is hidden again as the mists return.

"The Goddess," in which a goddess who is truth tosses the protagonist out of Lie Castle (no doubt the same "drowsy mansion" in which the wanderer of "Autumn Journey," written almost twenty years earlier, had lingered a while) is not based on a dream but on an actual waking vision, but is, I think, more than merely metaphorical—perhaps, if I am right about the active character of myth in poetry, because it is dramatic. (I want to re-emphasize the words *myth in poetry*, because obviously myth as such is not always dramatic or active: e.g., the idea of the world-tree Ygdrasil is myth but not drama.) The poem's energy arises from an experience of awakening to the truth and to the necessity for truthfulness—an experience sufficiently profound to produce the image of truth as a Goddess, to produce that

72

image spontaneously, and not by means of the conscious effort of allegory to find similes.

In "Xochipilli" the pre-Columbian God of Spring creates red flowers from the dung of a serpent that coils and preens in the heart of a fire in the God's hearth; he creates white flowers from the bones of small animals, sacrificed to serve as food for the snake; from the sound of the rain on his thatched roof and the spatter of raindrops falling into the fire, and from the hissing of the serpent, the God, stirring the fire, creates the grass "that shall sing when the wind blows." This I would call genuinely mythological. From looking at a small statue of Xochipilli, the actions of the God appeared in my mind as knowledge, rather than as uninterpreted visual images. The representation of Xochipilli, I mean, informed me of what his actions would be, and from this intuitive knowledge came visualizations and their verbal equivalents. One is obliged to describe the process as a sequence, when in fact the separate elements of it overlap and synthesize. Readers who are not themselves practicing poets often assume there is a hiatus between seeing and saying; but the poet does not see and then begin to search for words to say what he sees: he begins to see and at once begins to say or to sing, and *only in the action of verbalization does he see further*. His language is not more dependent on his vision than his vision is upon his language. This is surely one of the primary distinctions between poet and mystic.

In its very small way the poem about Xochipilli exemplifies what I meant when I once wrote: the hand of a god is felt on the writer's shoulder. I cannot say that I was "steeped' in Mexican mythology. I had lived in Mexico for two years, and had read a certain amount about it and visited some of the archeological sites; however, I had no special knowledge of the attributes of Xochipilli, and did not check my intuitions against any scholarly data. Yet I feel this swiftly written little poem is an authentic revelation of the spirit of this god, transmitted to me through a representation of him made at a time when the sculptor undoubtedly believed in him as a matter of course. Another example of how this may happen is "Psalm Concerning the Castle" (*The Sorrow Dance*, 1967). This was written after contemplating a Han dynasty funerary castle, made of pottery and measuring about two and a half feet high, which is in the Fogg Museum at Harvard. At the time I knew nothing about it, not even that it was tomb furniture, since the Fogg had it listed simply as "Pottery Watchtower, Han Dynasty." However, when I visited the Smithsonian, after the poem was published, I discovered an account of these objects which established their identity as, indeed, soul-dwellings. Something of the maker's intention had, in this case also, made itself known to me through the object contemplated. The myth of what the soul would do after death lived on in the work it gave rise to, and penetrated another work in a different medium and a different era. Though grammatically imperative, as an ordinance for what must be, and therefore somewhat static, yet as the record of a kind of mandala-landscape outside of time and inside the soul, as well as because of its origin in the enduring powerfulness of ancient belief captured in a sacred object, it seems to merit the term mythological.

In "The Well" my vision of the Muse resembles a certain actress, but the face of the actress resembled—in features, though not in coloring—that of the personage who occurs and reoccurs in the beloved fairy tales of George MacDonald—the young/old grandmother, demonic yet benevolent. And in a somewhat later poem, "To the Muse," this resemblance extends to the reference to her spinning room in a tower that is hard to find at will, even though it is part of the house one inhabits. Those familiar with "The Princess and the Goblins" and "The Princess and Curdie," as well as some of the shorter MacDonald stories, will recognize this image. The Goddess in the poem about Lie Castle also bears a genetic resemblance to the demonic aspect of MacDonald's archytypical figure as she appears in the often frightening guise of the North Wind in "At the Back of the North Wind."

In "The Well" the locus of the dream event the poem tells of is Valentine's Park, in England, which I have called "a place of origin." Though I have not seen this park for more than seventeen years I can still, if I shut my eyes, take walks in it. Its topography includes what was for me a Roman Road, though not authenticated as such; and the great cedar reputed to be 1,000 years old; and two mysterious stone seats, each on a knoll at opposite ends of a woodland glade, which would have fitted giants and were known as the thrones of Oberon and Titania. It was in this tract of woodland that my sister and I and our dog once saw an apparition. Alpheus enters the dream not as deliberate, recherché allusion, but because in the dream I was given, along with the visual images, the knowledge of the identity of the river Roding with Alpheus. "The Illustration," which is a sequel to "The Well," speaks for itself on the theme of "myth in poetry." The origins—in memory and forgotten experience—of dream, vision, and synthetic intuitions, are pulled together here and revealed in a moment of comprehension: Vision is a lake across which glide manifestations of truth, images of inner knowledge. The overt intent of a parable can mask other meanings. The parables are drawn from the complexity of Nature. The "Light of Truth" brings the traveling soul and its Muse together at the Place of Origin by way of a winding road. (And only now do I connect the "closed all-seeing eyes" of the Muse with those of "The Dog of Art," an earlier poem.)

In "A Letter to William Kinter of Muhlenberg," the profound Christian symbolism of the Stations of the Cross is dimly apprehended as the model for spiritual pilgrimage, which in turn is imaged forth in a reference to the peripatetic discourse of personages in *The Zohar*.

Zaddik, you showed me
the Stations of the Cross

and I saw
not what the almost abstract

tiles held—world upon world—
but at least

a shadow of what
might be seen there if mind and heart

gave themselves to meditation,
deeper

and deeper into Imagination's
holy forest, as travelers

followed the Zohar's dusty
shimmering roads, talking

with prophets and
hidden angels . . .

At the period of my childhood when my father was work-
ing on his translation of parts of *The Zohar,* he would come
to the midday dinner table with his morning's work in his
mind and quote from it, and the sense of the weather in
Palestine in which the rabbis walked and talked and met
with strangers of great wisdom was reinforced for me by
the hum of bees at the window and by the way the dining
room would look dark after the bright sunshine in which
I had been playing outside.[1]

In "From the Roof" the Hudson River is spoken of as

[1]Often the discourse in *The Zohar* is given a very concrete locus. Two
rabbis will be walking along a road talking with one another when they
are joined suddenly by someone else who enters their conversation, and
they will walk along for miles, discussing. And frequently this person
who has contributed the clinching argument, let us say, to what is being
discussed, disappears as suddenly as he has appeared.

perhaps the material manifestation of "the hidden river"—
and "who can say/the crippled broom-vendor yesterday,
who passed/just as we needed a new broom, was not/one
of the Hidden Ones?"—that is, one of those angels or
prophets. The mixture of Christian and Jewish references
is I suppose rather peculiar to me on account of my back-
ground—not the more frequently found "mixed marriage"
from which a child may pick up separate concepts from each
parent, but one in which, as well, one parent was both
learned Jew and fervent Christian. I remember one day on
a country walk when my sister and I half convinced our-
selves that a blue-eyed, black-bearded, handsome old tramp
or tinker we met at more than one crossroads, and who
smiled at us, was a Christian saint gathering deeds of charity
in his pack to take to the recording angel. (And perhaps
he was.) But we drew the idea, surely, from Hasidic
sources. However, though this is my particular combination
of cultural influences, it is typical in some degree of the
eclecticism of twentieth-century poetry, in which figures
from all manner of pantheons, some discovered by the poet
only late in his life, may enter and act without conflict:
for the modern poet is not infrequently a syncretist. It is
rare for him to subscribe to a single orthodoxy; but his
nature as poet is so essentially religious that, exposed as
never before to the knowledge of many faiths, many
mythologies, he instinctively takes from any or all some-
thing of his sustenance.

"Matins" is the one instance I can think of among my
poems where specific mythic reference is made but not
accounted for. In section vi of these meditations on the
idea of "the authentic," the Irish tale of Conn-Edda is
summarized, as it were, and in section vii referred to,
though the name of Conn-Edda is never mentioned. It
happened this way. One day when I had written most of
the rest of the poem but not finished it, I read the story as
recounted by Heinrich Zimmer in *The King and The
Corpse;* and that night I dreamt the story with myself as

77

Conn-Edda—dreamt it in the first person. I therefore believed myself justified in incorporating my dream-experience into the poem without a note, feeling that I had *made it my own,* and also that the tale was familiar enough for many people to recognize it anyway. But since then I've come to think a note would have been preferable to the explanation I have so often found myself compelled to give when I have read the poem to an audience.

"Song for Ishtar" did not arise, like "Xochipilli" and "Psalm Concerning the Castle," from contemplation of a ritual object. In writing it I took cognizance of the fact that the pig was sacred to Ishtar; yet that fragment of information should not be considered as the cause or stimulus of the poem, but merely as the chink through which the poet enters a work: reading that "the pig was held sacred to Ishtar" can—then or years later—set off a train of words and rhythms, become a poem, because it is a form of something already known: the poet's experience of the demonic, or possessed, nature of his or her role. This is the inwardness of myth. Ishtar is here equated with the Muse—not improperly, I think, for Ishtar is a Moon Goddess and symbolic of change, transformation, regeneration; a raingiver, "Master of Women," "Mistress of All Men"; and surely the Muse can be regarded as an aspect of such a power. (Robert Graves has of course documented some aspects of this relationship in *The White Goddess,* which I must confess I have never really read, only glanced through; but my impression is that he has narrowed it down far too much, virtually excluding—by implication, at least—all poetry other than men's love poems to women from the canon of true poetry, which strikes me as absurdly reductive and restrictive.)

"Into the Interior" is so direct a statement of my theme that I am amazed at my own unconsciousness of that dominance I have only been discovering in writing these notes.

"The Prayer" is again too direct a statement, I think, for comment on it to be useful. I shall say only that it is, quite simply, a true story. And also that it was only after I had visited Delphi and had later written this poem that I read in Jane Harrison of Delphi's often forgotten association with Dionysus (my name-patron, by the way . . .).

"The Film" is a kind of shorthand narrative of initiation, rites of passage. I was to be reminded of "the corridor of booths" when later I came to read *Steppenwolf*, for these booths were akin to the "Magic Theater" of Hesse's novel. It seems as if these scenes of life's possibilities are viewed by the Young Heroes only after their encounter with the Goddess. But the "Nothing" with which the film (though not the poem) ends seems to imply that once they have passed through the rites and are each embarked on their voyages through life, these glimpses go under into forgetful-ness just as prophetic dreams are put aside and forgotten. "The film is over/we're out on the street"—the film's abrupt end has its counterpart in the life of the people who have watched it, abruptly ejected from the theater and into the street of their continuing existence. One reaction to the work of art is that of the artist's wife, who sadly leaves him because she feels he has, in his art, presented psychic secrets, committed desecration. But the "I" of the poem, whom the "Maker of Visions" brings to the very door of Home (to her own starting place, that is to say) seems, through not rejecting the experience of the work of art, to experience in her own life a parallel to what she has wit-nessed. "Home" no longer contains the powerful figure of the archetypal dominating Mother: having seen the Turtle Mother represented in the film it is as if the "I" has passed beyond this enormous waiting presence. The house is occupied only by things, not by a psychic presence. The "So be it" implies an end and a beginning. This seems to me a small example of how the absorbed elements of shared myth can join in dream with personal fictions to form a possible basis for what in the beginning of these notes I called "invented" or personal myth. It is a curious example because of its involutions: just as the actual poem is based on dream, so *in* the dream the "real-life" actions are affected by a dreamlike film.

Among the poems which carry the recurrent theme of pilgrimage, the last I will mention is a cluster or cycle called the "Olga Poems" *(The Sorrow Dance,* 1967). These are a kind of elegy written after the death of my sister in 1964. It could be described as a fragmentary account of her life— fragmentary because I knew her only in a fragmentary way, our lives having completely separated us for years at a time.

Here is, for the first time (among all those poems I have cited which are based on the underlying conception of life as what Keats so beautifully called "A Vale of Soulmaking"), a poem that brings the pilgrim to the end of his pilgrimage, as it were. All the others are written, one might say, on the road; this one looks back at a life that has ended, or come full circle. But the purpose of pilgrimage that I hope emerges is not merely what is known as "a good death"; the candle doesn't just get relit at the end of all the darkness, but is somehow to be miraculously kept alight all the way through. The spirit of here-and-now I had learned from Williams is united here with the romantic spirit of quest, of longing to wander toward other worlds. In one section of the "Olga Poems," one of the first of such dreamed worlds is remembered: "In Valentines/a root protrudes from the greensward several yards from its tree//we might raise like a trapdoor's handle, you said/and descend long steps to another country//where we would live without father or mother/and without longing for the upper world." But that would have been to deny the "unfolding" of life, to stop the pilgrimage when it had barely begun, to cut off the growth of the soul. And for a poem called "Joy," written after the "Olga Poems," and which could probably not have been written without my having taken that long look at Olga's life, I took as epigraph these words from Thoreau:

80

"You must love the crust of the earth on which you dwell. You must be able to extract nourishment out of a sandheap. You must have so good an appetite as this, else you will live in vain."

The "Didactic Poem" is of course a variant of the Homeric incident of the blood-drink given to the souls in Hades who sullenly speak only in payment for this draught they thirst for. The poem began (without reference to Charles Olson's magnificent poems "Newly Discovered Homeric Hymn" or "As the Dead Prey Upon Us," which take off from much the same point, and which though I knew them I seem to have forgotten in writing—and indeed, had I remembered them I would probably not have written this poem at all) by my wondering why this story had such an impact. Thinking about what the dead are to the individual psyche, it occurred to me that only those dead desire the blood-drink (and therefore exercise a compulsion upon us) who were unsatisfied in their lives, and who find a foothold in our "unlived lives" (the phrase is Rilke's—"unlived life, of which one can die"). The blood is the blood of the living. When a man is still trying to satisfy his parents, who died in disappointment at their own lives, by deeds not done for himself or for the living but for them, they are drinking his blood. And when young men die in wars originated by their elders, those elders, whether literally dead or living in the present hell of their own sins, are drinking those young men's blood. The poem became didactic or hortatory as realization turned to warning. We ourselves must abandon what is dead in us and live the good of our lives if we would break the cycle.

Finally, there's the poem "A Vision" (in *The Sorrow Dance*) which does not originate in dream but, more fully than any of my other poems, was a waking vision, quite unprepared for by any conscious thought, but accompanied by that understanding of what is happening that one also has, at least sometimes, while dreaming. The "action" on the part of the angelic protagonists is almost entirely interior,

81

a matter of *becoming aware,* yet it *is* action and takes the poem, I think, out of the static into the dramatic. It can be called mythic, because in it personages of another order of being, and concerning whom the poet had no preconceived metaphorical intention, entered the consciousness and stirred the soul.

Examination of my own work for the presence of myth has confirmed me in my belief that myth arises from within the poet and poem rather than being deliberately sought. I think I may have shown that dreams may be a more frequent and—in an age when the Western intellectual, along with the rest of the people, is rarely in live touch with a folkloric tradition of myth and epic—a more authentic source of myth in poetry than a scholarly knowledge would be, unless that scholarly knowledge is deeply imbedded in the imaginative life of the writer.

I am thinking here of the contrast between the many academic set-pieces on mythological themes—usually on Greek or Roman ones—which read like exercises in the gentle art of saying nothing elegantly or of evading the here-and-now (and seem like the last echoes of the long period when every gentleman could construe a page of Vergil or Ovid, yet feel in his pulses nothing of what they meant) —between these on the one hand and the poems of writers like Duncan, Olson, Pound, David Jones, in whom scholarship is an extension of intuitive knowledge. That acquired knowledge of a pre-existing mythology or mythologies can produce great poetry we have only to think of Yeats to see (though not, in my opinion, in the famous sonnet upon Leda and the swan). Yeats's conscious deliberate intention in the beginning was to stimulate a sense of pride and national identity in the Irish people by reviving their legends, but the myths themselves took over and infused his life, waking and sleeping, with their presence. Similarly, H. D. began with homage to gods desired by the will but still remote (or so the Greek spirits of her earlier poems seem to me) and came, through the practice of her devotional art, to unsought visions of Our Lady and to the visitation of great Angels. Or again, there is the way in which the profound longing for, and striving toward, a language and a form with which life might be quickened, renewed, grasped, gave to William Carlos Williams the majestic image of Paterson.

My emphasis on the eclectic does not imply that I think Christian symbolism has lost its power to inform the poem. In a convinced and fervent Christian poet like Margaret Avison, for instance, who seems to me in her most moving poems the direct heir both of George Herbert and of Gerard Manley Hopkins, there occurs that synthesis of personal experience and the shared, or cultural, inheritance of a tradition of emotive patterns which is myth-in-poetry at its most penetrating (i.e., which can most deeply penetrate the feeling-life of an empathic reader).[2]

A great advantage the Christian poet has is a more vivid sense of the yearly cycle. We all have the seasons; and the procession of festivals in all the different religions has, as we know, reference, whether directly or vestigially, to the cycle of planting, harvest, apparent death, and the resurgence of life, enacting the correspondences between the vegetable and spiritual worlds, as well as commemorating historical events of spiritual significance. The subscriber to any orthodoxy is reminded of these patterns by rites and festivals, and the eclectic can have some share in them all; but the idea of the Christian Year, in which the universals are embodied in the life of a single person, is capable of being charged with an emotive force that I personally feel is unequaled, and which, because Western literature, and therefore the languages of Western literature (with the exception of Yiddish), has for so many centuries been so deeply affected by it, can still reach non-Christians in some degree. However, it is an undeniable fact that there are today far more non-Christian than Christian poets, as indeed there are few poets who are adherents of any religion in

[2]See her book, *The Dumbfounding* (New York, W. W. Norton, 1966).

particular, and many who are atheists or agnostics. Even the impact of the seasons is diminished for those who live all year in great cities. The urban poet who is also a skeptic or rationalist is thrown back, I think, upon personal relations in an unprecedented degree; perhaps, despite a conscious disavowal of the mysterious and the sacred in such poets, a future mythology will arise in their work out of the *experience* of the sacred in the love of person for person.

Myth remains alive only when it retains its capacity to provoke, at a deep level, the "shock of recognition" and a sense of personal relevance. For it to affect the reader, it must in some degree have "happened" to the poet, happened in a more far-reaching, unforeseeable way than an allegory which he may think out, or write out, without ever wholly involving himself in it even for the time it takes him to write it. The Jew on the Day of Atonement, the Christian on Good Friday or Easter Day, experience a profound crisis of which the religiously unattached poet is deprived. But he does have, if he will trust them, the sources of renewal and inspiration to be found—though not sought —in dream and vision and archetypal revelation not dependent on a set of conscious beliefs, and in the events and intuitions of his daily life. Man is the animal that perceives analogies. Even when cut off from tradition, the correspondences that, if he holds open the doors of his understanding, he cannot but perceive, will form images that are myth. The intellect, if not distorted by divorce from the other capacities, is not obstructive to the experience of the mysterious.

The prospectus for this conference notes that "modern theologians often assert that 'modern man' is not addressed by myth; contemporary poets often continue to assume that 'modern man' is spoken to by it directly and profoundly." Perhaps what it comes down to is that the forms of myth say nothing if not informed by direct experience on the part of those who tell them, and *do* speak directly and profoundly to the reader in direct proportion to the degree of inwardness they have for the writer. An essential I have not been able even to touch on, for the obvious reason that to do so adequately would take too much time and would lead into endless discussion of technique and aesthetics, is of course the energy, precision, and music of his language. Without that, there is nothing. The early poems of my own which I discussed fail as myth more from lack of artistry than from lack of conviction. Conviction that does not find its proper language is not poetry, for poetry, as Mallarmé reminded us, is not made of ideas but of words; i.e., if they fail as myth it is because they fail as poems, as verbal constructions. Kinetic works of art are informed by conviction and artistry working synergically.

I will conclude with that poem of D. H. Lawrence's which more than any other seems to sum up the *kind* of knowledge from which myth in poetry can grow:

THERE ARE NO GODS

There are no gods, and you can please yourself
have a game of tennis, go out in the car, do some shopping,
    sit and talk, talk, talk,
with a cigarette browning in your fingers.
There are no gods, and you can please yourself—
go and please yourself—

But leave me alone, leave me alone, to myself!
and then in the room, whose is that presence
that makes the air so still and lovely to me?

Who is it that softly touches the sides of my breast
and touches me over the heart
so that my heart beats soothed, soothed, soothed and
    at peace?

Who is it smoothes the bedsheets like the cool
smooth ocean when the fishes rest on edge
in their own dream?

Who is it that clasps and kneads my naked feet, till
        they unfold,
till all is well, till all is utterly well? the
        lotus-lilies of the feet!

I tell you, it is no woman, it is no man, for I am alone.
And I fall asleep with the gods, the gods
that are not, or that are
according to the soul's desire,
like a pool into which we plunge, or do not plunge.

I have always had a strong love for looking at paintings—a love for color, for the thickness or thinness of paint, and for the miraculous coexistence of sensuous surface reality—brush marks and the grain of canvas showing through—with illusion, the depicted world to be entered. And in thinking about the process of writing poetry, I have often drawn analogies with the painting process, feeling a correspondence, for instance, between the intuited need in one poem for a limpid fluidity of diction and rhythm and the intuited need for transparent color and flowing line in a certain painting; or again, between the compositional need for strong and harsh outlines or heavy thick paint in one painting and for halting rhythms and heavy thick words in a certain poem. The standing back to regard the whole canvas from time to time, then returning to the close embrace of details, also has its parallel in the experience of writing a poem. Yet I have come to see that the art of photography shares with poetry a factor more fundamental: it makes its images by means anybody and everybody uses for the most banal purposes, just as poetry makes its structures, its indivisibilities of music and meaning, out of the same language used for utilitarian purposes, for idle chatter, or for uninspired lying.

Because of this resemblance in the conditions of the two arts—because the camera, like language, is put to constant nonartistic use, quotidian use by nonspecialists, as the painter's materials (though often misused) are not—a poet finds, I think, a kind of stimulation and confirmation in experiencing the work of photographic artists that is more specific, closer to his poetic activity, than the pleasure and love he feels in looking at paintings. I can often turn to

---

Written in response to a request from the photographic magazine, *Aperture,* and published as a kind of advertisement for it in *Stony Brook.*

fine photographs to help myself discover next steps in a poem I am writing: almost it's as if I can respond to such photographs *because* I'm a working poet, while my response to painting, intense though it is, is in some degree detached from my life as active artist, is a more passive receptivity.

Even though one may never write a poem directly inspired by a photograph, these images drawn from the same sources the poet's own eye can see (photography having, even at its most individual, subjective, or transformational, a relationship to the optical far more basic than that of painting) and which are transformed into high art through a medium of unexotic availability, connect at a deep level with the poetic activity; and are, in fact, possible sources—as nature is source—for the poet, to a degree that paintings are not, even to someone who loves them as much as I do. Perhaps another way of saying it would be that photographs—and I don't mean only documentary photographs—teach the poet to see better, or renew his seeing, in ways closer to the *kind* of seeing he needs to do for his own work, than paintings do; while the stimulus of paintings for the poet *as poet,* i.e., their specific value for him aside from his general human enjoyment of them, may have more to do with his compositional gesture-sense (as music may) than with the visual.

"Songs are thoughts, sung out with the breath when people are moved by great forces and ordinary speech no longer suffices," said Orpingalik, the Eskimo poet, to Rasmussen.[1]

We are living in a time of dread and of awe, of wanhope and of wild hope; a time when joy has to the full its poignance of a mortal flower, and deep content is rare as some fabled Himalayan herb. Ordinary speech no longer suffices.

Yet much of what is currently acclaimed, in poetry as well as in prose, does not go beyond the most *devitalized* ordinary speech. Like the bleached dead wheat of which so much American bread is made (supposedly "enriched" by returning to the worthless flour a small fraction of the life that once was in it) such poems bloat us but do not nourish. "How could documentary realism have any value at all," Proust wrote in *Time Retrieved*,[2] "since it is *underneath* little details such as it notes down that reality is hidden—the grandeur in the distant sound of an airplane or in the lines of the spires of St.-Hilaire, the past contained in the savor of a madeleine, and so forth—and they have no meaning if one does not extract it from them. Stored up little by little in our memory, it is the chain of all the inaccurate impressions, in which there is nothing left of what we really experienced, which constitutes for us our thoughts, our life, reality, and a so-called 'art taken from

A lecture given for the Society for the Arts, Religion, and Contemporary Culture in New York, January 1970. Before the lecture I played a record of the Jefferson Airplane's "We Can Be Together."

[1]Quoted in Sir Maurice Bowra's *Primitive Song* (New York, New American Library, 1963).

[2]Quoted in *The Creative Vision* (New York, Grove, 1960), edited by Haskell M. Block and Herman Salinger, which cites the Random House edition of *The Past Recaptured* (1932)—adding, however, that the text of the selection has been revised "in accordance with" the 1954 Gallimard edition. I myself use the word "retrieved" in place of "recaptured" because of a personal preference.

life' would simply reproduce that lie, an art as thin and poor as life itself [as that superficial, lying life, that is to say] without any beauty, a repetition of what our eyes see and our intelligence notes [again I gloss this as meaning superficial intelligence as distinct from our *understanding*], so wearisome, so futile that one is at a loss to understand where the artist who devotes himself to that finds the joyous, energizing spark that can stimulate him to activity and enable him to go forward with his task. The grandeur of real art, on the contrary . . . is to rediscover, grasp again, and lay before us *that reality from which we become more and more separated as the formal knowledge which we substitute for it grows in thickness and imperviousness —that reality which there is grave danger we might die without having known and yet which is simply our life.*"

Rilke too spoke of that grave danger: "Unlived life, of which one can die," he called it.

Much of the prevalent poetry I find so inadequate to our needs (and which I sometimes think of, perhaps unfairly, as the Midwestern Common Style) derives its "documentary realism," ironically, from one of the greatest of modern poets, William Carlos Williams. What Williams said about the American idiom, about the necessity, for a live poetry, of drawing upon the diction and rhythms of the vernacular; and what he did himself, both in that respect and in revealing the neglected worlds that lie about us, has been appropriated, misunderstood, and banalized by innumerable published and unpublished poets, whether or not they know and acknowledge the source of their practices. What began as a healthy reaction, a turning away with relief from sterile academic rhetorics, has proliferated in an unexampled production of *notations:* poems which tell of things seen or done, but which, lacking the focus of that energetic, compassionate, questioning spirit that infused even the most fragmentary of Williams's poems, do not impart a sense of the experiencing of seeing or doing, or of the *value* of such experience—do not impart that keener sense of being alive

90

which Wallace Stevens claimed was one of the essential functions of poetry.

The lack of a unifying intelligence, of the implicit presence of an interpreting spirit behind the notation, is associated—and not accidentally—with a lack of music. By music I don't mean mere euphony, but that verbal music that consists of the consonance of sound and rhythm with the meaning of the words. These wizened offshoots of Williams's zeal for the recognition of the rhythmic structure of the American language have made the mistake of supposing he was advocating a process of reproduction, of facile imitation—whereas what he was after was origins, springs of vitality: the rediscovery, wherever it might turn up (in language or incident), of that power of the imagination which first conceived and grasped *newness* in a new world, though the realization was ever and again nipped in the bud, blighted, covered over with old habits and strangling fears. Read him—the short early and later poems, and *Paterson,* and the longer poems of the great final flowering, from *The Desert Music* on; and the prose: *In the American Grain,* and essays like "The American Background," as well as the specifically "literary" essays such as those on Pound, Sandburg, or Stein, and the unclassifiable pieces such as "The Simplicity of Disorder." It is all there, said many ways, but clear and profound. Williams emphasizes the necessity for the poet to deal with specifics, to locate himself in history—but never at the expense of the imagination. "They found," he wrote in "The American Background" of the first settlers, "that they had not only left England but that they had arrived somewhere else: at a place whose pressing reality demanded not only a tremendous bodily devotion but as well, and more importunately, great powers of adaptability, a complete reconstruction of their most intimate cultural make-up, to accord with the new conditions."

It is the failure, over and over, to make that adaptation—the timid clinging to forms created out of other circumstances—that he deplores, grieves over; the rare leap

91

of imagination into the newly necessary, the necessary new, that he rejoices in. When he blasts Sandburg (in 1948, when Sandburg's *Complete Poems* came out), it is for formlessness, for lack of invention. If he underestimated Whitman (and sometimes he did), it was because he believed Whitman had failed to go far enough and to provide a structural model others after him could have used to go further —so that Whitman, by default, set American poetry back rather than advancing it (though surely this was equally due to the unreadiness of any young writers of Whitman's time to recognize what he was doing and pick up from it). Williams criticizes Whitman and Sandburg, both of whom dealt with homespun "content" and whose diction was distinctively American; and praised Poe, Cummings, Pound, Marianne Moore, none of whom consistently, and some of whom never, wrote in simple imitation, reproduction, of the American idiom, as understood by some of those who today take Williams's name in vain in defense of their own banalities. Since the poetry I have in mind is widespread, and some of its perpetrators are still young (though usually not much under thirty) and perhaps will grow out of what may be charitably construed as a necessary phase in their personal development, I want to avoid quotations that single out one or two for attack; so instead I shall try to describe the *kind* of poem I mean, as if I were providing field marks as in an ornithological handbook. Usually one of these poems, inadequate to our need, begins with—or at least its first short sentence includes—the personal pronoun. This is, of course, far from being an impermissible thing under all circumstances; in poetry nothing is impermissible if it is alive and if it functions. But in the poetry I am identifying, this beginning with "I" reveals the quite unconscious egotism of the writer, who takes for granted our interest in him but fails, in what follows, to give us a contextual reason for that interest. The ubiquity of the personal pronoun in the romantic tradition is justified whenever the responses of the poet are unashamedly and overtly the subject of the

92

poem, but this validity is undermined when there is a pretense of objectivity. The kind of poems I am thinking of are banal, prosaic, even journalistic on the one hand, and on the other they thrust forward the person of the poet in a curious gesture compounded of self-pity and braggadocio, an unacknowledged manifestation of romanticism, but of a romanticism misunderstood and debased. The poet then proceeds to relate some incident seen, and frequently to inform us, more or less indirectly, that he is in his thirties, an instructor or assistant professor, has or had a wife, half wishes he didn't, and goes in for a good deal of beer drinking with other instructors and assistant professors. The incident described (and it is described rather than vividly presented) is of a trivially nostalgic nature and is treated, naturally enough, not with passion but with what is called "wry humor" (a euphemism for weak cynicism). These thoughts and impressions do not become songs, the images do not flare, because the deep unconscious sources of song and image are battened under hatches. In reaction to these banalities there exists an equally prevalent and equally inadequate poetry that I think of as *mechanical surrealism*—the appearance of surrealism without its genuine content: poems strung together out of notebook jottings saved for a rainy day, poems that do not explore but contrive, a fake, deliberate irrationality, works not of imagination, not of fancy—which has its genuine light charms—but of *spurious* imagination.

Underneath surface differences of content these two kinds of poetry are really very similar, and this underlying similarity is attested to in the lack of distinct formal differences between them. Whether the poet writes of beer cans, the Sunday funnies, and provincial malaise, or of strenuously strange and vague phantasmagoria, these competent jottings remain . . . competent jottings, rhythmically and sonically undistinguished, indistinguishable.

What then do we need? We need a new realization of *the artist as translator*. I am not talking about translation

93

from one language to another, but of the translation of experience, and the translation of the reader into other worlds. Let me quote Proust again: "I perceived that, to describe these impressions, to write that essential book, the only true book, a great writer does not need to invent it, in the current sense of the term, since it already exists in each of us, but merely to translate it. The duty and task of a writer are those of a translator." What did he mean? Let us examine the word. It comes from the past participle of the Latin *transferre*, "to transfer": to carry across, to ferry to the far shore. What Proust calls documentary realism at best only *relates;* that is, it carries us *back*, not forward; the process has that "photographic" fidelity he speaks of as insufficient for the complexity of our experience.[3] Since almost all experience goes by too fast, too superficially for our apperception, what we most need is not to *re*-taste it (just as superficially) but really to taste *for the first time* the gratuitous, the autonomous identity of its essence. My 1865 Webster's defines *translation* as "being conveyed from one place to another; removed to heaven without dying." We must have an art that translates, conveys us to the heaven of that deepest reality which otherwise "we may die without ever having known"; that *transmits* us there, not in the sense of bringing the information to the receiver but of putting the receiver in the place of the event—alive. *Transmit* (like *mission* and *missive*) in English comes from the same Latin root *(mittere,* "to send") as *mettre* and *mettere* in French and Italian, both meaning "to put." It is as if, therefore, in the English *transmit* one has the sense of being at the sending end and in the Italian *trasmettere* that of being at the receiving end; and I am now using the English word with this latter feeling, as if it said "transput." If a poetic translation, or attempted act of translation, is weak or an operation of mere fancy, it does not "increase our

[3]I'm using the term *photographic* idiomatically. For the art of photography I have every respect.

sense of living, of being alive," but instead removes us from reality in a lapse of perception, taking us not deeper into but farther away from the world—a kind of dying. We must have poems that move away from the discursively confessional, descriptive, dilutedly documentary *and* from the fancies of inauthentic surrealism to the intense, wrought, bodied-forth and magical—poems that make us cry out with Carlyle, "Ah, but this sings!"

A poetry that merely describes, and that features the trivial egotism of the writer (an egotism that obstructs any profound self-explorations), is not liberated from contingency and does not fulfill what David Jones has called the *sine qua non* of art, "the gratuitous setting up of sacred objects to the unknown god." "By that sort of paradox," he says also, "man can act gratuitously only because he is dedicated to the gods. When he falls from dedication . . . the utile is all he knows and his works take on something of the nature of the works of the termite."[4] Poetry that is merely "self-expressive" in the current sense of the term is not even ultimately utile to the greatest degree, for while it temporarily "relieves feelings" or builds ego, it does not, cannot, give the writer—and certainly fails to give the reader—the deeper satisfaction of a work of autonomy and gratuitousness.

Here I must stop to distinguish between the temporarily therapeutic self-expression which is equivalent to a gesture, expending its whole substance in the act—a simple function, a letting off of steam—and the disinterested expression of being, which Walter F. Otto (as quoted by Kerenyi in his book *Asklepios)* describes in the following passage: "Wherever a creature emits even the simplest sequence of musical tones, it evinces a state of mind entirely different from that which occurs in the uncontrolled outcry. And this state of mind is the essential when we ask about the nature

[4]See David Jones's essay "Art and Democracy" in *Epoch and Artist* (London, Faber and Faber, 1959).

95

of the primordial musicality. It is often unmistakable that the song, even of animals, is sufficient unto itself, that is not intended to serve any purpose or produce any sort of effect. Such songs have aptly been characterized as *self*-expressions. *They arise from an intrinsic need of the creature to give expression to its being.*" (my italics) It is clear, I think, that here the emphasis must be on the word *self—self*-expression, the expression of the creature's very being, not self-*expression,* the blowing off of steam. As Otto continues, it becomes clear too how *self*- expression relates to the dynamic, kinetic concept of translation: "But self-expression demands a presence, for which it occurs. This presence is the environing world. No creature exists for itself alone; all are in the world, and this means: each one in its own world. Thus the singing creature expresses itself in and for its world. In expressing *itself* [my italics] it becomes happily aware of the world, it cries out joyfully, it lays claim to the world." (And here I would add, "Or it becomes *un*happily aware of the world, but its cry of *self*-expression is still an affirmative act, for all awareness, all acknowledgment of self and world, is essentially affirmation." As Jane Harrison reminded us, "Aristotle said that poetry had two forms, praise which issued in hymns and heroic poetry, blame which yielded . . . satire. . . . We analyze and distinguish but at bottom is the one double-edged impulse, the impulse toward life."[5] "The lark rises," Otto goes on, "to dizzy heights in the column of air that is its world; without other purpose, it is at the same time the language of the world's reality. A living knowledge rings in the song. When man makes music he doubtless has a much broader and richer environment. But the phenomenon is fundamentally the same. He too must express himself in tones, without purpose and regardless of whether or not he is heard by others. But here again *self*-expression and

[5]The quote is from Jane Harrison's classic *Prolegomena to the Study of Greek Religion.*

revelation of the world are one and the same. As he expresses himself the reality of the being that enfolds him speaks in his tones."

It may be objected that if the reality of an individual's being is indeed banal, then his banal expression of it should be accepted as valid. I disagree because I do not believe in the intrinsic banality of any existence. I believe with Carlyle that "no most gifted eye can exhaust the significance of any object"[6]—and if this inexhaustible significance is to be found in things, inanimate and animate, how can it not be true of man? But, says Rilke, "If a thing is to speak to you, you must for a certain time regard it as the only thing that exists, the unique phenomenon that your diligent and exclusive love has placed at the center of the universe, something the angels serve that very day upon that matchless spot."[7] And the documentary realist, whether his material is external—say, the boredom of Midwestern highways—or more apparently internal—say, the therapeutic description of his feelings—produces banalities of form, of language, because he does not bring to that material the ecstatic *attention*, the *intensity*, that would penetrate to its reality.

The word ecstasy is the key here; but it must be recognized that I am not asking for a poetry *about* ecstasy, a poetry whose subject matter is unnaturally confined to what used to be called the sublime or lofty, nor for a new Symbolism that would again, like the Symbolism of the late nineteenth century, quench itself by disgust, a contempt for the material world that takes aesthetics down the road of disdainful asceticism and ultimately into an abstention even from words themselves, preferring silence to the blood and smell of language. No, what I am talking about is on the contrary an ecstasy of attention, a passion for the thing

[6]From "The Hero as Poet" in Thomas Carlyle's *On Heroes, Hero-Worship and the Heroic in History* (1841).

[7]Rainer Maria Rilke, *Selected Letters,* translated by R.F.C. Hull (London, Macmillan, 1946). p. 324.

known, that shall be more, not less, sensuous, and which by its intensity shall lead the writer into a deeper, more vibrant language: and so translate the reader too into the heavens and hells that lie about us in all seemingly ordinary objects and experiences: a supernatural poetry.

By *supernatural* something other than the *surreal* is meant —a penetration by the imaginative faculty through to the meaning of appearances. Many works of surrealist art do so penetrate, but surrealism as a mode of creation is only one of many aesthetic approaches.

Surrealism may attain to the supernatural (e.g., Magritte, Breton) but is only one of its forms, and not perhaps its most satisfying one: Rembrandt, Cézanne, Giotto, Homer, Shakespeare, Dante satisfy more deeply, they engage the reason *as well* as the unconscious and intuitive, and the more elements common to us all that a work of art draws upon the more totally it can move us. And that term "move" should be thought of very literally—i.e., parts, or all, of our being are *set in motion* by works of art.

Since I believe there is a most intimate relationship between the quality of a person's life, its abundance or sterility, his integrity, and the quality of his poetry, it is not irrelevant to say that, judging by some—not a few—I have met on my travels, the people who write banal poetry and, to almost the same extent, those who in desperation make up a fake surrealism, usually seem to be the same academics who talk a liberal line concerning education and politics (and often, as teachers, are genial and popular) but who, when it comes to some crucial issue, such as a student protest, will not commit themselves far enough to endanger their own security. Which comes first, the chicken or the egg? Is their poetry banal because their lives are banal, or vice versa? I think it works both ways. If these people committed themselves, took risks, and did not let themselves be dominated by the pursuit of "security," their daily lives would be so changed, so infused with new experiences and with the new energy that often comes with them, that inevitably their poetry would change too (though obviously this would not ensure better poems unless they were gifted in the first place). But on the other hand, if they could manage to put themselves in a new, more dynamic, less suppressive relationship to their own inner lives and to the language, then they might discover their outer lives moving in a revolutionary way. So the process is dual, and can be approached from either direction.

And for myself—not without anguish, not without fear, not without the daily effort of rousing myself out of the inertia and energy-sapping nostalgia that would cling to old ways, to that dying bird-in-hand that's falsely supposed to be worth two free ones chirping in the bushes—I believe our survival demands revolution, both cultural and political. If we are to survive the disasters that threaten, and survive our own struggle to *make it new*—a struggle I believe we have no choice but to commit ourselves to—we need tremendous transfusions of imaginative energy. If it is indeed revolution we are moving toward, we need life, and abundantly—we need poems of the spirit, to inform us of the essential, to help us *live* the revolution. And if instead it be the Last Days—then we need to taste the dearest, freshest drops before we die—why bother with anything less than that, the essential?

Wallace Stevens wrote, "The poet feels *abundantly* the poetry of everything."[8] We must not go down into the pit we have dug ourselves by our inhumanity without some taste, however bitter, of that abundance. But if there is still hope of continued life on earth, of a new life, the experience of that abundance which poetry can bring us is a revolutionary stimulus. It can awaken us, from our sloth, even yet.

It is time that I explained my title. I was asked for a title long before I had given one thought to what I might

---

[8]Quoted from "Adagia" in Wallace Stevens's *Opus Posthumous* (New York, Knopf, 1957).

want to say. Therefore I decided to consult the *I Ching*, and I obtained the hexagram Great Possessions, and sent that in as the subject of my lecture. However, it did not come clear to me what Great Possessions were until I was halfway through writing these pages. As I wrote I came to see that, to my understanding, what was meant by the term in this context was simply (going back to Proust again), "That reality from which we become more and more separated as the formal knowledge which we substitute for it grows in thickness and imperviousness—that reality which there is grave danger we might die without having known and yet which is simply our life." The fact that, on the very day I wrote this page, I picked up a copy of Thoreau's notebooks which happened to be lying around, and opened it at random to the following entry, is itself a part of our Great Possessions, for they are everywhere about us, neglected till we live at that pitch of attention that reveals them to us: "Thurs. Dec. 10 1840. I discover a strange track in the snow, and learn that some migrating otter has made across from the river to the wood, by my yard and the smith's shop, in the silence of the night.—I cannot but smile at my own wealth, when I am thus reminded that every chink and cranny of nature is full to overflowing.—That each instant is crowded full of great events." Artists must go more deeply into their dormant, unused, idle "great possessions." We must vary the structure and kinds of revelation—discover a verbal "magic realism" that will energize the understanding in many and precise ways. "You must change your life."[9] Perhaps all authentic art implies that need for change, i.e., it shows up the vagueness and slackness of ninety per cent of our lives—so that art is in its nature revolutionary, a factor instigating radical change, even while (giving "the shock of recognition," and naming and praising *what is*) it is con-

[9]Quoted from Rilke's poem "Torso of an Archaic Apollo."

servative in a real sense. As alternative titles I considered using "To Find the World" or "The Further Step."

That there is a hunger for *translation* is plain; and it is above all the young who are hungry. The attempt to use drugs not as an escape from the pain of life but as "expanders of consciousness" is clear evidence of that. And while with rare exceptions the many young men and women I know are not creating a poetry that would even begin to appease that hunger, they *are* making in their music an ecstatic and poetic world that can be genuinely magical. If one will listen freely and fully, one finds that the best of this music translates one into new realms of perception and performs the task Wallace Stevens said the poem must perform: it "stimulates the sense of living and of being alive." The words of these songs are important but they are not poems, they are the words of songs, inseparable not only from the melody-line but from the total orchestration. Rock music—like other forms of music—is not a substitute for poetry. But in its passion and vigor and incantatory effect it can show us, I think, some of what is lacking from a good deal of contemporary writing.[10]

But I don't want to give the impression that the whole poetry scene looks bleak to me. On the contrary, alongside the inadequate I do find much of what I crave—and perhaps indeed it is on the increase. The poetry of, for instance, Robert Duncan, has for twenty years been appeasing my own hunger. The importance of Allen Ginsberg is precisely that he has given us poems of ecstatic revelation (though sometimes they are limited structurally by a habitual rhetoric that leads to too many generalizations, perhaps). This poem by Hayden Carruth is a tribute to Ginsberg, to his authenticity and poetic power:

[10]This was in 1970. Rereading this in 1973, I find myself somewhat out of sympathy with my enthusiasm for pop music, which has waned, or at least changed its focus.

THAW

. . . *sonnet for Allen Ginsberg*

fuzz of snow browning in lastyear's haystubble,
    the pasture's winter-starved moss
lionskin flung rumpled, moist, eaten, crushed eyes in
    the mange-fur
old leaves, eddy and sparrow-dance, the world-flakes,
    get up they whimper
matter underfoot, sun's hairs, abandoned nests, coarse
    littleness, litter
mouse-cry, shrew-cry, snake-cry breaking against my
    ankles, set agony of small things, their glasslike sex
the stone's huge fame also, crevice-speaking, ancient
    in lichen, menhir for what slow generations gone—
and again I see the universe around me; decaying vision,
    mine so long, the filth of it so long
blowing, mindless trash of stars, comets gasping down,
    space-dust
clouds of broken magnetism, bones of god-eaten nebulae
stirred in this warmish foreign wind, futile, useless—
    what good in it, ice will come again!
say
allen-what-do-they-call-you
mindpetal, spectre, strangest jew, cityboy
farther from here than purple tao—far!—your little
    mousetrap books
clapping love insistent, my own fingers painted and
    pinched again after this time
look out, peer down, street under your high small window
greasy ginko, acacia, rubble, I don't know, not mine—
    do you see a wind?
straw-rasp of papers, twigs shining?—what flows in
    your city, what stirs?
speak of it one more time for me, heart's cataclysm in
    the worn riffs of my years

in the beat of rote-pulse this new, this lifting, my
    pure impulse here
litany cracked open, wind across distance,
    a poke-through, such long ways
so that ragged solitude be warm, this pasture right
    for being—
right, right and easy, some cognizance, humanly,
    anything but heart-gape, void of misplacement—
this wind's connection come growling now low in the hills
    like the cityvoice, many-toned, horns and angers,
        terrors,
    far echoes, proceedings, prowling this way in lethean
    twistings, whispers among firs, spruces
or like smoke on the long wind, or like pieces of the
    rims of circles come rippling up this long inlet—
yours dominantly there now, gingerly, your tender
    cupbearings, self-song, not strange to me
soft breathings hard against fact, sudden, like ben
    webster once, and valid, magnanimous—
o poet, ragged heartsinger, wind-fellow, friend of mine!

The poetry, especially the recent poetry, of Galway Kin-
nell, is another instance of the kind of revelation in language
that I hunger for:

Excerpts from *The Book of Nightmares:*

5
Sancho Fergus my boychild was born
with such great shoulders
his head
came out, the rest of him
stuck, and he opened his eyes, his head
all alone out in the room, he squinted

103

with pained, barely unglued eyes on the
          nine-months blood
splashing beneath him
on the floor
and almost smiled,
I thought, almost forgave it all in advance.

And when he came wholly forth
I took him
in my hands and held him up and bent over
and smelt
the black, glistening fur
of his head: as the figment
of her unborn children's bewilderment bent over
the new-born planet *Earth* and smelt
the grasslands, and the ferns.

From another section:

2

I know there is so much of me
wasted,
so much we could have been or done
that we held ourselves back from,
out of fear,
or out of the dream we had but one thing to be or to do,
or out of the faith a life is richer lived among paths
          not taken.

Yet now
it seems nothing,
nothing that once touched the web of the possible
could keep itself
right down to the last, beyond knowing.

And how clear the air becomes, before dark.

7

Sancho Fergus,
don't cry!

Or else, cry.

On the body,
on the blued flesh, when it is
laid out, see if you can find on it
the one flea,
which is laughing.

Such poems are not narrowly "political" in content, cer-
tainly, yet a strong political awareness operates in them
as a subcurrent. And both of these poets are among those
who believe poetry and politics need not, and indeed
cannot, be kept apart. Galway Kinnell worked in Louisiana
as a civil rights activist and later toured the country in sup-
port of Resist. Hayden Carruth's health has made it impossi-
ble for him to engage in similar actions, but he is a lifelong
radical who has recalled recently that "Twenty years ago
I was greatly puzzled by the question of how to break into
the autonomous poem of the 1940s and early 50s with my
radical concerns. . . . My own early political experiments
were mostly dismal, not poems at all but rants and curses.
Now we have had a decade rich in further experiments. . . .
The political content of poetry is seen to be quite at ease
in its esthetic function. We wonder why we were ever
puzzled." What has happened in this decade is that just
those poets whose work is least banal, who most frequently
and wonderfully avoid "documentary realism" and achieve
the "supernatural" are the most politically aware, also, and
consequently there are no sharp dividing lines in their work
between "political" and "private" content. Ginsberg and
Duncan, Gary Snyder and (in his recent work) Robert Bly,
as well as the two poets I have quoted, provide notable

examples of this interpenetration—but it is also true of many other poets who give us what I think we need when "ordinary speech no longer suffices." The poet in our time, "moved by great forces," must live in the body as actively as he lives in his head; he must learn to extend himself into whatever actions he can perform, in order to be "part of the solution and not part of the problem"; he must do whatever he can see to do to bring down the World Federation of Death, Inc. If he does not struggle against war and oppression, he will negate whatever his words may say, and will soon have no world to say them in.

But for a poet the attention to things and people, to the passing moments filled to the brim with past, present, and future, to the Great Possessions that are our real life, is inseparable from attention to language and form. And he must recognize not only that poetry is intrinsically revolutionary but that it is so not by virtue of talking *about* any one subject rather than another (though if he has political concerns they may not be excluded, and *not* to have political concerns—in the broad and deep sense of the term—is surely impossible to the aware adult in the last quarter of the twentieth century). But whether content in any poem is huge or minuscule, funny or sad, angry or joyful, it can only be deeply and truly revolutionary, only *be* poetry, *"song that suffices our need,"* by being *in its very substance of sound and vision* an ecstasy and a giving of life.

The poet is in labor. She has been told that it will not hurt but it has hurt so much that pain and struggle seem, just now, the only reality. But at the very moment when she feels she will die, or that she is already in hell, she hears the doctor saying, "Those are the shoulders you are feeling now"—and she knows the head is out then, and the child is pushing and sliding out of her, insistent, a poem.

The poet is a father. Into the air, into the fictional landscape of the delivery room, wholly man-made, cluttered with shining hard surfaces, steel and glass—ruthlessly illuminated, dominated by brilliant whitenesses—into this alien human scene emerges, slime-covered, skinny-legged, with a head of fine black hair, the remote consequence of a dream of his, acted out nine months before, the rhythm that became words, the words that were spoken, written down.

The poet is being born. Blind, he nevertheless is aware of a new world around him, the walls of the womb are gone, something harsh enters his nose and mouth and lungs, and he uses it to call out to the world with what he finds is his voice, in a cry of anger, pathos, or is it pure announcement?—he has no tears as yet, much less laughter. And some other harshness teases his eyes, premonition of sight, a promise that begins at once to be fulfilled. A sharp smell of disinfectant is assaulting his new nostrils; flat, hard, rattling sounds multiply, objects being placed on glass surfaces, a wheeled table pushes out of the way, several voices speaking; hands are holding him, moving on his skin, doing things to his body—wetness, dry softness, and then up-ness, downness, moving-along-ness: to stillness in some kind of container, and the extraordinary experience, lasting an eternity,

Written for a symposium on the question, "Is There a Purely Literary Study?" held at Geneseo, New York, in April 1967.

of lying upon a permanently flat surface—and finally close-ness to something vaguely familiar, something warm that interposes a soothing voice between him and all else until he sleeps.

It is two years later. The poet is in a vast open space covered by rectangular gray cobblestones. In some of the crevices between them there is bright green moss. If he pokes it with a finger it feels cold, it gives under pressure but is slightly prickly. His attention is whirled away from it by a great beating of wings around him and a loud roucouing. People with long legs who surround him are afraid he will take fright at the flock of pigeons, but he laughs in wild pleasure as they put lumps of bread into his hands for him to throw to the birds. He throws with both hands, and the pigeons vanish over his head and some-one says, Cathedral. See the big building, it's a Cathedral. But he sees only an enormous door, a mouth, darkness inside it. There is a feather on his coat. And then he is indoors under a table in the darkish room, among the legs of the table and of the people, the peoples' feet in shoes, one pair without shoes, empty shoes kicked off nearby. Emerging unseen he steps hard on something, a toy train belonging to another child, and it breaks, and there is a great commo-tion and beating of wings again and loud voices, and he alone is silent in the midst of it, quite silent and alone, and the birds flying and the other child crying over its broken train and the word cathedral, yes, it is ten years later and the twin towers of it share the gray of the cobble-stones in the back of a large space in his mind where flying buttresses and flying pigeons mean cathedral and the silence he knows is inside the great door's darkness is the same silence he maintained down among the feet and legs of adults who beat their wings up above him in the dark air and vanished into the sky.

It is Time that pushed them into the sky, and he has been living ten, twenty, thirty years; he has read and forgot-ten thousands of books, and thousands of books have entered

108

him with their scenes and people, their sounds, ideas, logics, irrationalities, are singing and dancing and walking and crawling and shouting and keeping still in his mind, not only in his mind but in his way of moving his body and in his actions and decisions and in his dreams by night and by day and in the way he puts one word before another to pass from the gate of an avenue and into the cathedral that looms at the far end of it holding silence and darkness in its inner space as a finger's-breadth of moss is held between two stones.

All the books he has read are in the poet's mind (having arrived there by way of his eyes and ears, his apperceptive brain-centers, his heartbeat, his arteries, his bones) as it grasps a pen with which to sign yes or no. Life or death? Peace or war?

He has read what Rilke wrote:[1]

> . . . verses are not, as people imagine, simply feelings (we have those soon enough); they are experiences. In order to write a single poem, one must see many cities, and people, and things; one must get to know animals and the flight of birds, and the gestures that flowers make when they open to the morning. One must be able to return to roads in unknown regions, to unexpected encounters, to partings long foreseen; to days of childhood that are still unexplained, and to parents whom one had to hurt when they brought one some joy and one did not grasp it (it was a joy for somebody else); to childhood illnesses that begin so strangely with such a number of profound and grave transformations, to days spent in rooms withdrawn and quiet and to mornings by the sea, to the sea itself, to oceans, to nights of travel that rushed along loftily and flew with all the stars—and still it is not enough to be able

[1]From *The Notebooks of Malte Laurids Brigge* (1908).

to think of all this. There must be memories of many nights of love, each one unlike the others, of the screams of women in labor, and of women in childbed, light and blanched and sleeping, shutting themselves in. But one must also have been beside the dying, must have sat beside the dead in a room with open windows and with fitful noises. And still it is not yet enough, to have memories. One must be able to forget them when they are many and one must have the immense patience to wait till they are come again. For the memories themselves are still nothing. Not till they have turned to blood within us, to glance and gesture, nameless and no longer to be distinguished from ourselves—not till then can it happen that in a most rare hour the first word of a poem arises in their midst and goes forth from them.

This the poet has known, and he has known in his own flesh equivalent things. He has seen suddenly coming round a corner the deep-lined, jowled faces and uncertain, unfocusing eyes, never meeting his for more than an unwilling second, of men of power. All the machines of his life have directed upon him *their* power, whether of speed or flickering information or disembodied music. He has seen enormous mountains from above, from higher than eagles ever fly; and skimmed upstream over the strong flow of rivers; and crossed in a day the great oceans his ancestors labored across in many months. He has sat in a bathtub listening to Bach's *St. Matthew Passion*, he has looked up from the death of Socrates, disturbed by some extra noise amid the jarring and lurching of the subway train and the many rhythmic rattlings of its parts, and seen one man stab another and a third spring from his seat to assist the wounded one. He has seen the lifted fork pause in the air laden with its morsel of TV dinner as the eyes of the woman holding

110

it paused for a moment at the image on the screen that showed a bamboo hut go up in flames and a Vietnamese child run screaming toward the camera—and he has seen the fork move on toward its waiting mouth, and the jaws continue their halted movement of mastication as the next image glided across the screen.

He has breathed in dust and poetry, he has breathed out dust and poetry, he has written:

> Slowly men and women move in life,
> cumbered.
> The passing of sorrow, the passing
> of joy. All awareness
>
> is the awareness of time.
> Passion,
> however it seems to leap and pounce,
> is a slow thing.
> It blunders,
> cracking twigs in the woods of the world.

He has read E. M. Forster's words, "Only connect," and typed them out and pasted them on the wall over his desk along with other sayings:

> The task of the poet is to make clear to himself, and thereby to others, the temporal and eternal questions which are astir in the age and community to which he belongs.
>
> —Ibsen

> We have the daily struggle, inescapable and deadly serious, to seize upon the word and bring it into the directest possible contact with all that is felt, seen, thought, imagined, experienced.
>
> —Goethe

The task of the church is to keep open communication between man and God.

—Swedenborg

And below this the poet has written, "For *church* read *poet*. For *God* read *man and his imagination, man and his senses, man and man, man and nature–well, maybe "god," then, or "the gods"* . . ."

What am I saying?

I am saying that for the poet, for the man who *makes* literature, there is no such thing as an isolated study of literature. And for those who desire to know what the poet has made, there is therefore no purely literary study either. Why "therefore"? Because the understanding of a result is incomplete if there is ignorance of its process. The literary critic or the teacher of literature is merely scratching a section of surface if he does not live out in his own life some experience of the multitudinous interactions in time, space, memory, dream, and instinct that at every word tremble into synthesis in the work of a poet, or if he keeps his reading separate from his actions in a box labeled "aesthetic experiences." The interaction of life on art and of art on life is continuous. Poetry is necessary to a whole man, and that poetry be not divided from the rest of life is necessary to *it*. Both life and poetry fade, wilt, shrink, when they are divorced.

Literature—the writing of it, the study of it, the teaching of it—is a part of your lives. It *sustains* you, in one way or another. Do not allow that fatal divorce to take place between it and your actions.

It was Rilke, the most devoted of poets, the one who gave himself most wholly to the service of his art, who wrote:

> . . . art does not ultimately tend to produce more artists. It does not mean to call anyone over to it, indeed it has always been my guess that

112

it is not concerned at all with any effect. But while its creations, having issued irresistibly from an inexhaustible source, stand there strangely quiet and surpassable among things, it may be that involuntarily they become somehow exemplary for *every* human activity by reason of their innate disinterestedness, freedom and intensity. . . .[2]

For as much as the artist in us is concerned with *work*, the realization of it, its existence and duration quite apart from ourselves—we shall only be wholly in the right when we understand that even this most urgent realization of a higher reality appears, from some last and extreme vantage point, only as a means to win something once more invisible, something inward and unspectacular—a saner state in the midst of our being.[3]

He is saying, in these two passages from letters, that though the work of art does not aim at effect but is a thing imbued with life, that *lives* that life for its own sake, it nevertheless *has* effect; and that that effect is ultimately moral. And morality, at certain points in history, of which I believe this is one—this year, even if not this day—demands of us that we sometimes leave our desks, our classrooms, our libraries, and manifest in the streets, and by radical political actions, that love of the good and beautiful, that love of life and its arts, to which otherwise we pay only lip service. Last spring (1966) at a Danforth Conference, Tom Bradley, one of the speakers, said (I quote from my notes): "Literature is dynamite because it asks—proposes—moral questions and seeks to define the nature and worth of man's life." (And

[2]From a letter to Rudolf Bödlander, *Letters of Rainer Maria Rilke*, Vol. II, p. 294.

[3]From a letter to Gertrude Oukama Knoop in Rilke, *Selected Letters*, p. 330.

this is as true of the most "unengaged" lyric poem, intrinsically, as of the most didactic or discursive or contentious). Bradley continued, "The vision of man we get from art conditions our vision of society and therefore our political behavior.... Art and social life are in a dialectical relationship to each other that is synthesized by political action."

The obligation of the poet (and, by extension, of others committed to the love of literature, as critics and teachers or simply as readers) is not necessarily to write "political" poems (or to focus attention primarily on such poems as more "relevant" than other poems or fictions). The obligation of the writer is: *to take personal and active responsibility for his words, whatever they are, and to acknowledge their potential influence on the lives of others.* The obligation of teachers and critics is: *not to block the dynamic consequences of the words they try to bring close to students and readers.* And the obligation of readers is: *not to indulge in the hypocrisy of merely vicarious experience, thereby reducing literature to the concept of "just words," ultimately a frivolity, an irrelevance when the chips are down.* ... When words penetrate deep into us they change the chemistry of the soul, of the imagination. We have no right to do that to people if we don't share the consequences.

People are always asking me how I can reconcile poetry and political action, poetry and talk of revolution. Don't you feel, they say to me, that you and other poets are betraying your work as poets when you spend time participating in sit-ins, marching in the streets, helping to write leaflets, talking to people about capitalism, imperialism, racism, male chauvinism, oppression of all kinds? My answer is no; precisely because I am a poet, I know, and those other poets who do likewise know, that we must fulfill the poet's total involvement in life in this aspect also. "But is not the task of the poet essentially one of conservation?" the

114

question comes. Yes, and if I speak of revolution it is because I believe that only revolution can now save that earthly life, that miracle of being, which poetry conserves and celebrates. "But history shows us that poets—even great poets —more often fulfill their lives as observers than as participants in political action—when they do become embroiled in politics they usually write bad poems." I answer, good poets write bad political poems only if they let themselves write deliberate, opinionated rhetoric, misusing their art as propaganda. The poet does not *use* poetry, but is at the service of poetry. To *use* it is to *mis*use it. A poet driven to speak to himself, to maintain a dialogue with himself, concerning politics, can expect to write as well upon that theme as upon any other. He can not separate it from everything else in his life. But it is not whether or not good "political" poems are a possibility that is in question. What is in question is the role of the poet as observer or as participant in the life of his time. And if history is invoked to prove that more poets have stood aside, have watched or ignored the events of their moment in history, than have spent time and energy in bodily participation in those events, I must answer that a sense of history must involve a sense of the present, a vivid awareness of change, a response to crisis, a realization that what was appropriate in this or that situation in the past is inadequate to the demands of the present, that we are living our whole lives *in a state of emergency* which is—for reasons I'm sure I don't have to spell out for you by discussing nuclear and chemical weapons or ecological disasters and threats— unparalleled in all history.

When I was seven or eight and my sister sixteen or seventeen, she described the mind to me as a room full of boxes, in aisles like the shelves of a library, each box with its label. I had heard the term "gray matter," and so I visualized room and boxes as gray, dust-gray. Her confident description impressed me, but I am glad to say I felt an

115

immediate doubt of its authenticity. Yet I have since seen lovers of poetry, lovers of literature, behave as if it were indeed so, and allow no fruitful reciprocity between poem and action.[4]

"No ideas but in things," said William Carlos Williams. This does not mean "no ideas." It means that "language [and here I quote Wordsworth] is not the dress but the incarnation of thoughts."[5] "No ideas but in things," means, essentially, "Only connect." And it is therefore not only a craft-statement, not only an aesthetic statement (though it is these things also, and importantly), but a moral statement. *Only connect. No ideas but in things.* The words reverberate through the poet's life, through *my* life, and I hope through your lives, joining with other knowledge in the mind, that place that is not a gray room full of little boxes. . . .

[4]At this point in the talk as originally given, I inserted the poem, "O Taste and See," from my book of the same title.
[5]See note on Wordsworth's statement, p. 16.

SECTION II:
LIFE AT WAR

From "Writers Take Sides on Vietnam," 1966

I am absolutely opposed to the U.S. war of aggression in Vietnam. Not only is it an unjustifiable interference hypocritically carried on in the name of "freedom" while in fact its purpose is to further the strategic ends of a government whose enormous power has destroyed the morality of its members; but it is being waged by means of atrocities. This is a war in which more children are being killed and maimed than fighting men. Napalm, white phosphorous, fragmentation bombs, all used deliberately on a civilian population; poisoning of crops, defoliation of forests; not to speak of the horrendous blight of disease and famine that follows, the corruption, prostitution, and every kind of physical and moral suffering—nothing whatsoever could possibly justify these crimes.

Violence always breeds more violence and is never a solution even when it temporarily seems to be. Violence of this magnitude, even if the ultimate holocaust it is swiftly leading to is averted—i.e., if we at least stop in time to avoid a still larger war—promises a dreadful future for America, full of people tortured and distorted with the knowledge (conscious or unconscious) of what we have done. One does not need to be a bomber pilot to feel this; one need only be an American who did nothing to stop the war, or not enough; one has only to be a human being. It is hard to be an artist in this time because it is hard to be human: in the dull ever-accumulating horror of the war news, it is more difficult each day to keep remembering the creative and joyful potential of human beings, and to fulfill that potential in one's own life, as testimony. Shame, despair, disgust, these are the reverberations that threaten to silence poets thousands of miles away from where the bombs are falling. The struggle of all artists and all pacifists

From *Writers Take Sides on Vietnam* (New York, 1967).

is to overcome their nausea and actively hold to what their work has caused them to know—the possibility of beautiful life.

I believe that cessation of all violence and withdrawal of all troops from Vietnam is the only right action for the U.S. I would like to see this withdrawal followed by the penitent presentation to the people of Vietnam by the U.S of huge quantities of food and supplies—such quantities that people here would feel the pinch, actually sacrifice something, not merely donate a surplus. I would like to see this given absolutely outright, and unaccompanied by U.S. "advisers," though large numbers of doctors, nurses, and other people who might really be of use in reconstructing the ravaged country might humbly offer their services to work under Vietnamese supervision. Such acts of penitence, distinct from the guilt that stews in its own juice, would do something to make the future more livable for our children.

I'm one of those people whose first participation in the peace movement began in New York way back when we demonstrated in City Hall Park against compulsory air-raid drills and our slogan used to be, "Peace Is Our Only Shelter." We wore buttons that said, "Stop the Testing" and "Strontium 90 Builds Bones." With others of my generation, I moved along to organizing "Writers-and-Artists-Protest-the-War-in-Vietnam" ads in *The New York Times*, in emulation of the French intellectuals' protests about Algeria. Rallies and demonstrations became more and more frequent; veterans destroyed their honorable discharge papers, and we took them to the White House in a little coffin; we organized poetry readings and art exhibits and anthologies, and showed slides of napalmed children. We moved into the support and encouragement of draft resistance. And the war dragged on and at home poverty continued and racism intensified. And the demonstrations got bigger and bigger, but they still were one-issue efforts—Stop the War in Vietnam. And at last a better understanding of the futility of this one-issue campaign began to get through my thick head and some other thick heads. Today, I believe we cannot bring the wars to an end—and I use the plural "wars" because there are wars going on in many countries, and in all these wars the United States has a hand—we cannot bring the wars to an end without bringing the capitalist-imperialist system to an end. These wars, whether in Asia or in Latin America or wherever they erupt, are wars of national liberation, in which people are fighting for self-determination against America's puppet governments, America's CIA and its "advisers," America's napalm, America's giant corporations, even when American troops are not involved. Now the peace movement must

Delivered at the University of Massachusetts, Amherst, April 15, 1970, at an outdoor rally.

become the revolutionary movement, must work to educate people to the realization that the struggle of black people *inside* the U.S. is a struggle for self-determination parallel to those *outside* the U.S., and that it will become a race war if we, white radicals, do not act toward revolution. A one-issue peace movement attempts to deal with only a single symptom of the disease that infects every aspect of our society; just as people concerned about the ecological disasters and threats of yet greater disaster attempt to deal with symptoms only if they do not realize that the greed of a profit system underlies the pollution of our resources. We must get together to uproot the cause, even while we continue to struggle against the effects—and we must not confine our struggle to any single effect. Anyone who works to end the war in Vietnam but does nothing to stop the political and racial oppression that is happening around us simply does not understand where it's at. Everyone who's out today to demand an end to the war has a moral and rational obligation to be out demanding that the trial of Bobby Seale and the other Panthers be stopped too. As many people must flock to New Haven when that trial begins as flocked to Washington in November. More and more, people must be prepared to act militantly. The days of mere protest are over, and the days of separating war, and racism, and pollution of natural resources, and social injustice, and male chauvinism, into neat little compartments are over. I say this with the conviction—and if it sounds apocalyptic, o.k., it *is* apocalyptic—that unless all men and women of good will realize this very, very soon, and act on it, there will be no future, but an increasing horror followed by annihilation. Even at best we are not going to escape a period of terror, of increased repression, of bloodshed. It is happening already. But our one chance of survival, and not of mere survival but of a decent and humane life for ourselves and our children and our children's children, lies in solidarity and in the recognition *now* of the necessity of revolution.

Statement for a Television Program

The following statement was written in response to an invitation to "comment on any topic, e.g., poetry, women, the war," on a program taped weekly by a major TV network (NBC). I could not in these times choose any "topic" but the war; however, my text (which had to be submitted a week before being taped—and which was written during the interval between Nixon's two televised speeches in May 1972—was rejected. "I feel," wrote the producer, "that, deep as my own emotions are about this futile war, it would be inappropriate for me to use it at this time. My decision is shaped not by your piece—you write so very movingly —but by the number of Vietnam statements we have already had on the program. They cover a wide range of attitudes and angles, and with them I effected a coverage and balance which I think best to let stand."

It seems to me that a "balanced" view of genocide and of actions which are leading directly toward the extinction of life on earth is itself a kind of insanity. It is evident, moreover, that a program that first invites people to speak on whatever they feel it is important to say, and then rejects their words in the name of "balanced coverage," is a little short on sincerity. Here is my statement:

I have been asked to speak on this program because I am a poet. One of the obligations of the writer, and perhaps especially of the poet, is to say or sing *all* that he or she can, to deal with as much of the world as becomes possible to him or her in language. I and most of my fellow American poets nowadays find ourselves inevitably—of necessity—writing more and more poems of grief, of rage, concerning the despoilment of the earth and of all life upon it, of the systematic destruction of all that we feel passionate love for, both by the greed of industry and by the mass murder we call war. We are living at war: the shame and horror of being citizens of the country which, in its ruthless imperialism, is not only ravaging Southeast Asia but, with its military bases, its Polaris submarines, the machinations of its CIA, and the tentacles of its giant corporations, is everywhere the prime force of antilife and oppression—this shame and horror cast their shadow over all we say, feel, and do. The spring sunshine, the new leaves: we still see them, still love them: but in what poignant contrast is their beauty and simple goodness to the evil we are conscious of day and night. And this evil, this blight, this war in which our whole lives are being spent, is present at home, here in the U.S., as well as abroad, in the form of racism, of gross injustice, of poverty and hunger in the midst of the very richest country in the world. As corrupt and self-seeking politicians erode the Constitution and bring us daily closer to outright fascism, the poet is turned away from his impulse to sing, to testify in patterns of words to the miracle of life, and is driven willy-nilly to warn, to curse, to gnash the teeth of language; and at the same time, living always in the war shadow, to celebrate the courage and high spirit of all who dare to struggle, Davids to the Goliaths of capitalism (the expression of man's greed) and imperialism (the expression of man's lust for power); to celebrate the courage and tenacity of the so-called "enemy" in Southeast Asia, and of all who here at home resist the system—people like Angela Davis, Dan and Phil Berrigan, Cesar Chavez; and to declare solidarity with them and with all who share their struggle.

Poets differ from other people only in having a specially intimate relation to words. When I say I speak as a poet, it is the same as to say I speak as a human being. In the name of humanness, then, I call on my fellow humans to *stop the war;* but not to think that by stopping the present slaughter in Vietnam we will have done the job—for that slaughter is only one manifestation of the total war that surrounds us. We could *begin* if we wanted to: we could stop the bombing tomorrow if every individual who would like to see an end to U.S. involvement would say *No Business as Usual* and ACT on those words. It is our own timidity that makes us feel powerless. If we acted to bring about a general strike and economic boycott, we would see we have more power than we think. But even if we stop the bombing and get rid of Nixon, let us understand that though it would be a beginning—and a good one—it would be ineffectual unless it led to a thorough change—outward and inward, institutional and personal—of the system Nixon and his bombs are part of. Stop the bombing. Declare peace. Change the system.

Think about elm trees . . .

Fountains of green in summer, their shade striping the roads of small towns with pleasant islands of coolness; in winter, the other beauty of their leafless grace, the basic form revealed.

Maybe it seems strange that we should be talking about elm trees at this time when we all have the war on our minds, and all the powerful and evil political and social system that lies back of the war.

But it is not irrelevant. Our elm trees are sick, and have been for many years now. More and more streets and gardens in the northeast and those parts of the Midwest where the elm grows, the character and charm of which once depended more than we realized on their bordering trees, are now edged only with great stumps, melancholy reminders . . . Maples and other species grown by the roadsides die too, from the effects of salt and of various other kinds of pollution; but the elm is affected not only by these deplorable causes but by its own disease, the Dutch elm disease. However, there are people working at a cure for the disease. Even now, trees that are very well cared for can be kept going, just like human beings with chronic diseases; but unfortunately this is very expensive. The tragedy is that if people—mostly city councils—keep on simply cutting down the sick trees and not planting others, then by the time a cure is found it may be too late—the species will have become extinct (as happened with the native American chestnut tree). It takes sixty or seventy years for an American elm to reach maturity. So we believe people should collect or obtain elm seeds from the remaining healthy elms and plant them. We ourselves, unless we are

---

An adult puppet theater, created in Cambridge, Mass., by Art Wood. Healthy elm seeds are given out to the audience at its performances.

under ten years old or so, will not live to see them reach their full, lovely, outreaching height, but we will have given them a chance to reach it, a chance for people now unborn to enjoy them.

The relevance of this to the other problems that are so heavily weighing on our minds and feelings is quite simple, for there is a clear analogy.

Policies of "brinkmanship," the machinations of insanely greedy and arrogant men, may at any moment push us into a final holocaust; our hopes and efforts for radical social change may never have time to take effect. Or the ecological disasters which greed and ignorance have already created may "do us in" before we can make a genuine effort to reverse or even to halt them. BUT—*we do not and cannot know for sure that there is no hope.* And even as we fear the worst, the life-spirit in us and in our brothers and sisters keeps us moving and acting, loving one another, creating, working. "What if there is a future after all, however unlikely that looks right now? What if it arrives after I've given up on it? What if I have done nothing toward creating that future, but just abandoned it while others worked?" As far as political action is concerned, it is the strong desire not to have to ask oneself these questions that keeps a lot of us going even at the most depressing times. If there is to be life on earth, a life worth living, we want to share it and *to have helped make it possible.* We have nothing at all to lose by trying.

In the same way one could easily forget the elm tree, both because so far the cure for its sickness has not been found and because one fears that World War III and/or the destruction of the essentials of life—air, water, the soil—will have occurred long before healthy elms could grow tall again anyway. But what if we avert the calamities, what if a livable future does exist for our children and grandchildren? Let us do this small thing, plant these small seeds. Just as we continue to struggle in other areas of our lives—to struggle *for* what we believe in as well as *against* what we loathe

127

and despise—let us struggle to make that small act of faith; a token of defiance, but maybe more than a token. There is always, still, the chance that the seed you take a few moments to plant now may some day be a branchy, whispering fountain full of birds, while the people strolling under it will think back to our times as to a remote nightmare only—a nightmare in which someone had the audacious imagination to plant elm trees, to plant joy, to plant love.

Glimpses of Vietnamese Life

Part I

The overwhelming impression I brought back from my visit to North Vietnam two months ago was of a people who were not only unalienated from their society but who enthusiastically identified with it; a people whose striking grace and gentleness is both a characteristic shared with other peoples of Southeast Asia and a result of the sense of security given them by their genuine revolutionary solidarity.

I have spent the last few days typing page after page of factual material accumulated during my stay. I was beginning to feel I would never get it all down and to despair of conveying a feeling of the place, even with all my facts, or perhaps just because I had too many facts. So I began over, reliving impressions.

Flying in from Vientiane, looking down at the great range of thickly forested mountains, relieved to see they were not pocked with craters but seemed endlessly green and impenetrable. Then the descent, green, lake-like rice paddies, little thatched houses, the broad curve of the river —and at last after our three-day journey stepping out into the Vietnam that has been in our thoughts daily for years now, but has seemed almost mythical in its remoteness.

Brilliant sunshine, smiling faces, and flowers at the barrier—yes, for us, from our hosts, the Union of Women and the Committee for Solidarity with the American People, and three young interpreters. We all hug each other, there is laughter, and a few tears of excitement.

Published in *American Report* (Part I, February 26, 1973; Part II, March 12, 1973), and written following my visit to Hanoi, together with fellow poet Muriel Rukeyser and Jane Hart, war-resister and wife of U.S. Senator Philip Hart (D-Mich.), just before Nixon's re-election.

While a young administrative assistant from the Solidarity Committee, who has one of the most memorable warm smiles I've ever seen, goes to see to our luggage, we all repair to a little waiting room where we are served the first of the innumerable cups of delicious green tea we drank that week. As we walked to the waiting room I found myself next to Lien, one of the interpreters. My arm around her, I felt the silkiness of her long black hair and her fragile, almost childlike shoulders. All three of us feel huge all the time we are in Vietnam.

With free use of the horn to warn the many bicyclists, the water buffaloes, and oxen, the people with one-shoulder yokes moving with the swift balancing step that reminds me of Mexican tortilla sellers coming down into Oaxaca from San Felipe, we drive into the city of Hanoi. (Now, in January 1973, I shudder as I think how that whole across-the-river district, half urban, half rural, has been blown to smithereens. How many of those very people, the first passers-by I saw in Vietnam, died among those ruins?) It is not only the gait of the people carrying goods to market that reminds me of Mexico, but the thatched small dwellings, the banana, jacaranda, palm, and *tabachin* trees, red-blossomed with feathery leaves.

On arriving at the hotel, what joy! I find my "brother," Nguyen Cong Hoan, waiting to greet me and meet my companions. He is the elderly novelist I met in Moscow in December 1971. He was there to visit a granddaughter studying (as many Vietnamese students do) at a Soviet university. I had been invited to Russia to meet some poets.

We made friends quickly and deeply, and he honored me by saying we were henceforth brother and sister. There were tears at our parting; he was not young, and was going back to the air raids, and at that time it had seemed unlikely I would have the chance to visit Hanoi in the foreseeable future.

Now we meet joyfully. I find that he is very famous and revered, and is loved above all as a humorist. Other members of our third host organization, the Writers' Union, who are at the hotel to welcome us, tell me this and add that he is considered a "national treasure."

The hotel rooms: very clean, simple, well-equipped, each with bathroom and balcony. There are rubber sandals by each bed. The style of the room reminds me of Italian moderate-priced provincial hotels. There are *jalousies* at the balcony doors and mosquito nets on the bed, which make a curious kind of little tent when unfurled. However, there don't seem to be any mosquitos.

A feature of the rooms—and nearly all Vietnamese rooms I was in—is a table set with a teapot, two small tea-cups, a tea caddy full of green tea, and a thermos full of hot water! Brought up to believe tea-water must be at a rolling boil, I am amazed.

Sensitive to our possible travel fatigue, which we are too excited to feel, they have arranged that our first outing be to peaceful lakes and parks. There is some bomb damage visible on the way. We are embarrassed at being V.I.P.'s driving fast through the almost carless, bicycle-filled streets of a country that *our* country is blasting. But there is no other way for us to see all that we are to see in a week, and we come to accept it.

It seems strange to be strolling by the shore of one of several lakes within city limits (among them the legendary lake in which a hero of old found the golden sword by which he put the Chinese to flight—a sword which, when he later returned it with gratitude to the water spirit, changed to a jade-green dragon and vanished beneath the waters).

Yes, it seems strange, watching men and boys fishing, children at play in the late afternoon amber light, to be experiencing so much peace here, where I expected to share in some of the physical struggle of a land that has indirectly

131

changed my life. The peace we experienced in Vietnam, not only this day but also in so many moments and hours during our stay, was the peace at the heart of the storm.

An apricot sunset, relaxed, slightly hazy dusk, mild air. Temples, pagodas. Superb topiary—tamarisk bushes cut into elephants, lions, birds. And everywhere the man-sized cylindrical holes, lined with concrete, that are the highly effective air-raid shelters we have seen in photographs. There is a little water in the bottom of them; gardeners have been sprinkling the grass and flowers. Lids lie ready by the holes.

All this relaxation is of course because no raids have occurred in over two weeks. Many children have been temporarily brought back to the city from the rural areas to which they were evacuated, though no schools at any level up through university are open in Hanoi. "We missed them so," some parents say to us.

Vigorous cockcrows in the center of town wake us in plenty of time for early Sunday Mass. Our hosts want us to see that religious observances are not suppressed here.

The large cathedral is full. The congregation is divided, men on the left, women on the right, and the men's side is as full as the women's. Moreover, there is a surprisingly high proportion of young people. Also a few gray-habited nuns.

The music is European. We are late, and stand near the back, so I don't hear if Mass is said in Latin; a hymn is sung in Vietnamese.

Coming out into the square before the cathedral with the rest of the congregation, we find others waiting to come in to the next Mass. Near the church doors, at the tops of the steps leading down to the square, were the only two beggars we saw the whole time we were in Vietnam, old men with "mandarin" beards like Ho Chi Minh's beard in his later years. People over sixty-five are pensioned, but some few, I was told, who had always been beggars—

perhaps since childhood—still beg out of habit. I did not see anyone give to them.

Ho Chi Minh's picture hangs in all official buildings and public places such as the hotel lobby, and in people's homes too. But there are no giant-sized posters of him, like the representations of Mao one sees in pictures of China, or of other leaders elsewhere. These pictures, usually photos, not idealized representations, are never larger than the pictures one sees in America of John Kennedy for instance; and they don't show him in heroic poses but as Uncle Ho, very human, no taller than anyone else, often with others beside him, often with children.

Similarly, there is no equivalent of the Little Red Book or of North Korea's similar book; when the words of Uncle Ho are quoted, they are lines from his poems, or sometimes ancient proverbs he liked to use. No heavy leadership cult, but pride and affection, personal as if he were each person's beloved uncle.

I go with Muriel to the St. Paul Hospital, where she has to get a foot infection treated. The nurse in charge is very gentle. In the visitors' book in the waiting room I read notes of thanks, in French and English, from various foreign visitors who have been treated there.

In the treatment room I watch the witty, patient, French-speaking doctor, a man I'd love to talk with longer, carefully scrub up and attend to the infection on Muriel's foot, and I note that student nurses as well as the head nurse address the doctor directly and without the fear of authority that is traditionally instilled in the minds of "probationers" (as they are called in England, where I was once one myself.)

Later we are at the Bach Mai Hospital (yes, the same one on whose very existence the despicable Jerry Friedheim of the Pentagon cast doubt—before he had to admit grudgingly it had indeed been hit). The tall thin director—recently described in a French journalist's report after the terror

133

bombing as running desperately from area to area of what had been his hospital, organizing the digging out of whoever was still alive under the rubble—escorted us on a tour that included those parts of the hospital that had already been bombed before our visit (late October) and the busy wards in full use. Even in these there are signs of damage—cracked plaster is being repaired by groups of workers, male and female, and there's a sound of hammering and sawing.

We are stunned by the encounter with two patients' cases in particular. One is never fully prepared for the sight of suffering. These are two children, boys, each in small separate rooms, each with a silent, stony-faced mother sitting by his bedside.

One has lost both legs from just below the knee. His left arm and his body are bandaged, too. He lies on his back, expressionless, toying and toying with a little spool of some kind he holds in his hands. The nurse tells us it is good he exercises his fingers—the arm injury has partly paralyzed the arm but the full use of it may return. We think of how his feet will never return, and even if he can be fitted with artificial legs eventually, he will never run and jump again. He is only eight years old.

The other is a couple of years older. Bomb fragments[1] have lodged in his brain, as well as elsewhere in his body. His head is swathed in bandages—his face looks out of its turban with a strange expression, disoriented. It is probable the brain damage is irreversible. We cannot speak. Going out into the sunlight again, we take photos of bomb craters in the gardens.

At the Writers' Union we read poems to each other in our own languages, then our wonderful chief interpreter

[1]I.e., pellets from an antipersonnel weapon, of the type which has over three hundred pellets to a "bomblet" and over six hundred "bomblets" to each "mother bomb." Formerly made of metal, these pellets were "improved"; that is, are now made of a plastic undetectable in the victim's flesh by X-ray.

134

Quoc, who is twenty-eight and has a wife and two young children but looks about sixteen, gives instant paraphrases of them, which from Vietnamese into English, at any rate, are remarkably poetic. Those of us, both Vietnamese and American, who speak French amplify his versions. Mr. Quat of the Solidarity Committee, who speaks English well, is there to help out also.

A marvelous atmosphere of good fellowship, not only from them toward us but *between* them. None of the rivalry one can too often feel at writers' gatherings.

Huy Can reads a poem about the messages hastily scrawled on the walls of his home town of Haiphong after the bombardment—"I have the baby safely and have gone to Tu's house," or "Our son was hurt and I have gone to the hospital. Look for us there," or "Don't go into what's left of the house. It's dangerous."

I'm reminded, by his use of the vernacular, his collage—but more than collage—of things actually seen and heard, of the spirit and practice of William Carlos Williams, and I tell them a bit about him. (Later I find a French translation of "An Ode to Whitman" by Huy Can.) They listen with close attention. They don't want to hear as much about the politics and the antiwar efforts and "protest poetry" of American poets as about poetry itself.

There are more men than women at these gatherings at the Writers' Union, but women are represented, too. One of the women poets is very young and pretty. She brings her little boy with her and I draw him a picture. Later she brings me a gift—a large earthenware pig and piglets, symbol of many good things.

Secretary General of the Union is Nguyen Dinh Thi, poet and novelist, born in 1924, whose first books were printed on jungle presses during the struggle against the French. He was twice imprisoned, and commanded a battalion of the Liberation Army.

He's a man whose physical beauty and grace of presence are inseparable from his moral and spiritual beauty and grace. He speaks to us of how he sees the war not only as the clash of forces, two national identities, but as an experience that reveals clearly the worst and the best on both sides.

Like a storm, he said, it blows the lid off things, it reveals the garbage of bestiality hidden by the cloak of civilization. The horror of uncontrolled technology has been shown us, technology in the service of immoral men. "And," he told us, "we in Vietnam can understand your shame because we have *our* shame too, that people like Thieu, going further than any other puppets, actually invite the U.S to come and bomb their own country." He said this is not only because it was true but because in the kindness of his heart he wanted to alleviate our burden of shame at being members of what has become the Monster Race.

That same storm, he continued, has also revealed the best—in America as well as in Vietnam. It was interesting to me that he cited Norman Morrison as a paradigm of that best. Communism in the D.R.V.N. is characterized by its humanity, exemplified in this instance by the reverence in which Morrison, a Quaker, a pacifist, whose political action took the ultimate Buddhist form of self-immolation, is held, and not by Thi alone but by many people. Later we were to hear a poem famous in Vietnam, written by To Huu, one of the best-known poets, born in 1920, which is a monologue spoken by Morrison to his baby daughter. And I find his name in other poems too. His life sacrifice burns on in Vietnamese hearts.

The goodness of America, Thi went on, is not in the ascendant; yet the catalyst of the war has brought about the coming together for a common goal of many people of different backgrounds. "Don't think all your actions are in vain. Your support is important to our morale. And we have a proverb, *Many breezes make a big storm.* If peace comes, we will thank not whoever is in power in America, but the steadfast peace movement. The green bud has more potential than the yellow leaf."

136

Thi speaks of the ancientness of Vietnam. Pottery has been found there two thousand years older than any from India and China. There is evidence that rice was first cultivated in the Red River and Mekong Delta. He speaks of how, always under pressure from large and oppressive foreign powers, the Vietnamese survived as a people, retained and developed their identity, by developing a strong sense of mutual aid, of personal relations. "We can sacrifice all for independence, but we are also an openhearted people. We cherish life but are fearless of death." As I listen to him I realize that profound truth is being spoken, not a rhetorical statement:

The American fear of death, with America's resulting funeral industry, America's obsession with the "new," even America's racism which ties in with the Western equation "white equals purity, light, and life; black equals corruption (sin), darkness (of the grave), and death," (followed by "black as hell")—surely, I remind myself (for it is not an original idea) this is the same fear that erupts in American violence and—ultimately—genocide.

And conversely, the amazing ability of the Vietnamese not merely to fight on under such material odds but to be so generous, so discriminating between culprits and victims, between one American and another, and to be so cheerful and kindly in their relations with each other—surely it does indeed stem from their simply not having the obsessive fear of death.

They don't *court* death but they accept it, and *thereby* are able to truly "cherish life." "My people," says Thi in his soft but clear voice, "are gentle and merry." And later, "As a writer, I don't find the regime a *perfect model*, I see it rather as a slow accretion that is *in process*. As a poet, that is a joy to me—to witness and participate in that process. We are *finding the way*. Each day must be a new invention."

This is the life that our government, in our name, has been attempting to pulverize.

Part II

I begin the writing of this second group of recollections of my fall visit to North Vietnam after the cease-fire has been announced. Though there is relief in knowing that, for the moment at least, the people and scenes I am describing are not subject to constant threat, nevertheless with each word, with each face or field that comes into the mind's eye, comes the thought, "Are they still there? Did they survive the December terror bombings?"

We drive in a jeep, followed by two others, south from Hanoi. Jane Hart and I are in different jeeps, each with guides and interpreters.[2] In the third jeep ride our accompanying photographer and some aides. We are soon out of the city and into a landscape of tender, moist shades of green, full of the "water-mirrors" I had imagined in a poem, "What Were They Like?," written in 1966.

The growing of rice is staggered so that one sees it concurrently in many different stages of development: some fields are flooded, with no shoots visible above the water, in others the vivid young rice looks quite short, and in others it grew taller than I had realized; it looks similar to other grains, high and tasseled.

The roads are fairly straight in this flat country, and not dusty even when unpaved, for the soil seems to be a wettish red clay. Indeed the colors are reminiscent of Devonshire or parts of North Carolina, but with the luxurious vegetation of these latitudes. Many clusters of banana and other fruit trees and lines of palm trees give variety to the wide terrain. Sometimes we see a range of mountains on the horizon, clear-cut, manifold. The sky's light, joyful blue deepens as the sun mounts; two or three indolent clouds are reflected in the rice paddies, again giving me a feeling of *déjà vu*.

Buffalo, slow as clouds, ruminate here and there by the roadside; others, with their masters, plunge vigorously through the watery fields; sometimes both man and beast

[2]Muriel Rukeyser remained in Hanoi during this excursion.

are under water up to their chests, but one of my guides tells me land that is this wet is not desirable. Along the roads go pedestrians and cyclists—men and women and sometimes children—some not riding but pushing the bicycle, loaded with heavy but manageable sacks of produce or other materials, tied to a central pole.

Every now and then an oxcart passes; more rarely, carts drawn by small horses—or an army vehicle, camouflaged not with paint but with real branches. Many of the military personnel we see, even in Hanoi, wear wreaths of green branches around their helmets—perhaps for coolness rather than for camouflage. It gives them a bucolic appearance eminently suitable to soldiers who are basically and deeply attached to rural areas.

As we pass through hamlets strung out by the roadside we often notice families eating just outside their small thatched houses, sitting at tables placed under a tree or a palm-leaf shelter. Sometimes we see little restaurants in the same style, and shops. For some reason there are an enormous number of barbershops, all thriving. I laugh with my interpreters and guides about this. We are very gay.

Even as we laugh I think to myself how strange it is to be having such a good time in this war-scarred country, the idea of which has been like a heavy lump in my chest day and night for years. But not just this day in the country, *every* day I experienced from my Vietnamese friends the swift-flowing movement of feeling from laughter to tears, from grief to joy, and back again. And I came to feel that while I personally may be volatile, that is not what the Vietnamese are: it was not anything shallow or easy I was witnessing but the free play of genuine emotion possible only to a people with deep roots in their culture, their soil, and at the same time with the abundant flowering branches of security and hope that their revolution has given them.

With the same companions in laughter I share the tears of extremely painful experiences. I have a photograph that commemorates the first: it shows me holding hands with a woman who looks at me sorrowfully. Sunglasses hide my own expression, but in fact I was crying. Around us, looking concerned, are other people—some of my companions, some of her neighbors. We had just come out of her tiny house built on a dike, its floors beaten earth but all within immaculate.

Much of its space was occupied by two large platform beds, plain but solid-looking. And on one of them sat her eleven-year-old daughter. The father had ushered me in, graciously but humbly. The little girl, silent, patient, and otherwise perfectly formed, had had a foot blown off by yet another antipersonnel bomb. Nothing, nothing to say. I stumble out into the noon heat, the mother follows. We stand there gripping each others' hands tightly. Her neighbors crowd around—a murmur does not alter the basic silence. And at last we unclasp our hands and I depart. Three months have gone by since that day, but I feel I am still standing there within that moment.

We are crossing a river on a ferryboat. Mme. Bé, of the Union of Women, and I get out of our jeep and stand gazing downstream. Mme. Bé is conversing with one of the many other ferry passengers—most of them pedestrians. When we get back in and drive on, up the dike on the far shore and over onto the ongoing road, Bé tells me of what had passed between her and the old woman with whom she had spoken.

"Who are the women from the distant place with whom you are traveling?" inquired the old lady—dressed in blouse and trousers dyed to a shade of powdery brick red, a color much worn in the Delta, the very color of its earth. "They are Americans—visitors from America," Bé told her. "Americans! Yanquis!" exclaimed the old lady, horrified, shifting the weight of the carrying pole balanced on her shoulder, a bundle or basket dangling from each end of it. "Why do you want to bring such evil people here?" "But these are friends—friendly Americans, not those who come to kill us."

140

"Ah, good then; it is good that they come."

Immediately appeased, immediately ready to believe we are indeed friends, not the enemy. Mme. Bé laughs as she tells the tale—but I can't laugh. It seems to me too important, too moving, not funny at all. The old lady is probably illiterate—one of the small minority, all in the over-sixty age group, to whom the revolution's work in education, which reversed the literate/illiterate ratio, came too late.

Her reactions are direct, not filtered through any medium but her own experience. She has seen the cruel and rapacious landlords go, justice and self-improvement and mutual aid established in village life, the tragic, arranged marriages of her younger days become history, along with famines, diseases, and the high rate of infant mortality.

She has seen the growth of the Women's Union, which promotes and safeguards the rights of all women, young and old, married and single, and which has a branch in every town and village of the North. She has seen happy children going to schools that simply did not exist except for a tiny elite when she was young, and students returning from the universities to share their knowledge—as nurses, doctors, agronomists, teachers—with the people of their home villages.

And she has seen the huge bombers from a country half the world away fly over implacably, wave after wave, year after year, attempting to smash all this happy activity with mysterious, inexplicable brutality. Yet when these strange, tall, pink-faced women appear out of nowhere and she is told they are Americans, how quickly and how trustingly her initial horror is succeeded by a friendly acceptance of their being some other kind of American, not the destroyers.

This generosity of spirit, typical of what I observed, results from what I so frequently felt was an embarrassing overestimation, on their part, not only of the strength and dedication and size of the antiwar movement in America but of the degree of general good will existing among the mass of people in the U.S. toward the people of Vietnam.

141

At the village guesthouse where we spend the night, we sleep in one spacious room. The large platform beds, two on each side, are almost like separate rooms once the mosquito nets are drawn down. The beams of the high roof are beautifully carved. This was once part of a Buddhist temple. The sleeping room is entered through a large living and dining room, where we were served a delicious supper and breakfast. Outside, a long veranda runs the length of the building (the men in our party sleep in an identical set of rooms further along it) and on the veranda, flanked by flowerbeds and potted plants, are washstands with jugs of water, towels, and soap.

In back of the building is a set of outhouses. Returning to the main building from the outhouse early in the morning, I stop to watch the mist rising over a nearby pond. Across the water, beyond the water lilies, a path adjoins the bank. I glimpse children leading water buffaloes out for the day, an older schoolboy with books and bicycle, women with baskets talking to each other. Smoke from morning cooking fires rises with the mist. Birds are singing.

Last night an air-raid siren had sounded in the far distance, but this morning there are only pleasant, mild, life-sounds in the quietness. Someone is playing a bamboo flute under the persimmon trees. This is a glimpse of the immemorial village life so many Vietnamese poems and stories celebrate—what Thi, our poet friend in Hanoi, hoped we would see, calling it the root, the core of all things Vietnamese.

"Explain to the American people," said a worker at the Collective Farm later that day, "that life here is not turned upside down: the bombing is useless as well as savage."

Mr. Quat (Chairman of the Committee for Solidarity with the American People): "As long as the war goes on we are neither happy nor sad. Revolutionaries are simply people who want a better society and try to create it. When one has walked ten thousand miles one does not turn back before the last one hundred."

A wonderful concert had been prepared for us on our last day. Thi has arranged it, and it takes place in a large reception room at the Writers' Union. The folk and traditional music is enchanting, including such instruments as the monochord (which weeks later in Boston I look up in my 1885 Grove's *Dictionary of Music,* and find that it is reputed to have been invented by Pythagoras, but that he probably learned of it from the Egyptians, and that Euclid wrote of it in defining the intervals of the ancient Greek scale!), the bamboo flute, a bamboo xylophone or marimba, and a most ingenious kind of rattle the use of which involves dancelike movements of arm and wrist.

European-style music is performed well also, and poems are recited. Perhaps the most memorable of all the pleasures of this concert, and the most difficult for me to describe, is a skit performed by two little girls, daughters of a famous theatrical couple. Their older sister acted as announcer for the whole concert. Dressed as Saigon street boys, they mock the clumsy G.I.'s whose shoes they shine. Their sense of comedy, their expressive and charming little faces, their professionalism, and at the same time the fun they were obviously having, are beyond my skill to describe.

Mme. Nguyen Khanh Phuong, of the P.R.G. delegation in Hanoi—a beautiful woman who suffered unspeakable tortures in Diem's prisons and does not know the fate of her husband, arrested in 1959, nor has she seen her daughter since she was wrenched away from the year-old child in 1955—tells us how she survived "only thanks to the care and love of my comrades in the N.L.F."

We sit around a long coffee table in an elegant room at the delegation's house in the area of Hanoi where the embassies are clustered and where the well-to-do French once lived in luxury. Two young women from the South, brought to Hanoi for medical treatment of unhealing wounds and other results of torture under the Thieu regime, tell us their terrible stories. They don't weep. But they are deeply angry, and hurt as much emotionally as physically. Mme.

143

Phuong rises from time to time to replenish our cups and plates with tea and fruit.

I slip a paper napkin she hands me into my notebook to keep as a memento. "After twenty years of struggle," she says, "who could imagine we could give up? We are sustained by our deep belief in the justice of our cause. We suffer and fight in order to bring a time of happiness."

The two young women—who were not political when they were first arrested—sip tea and sit proudly upright. One has a colostomy, the other a complicated and painful hernia requiring a series of operations. Mme. Phuong, dressed in the long silk tunic worn for occasions of ceremony or festival, smiles at us with her sad eyes, a smile of pride and hope.

As we leave, each woman takes our hands in both of hers and holds them a long moment—and at the last minute I venture to embrace them, and each returns the embrace with warm sisterliness. They come out to wave to us as we drive away.

I write in my notebook, "All that we have known about and have been trying to spread among other people seems unreal compared to seeing mothers at the bedsides of their half-destroyed children, or hearing the stories of women like these. I cling to the need for revolutionary optimism, I yearn for it; and we *see* it, we feel inspired by it—but we have a long struggle before us in order to really *share* it. It seems to me such hope, faith, charity, can only emerge out of a suffering we have yet to experience."

Epilogue

I feel this is an appropriate place to end, because it will serve to remind readers and myself of the ongoing struggle, both in Vietnam—where at this very moment, despite Nixon's vaunted "peace," political prisoners are being murdered by America's puppet Thieu and his henchmen, and in the U.S. where we who do want true peace and justice for all, and who do at least *try* to work for it, have so much to learn and so far to go before we can offer any effective resistance to the continuing outrages our country perpetrates (and the U.S. is bombing Laos even as I write[3]) or any strategy for dealing with the next major outbreak of U.S. aggression, wherever it occurs.

Self-reproach can be a form of self-indulgence. That was something I began to learn in Vietnam, even though I experienced more self-reproach there than I ever had before: not because we do nothing, but because we don't push ourselves to do just a little bit more. I came to see, during that week, that revolutionary optimism is the *fruit* of serious struggle; that for us—at such a different point of moral and political development, and so deeply enmeshed and confused among the gross material and technological manifestations that surround us from birth—there is possibly far more strength and impetus to be drawn from contemplation of the *positive* quality of life in the Democratic Republic of Vietnam than from contemplation of the sufferings its people have endured.

In other words, the impetus to our own development toward the social change which alone can bring peace, can come more strongly from the knowledge of how humane, kindly, joyful, and constructive it is, after all, possible for human beings to be, than from grief, anger, and remorse when these emotions are separated from such positive knowledge.

Courage is patient.

[3]And now (April 1973) Cambodia.

145

Introductory

I came to teaching from the peculiar standpoint of one who has never been to school. As a child I "did lessons" at home under the tutelage of my mother and listened to the BBC Schools Programs. For French, piano, and art I was sent to various teachers for private lessons. My only experience of classroom work was in ballet school, from the age of twelve through to seventeen; in a year of nursing school when I was twenty-one; and in a Russian language class I attended at the New School in New York a few years ago.

My lack of experience of what it is like to be a student seemed to me, when I began to teach, to be a disability. I had plenty to say, plenty I was eager to impart if I could, but no models of procedure, no memories to draw on of how much a student could reasonably be expected to study in a given period of time. Afraid of boring my students, I talked too much and both bored and frustrated them. Work which they could have profitably done themselves—a kind of summary of each week's class (this was a poetry workshop at the N.Y. Poetry Center)—I did myself, in my uncertainty that I had really put across in the two-hour period all that I had intended to cram into it. But as time went by—both in that course and in my subsequent college teaching ventures—I came to see my inexperience as something of an advantage, even if it made things harder for me; it has meant that so far, at least, I have inevitably brought to teaching a freshness, a quality of improvisation, that I believe my students have found stimulating. Too many of them have been disillusioned by finding that a teacher has been using

Written for the anthology, *Writers as Teachers, Teachers as Writers,* edited by Jonathan Baumbach (New York, Holt, Rinehart & Winston, 1970).

some familiar trickery upon them—professional gimmicks, fake spontaneity, ploys.

What the nonprofessional teacher—the artist who is invited to teach *his thing*—has to offer must surely be precisely a fresh response to the individual group of students and his passionate interest in the art he is teaching, free from habits picked up from his own former teachers or in courses on pedagogy. Obviously the gifted and dedicated professional teacher is not going to impose tricks on his students either, if he can help it. But it must be difficult indeed for the professional, often overworked and perhaps longing for a sabbatical, to avoid almost unconsciously reusing gambits which worked the year before, not to speak of old notes rehashed. The artist who is a part-time teacher, especially if like myself he has taught each year at a different school, can more easily, confronted not only with new faces but with a different style of student in each place, forget what he did last time, or if he remembers it, find it inappropriate to this new group and new surroundings, and so start out with a genuine sense of adventure; while if my peculiar lack of formal education has at times caused me to demand too much or too little of my students, it has at least helped me, I think, to recognize how much there was for me to learn from them and for them to learn from each other.

Poetry Center Workshop, 1964

My first teaching assignment, the course traditionally called The Craft of Poetry, has been taught at the Poetry Center of the Y.M.H.A. in New York by many different poets over the years. It is held in the evening, once a week for twelve weeks, and the teacher has the opportunity of seeing poems and statements by a very large number of applicants (fifty or sixty) well beforehand and limiting the number of students to what he considers the optimum for the kind of course he intends to teach—which is entirely

150

his own decision. I chose twelve students, varying in age from seventeen to perhaps forty-six, though most of them were between perhaps twenty-three and thirty-five. At the last moment I took in a thirteenth; but with one student dropping out after the first few classes, and irregular attendance by some others, eight students became the regular core of the class. Several of these were already very accomplished poets.

My hope was not to teach anybody to write poetry—indeed, I had deep suspicions of the very idea of poetry workshops—but to attempt to bring each one to a clearer sense of what his own voice and range might be and to give him some standards by which to evaluate his own work. My major emphasis was on the poem as a sonic entity, not fully experienced if not heard as well as seen; and so each poem under discussion was always read aloud—preferably several times, and by several persons as well as by its author—before we began to talk about it. There were usually mimeographed copies for everyone to scrutinize, though as the course progressed and people kept bringing in new poems this wasn't always successfully organized, and indeed many poems were mimeographed which we never had time to discuss. Each week I would prepare what amounted to a short lecture on some particular aspect of poetry, such as the use and abuse of rhyme, the function of the personal pronoun and its nonfunctional intrusion, the relation of form to content, and so forth, and try to find among the students' work a poem or poems that would aptly illustrate my point. This would take perhaps half the period, and the second half would usually be given to the reading and criticism of some other poems. In my overanxiety, at that time, to keep control of the situation, I often maintained this structure perhaps too rigidly.

Assignments were few and consisted almost entirely of reading; writing assignments were confined to keeping a notebook which would include notes on the class, but these were "on trust" and I did not ask to see them. I wanted

151

above all not to have anyone writing poems "for the class," forcing himself to write when he had nothing to say. My assumption was that if they were poets (and some most certainly were) they would write when they had to, and show me what they wished to show. If any one of them, though a poet, happened during part or all of those twelve weeks to be in a period of not writing, it was my hope that the general principles I was trying to formulate and instill would be of future use to him in any case; and I certainly didn't want any who turned out not to be poets at all to be artificially stimulated, by mere emulation and by assigned work, to a deceptive efflorescence, if I could help it. (This has remained a firm principle in my later teaching experience, though I have somewhat modified its application, as I shall detail on a later page.) I myself, however, as I have already noted, was doing a good deal of homework. I used to rush back home each week and write my summary of the class—not only of what I had said or intended to say, but what everyone else had contributed too—plus axioms and apposite quotes from the Masters— from Pound, Rilke, William Carlos Williams, etc.—and from my own current reading. I would hurry this into the mail, to be mimeographed at the Poetry Center along with the week's batch of new poems for distribution at the next class. My idea was that even if the evening's discussion had become a muddle, each student would have at the end of the course a sort of little book of principles that he could go on using forever. Some of the students have assured me that they do indeed refer back to those summaries from time to time, and value them; but I myself later came to realize that I was spoon-feeding them. Because these were more mature people than the average college class and were for the most part not in need of prodding, some very fine work was written during the course; and when I began to sit back and listen to some of them discuss each other's poems, I found myself learning that I did not have to undertake *all* the teaching—that they had as much to learn from each other as from me. Richard Lourie, for instance, often could put his finger on exactly what it was that was wrong in a poem about which I had only felt an unfocused dissatisfaction; or Emmett Jarrett would come to my aid with a knowledge of prosody far exceeding my own. (These are two young men whose work is beginning to become known since that time.)

Probably the most important benefit of the course for teacher and students alike was in the stimulation of each other's company and the still-continuing friendships that developed from our association in class.

Drew University, 1965–66

My next two teaching assignments were concurrent. Drew University, in New Jersey, asked me to teach a weekly poetry class along the same workshop lines as the one at the Poetry Center; and C.C.N.Y. invited me to become the nonresident equivalent of a "poet in residence." The two groups of students were quite dissimilar.

At Drew—a class of about fifteen students—attitudes, or at any rate behavior, tended to be, with one or two exceptions, trusting or even docile, with an expectation of being told what to do by the teacher; whereas my C.C.N.Y. students that first term were mistrustful of anyone over thirty, in typical big-city style. Drew students for the most part shared a middle-middle-class, more or less suburban background—most frequently in New Jersey—and their ethnic origins were predominantly Anglo-Saxon. They were mostly sophomores and juniors, with one or two seniors and, I think, one freshman; there were a few more girls than boys. Once again I had had the opportunity of choosing among the applicants; but here there was neither a large number to choose from nor were there more than three or four whose precourse work showed unmistakable talent. My greatest difficulty, during the first semester, was that I felt bored and exasperated at lengthy discussions of bad poems and yet did not know how to avoid them without utterly discouraging the beginners who had written them. The more talented and sophisticated students shared my boredom. But I had genuine liking and concern for each of these kids, and my pleasure in seeing whatever development took place in them during the year outweighed the frustrations.

I was under no illusions about how many of them might go on to write poetry of value after the year was over; but there is justification in such a class if—by writing even one or two poems that are not mere doggerel on the one hand, or purely private "self-expressive" effusion on the other, and by recognizing the shortcomings and achievements of others—each student becomes a better *reader* of poetry than he might otherwise have been. I believed my own enjoyment of paintings derived some of its acuteness from my early attempts to be a painter myself; and it seemed reasonable to suppose that just as my memory of what it feels like to hold a brushful of paint or to see the need, in a composition, for a stronger line here and a lightening of tone there, enters into my appreciation of what a painter has done with his canvas, so a nonpoet temporarily engaging with the process of writing a poem would retain forever something of an insider's view when reading, and thereby deepen his satisfaction and the intelligence with which he read.

The structure of each week's class was not very different from that of the Poetry Center classes the year before, but with the addition of several elements: the reading and discussion of poems by good poets of various periods (mainly modern, since, as in most colleges, the students' knowledge of twentieth-century poetry was poor)—so that they had something with which to contrast their own work; a good deal of emphasis on their learning to read aloud properly (God knows what speech departments do, if anything—certainly the average American student has little concept even

154

of how to produce his voice, not to speak of how to read a poem aloud); and a small but regular amount of assigned reading. Writing assignments did not consist of poetry but of notebooks. Since I didn't want to intrude on their privacy, I asked them to make these loose-leaf notebooks, so that though I would periodically ask to see them, any personal revelations they did not wish me to read could be removed before they handed their books in. I believe notebooks to be perhaps the only sure and honest way a writer can stimulate his creativity—that is, can find out that he has more to write than he thought, as distinct from forcing himself to write when he has nothing to say. To be useful, they must not be either mere "backwards engagement books" or the kind of lengthy self-analytic confessionals that become substitutes for living. A useful *writer's* notebook typically consists of brief descriptions (in prose) of things seen or heard; a word or phrase that is haunting one; dreams; transcriptions from relevant current reading; and occasionally—when it happens—perhaps the beginning of a poem. I also required that they "write up" each week's class, much as I myself had done for my Poetry Center students. This practice proved to be exceedingly useful to me, for in checking these over I was able to correct many misunderstandings of which I might never otherwise have become aware. They served, in fact, as a useful measure of my own clarity in explication, or lack of it.

The only poetry-writing assignment in the class consisted of work in translation; and it was interesting to me to discover that the level of writing was uniformly higher when the students were working from another language than it was when they were attempting to write original poems. I have since seen the same thing happen with other groups of students. The explanation is simple: students, especially young ones, unless quite exceptionally gifted, simply don't have the technical equipment to deal verbally with the tumult and confusion of their own thoughts and feelings. When they find a poem in another language (with or without a prose literal to help them understand it) that seems to speak for them or for which they feel some empathy, the relief at discovering the groundwork already done, the experience already in focus, the image emerged, releases untapped reserves of language in them so that even if their translation is quite free, quite a personal interpretation or adaptation of the original, it will usually show a competence, a craftsmanship, far in advance of their other writing.

We had the advantage of holding our three-hour sessions in a small secluded building. A kitchen adjoined the classroom, so that when we took our break we could make coffee. This helped the students feel there was something special, intimate, and exclusive about being in the poetry course (the first of its kind at Drew), which they enjoyed. However, I overestimated the degree to which this feeling of intimacy and of shared experience would extend through the rest of each week for them. Because it was a residential campus, and not a very large school, I assumed, in my ignorance of college life, that they would surely meet frequently in the course of their daily activities; but since they were of different academic years, and not all English majors, this was not true. Moreover, since poetry was of supreme importance to me I presumed it was so for them also and that they would therefore create opportunities to meet and talk about each other's work between classes; but in fact, while for a few writing was a major interest, for the majority it was quite naturally only one among several equal preoccupations. It was not until the tragic death of one member of this class the following summer that I realized how much less all of them had known about each other (except in the case of one or two close friendships that had existed before the class began) than I did about each one. I wrote a letter to the whole class and sent Xeroxed copies to each member, thinking that the boy's death would have been the grief and shock to them that it was to me and that such a letter might be helpful and even necessary; but though their replies did express sorrow, it was for someone almost a stranger to all but one.

Retrospectively I felt that though most of these students worked hard, were interested, and showed definite, if varying, degrees of development in their work during the year—some, indeed, writing poems I thought extremely beautiful, and others "getting at things," making discoveries in their notebook writing that were of undeniable value—yet if they had had the kind of extracurricular interchanges—the hours over coffee, or late at night in someone's room, reading poems aloud, arguing, dreaming together—that I naïvely imagined were the heart of student life (as they are in books—old or European books, alas!) and would be especially prevalent among a bunch of hopeful poets—if they had had this they might have gone much further in their understanding of poetry, further both as readers and writers. Even if we had met twice, instead of once, a week, it would have helped. Or if I had been living on campus instead of merely taking the train from New York just in time to eat lunch and go to class, returning directly after it was over, laden with papers which I began to read in the train—consumed, I may add, with the kind of curiosity about *what had the kids produced this week* that only a noncareer, part-time teacher is prone to . . .

C.C.N.Y. I, 1965.

Meanwhile different things were happening for me at C.C.N.Y. Physically, to begin with, the setup could not have been more different. My trips to Drew included a delightful ferry ride and a train ride which—though I used to return home spent—I always found agreeable, much of it running between old backyards full of trees; and the Drew campus is spacious and green. My C.C.N.Y. class was scheduled early enough in the morning so that it was impossible to avoid the subway rush hour; then, always overloaded with books, a steep uphill walk through a housing project and a slum street to the Old English building, where the elevator was usually out of order or hopelessly crowded and the

157

corridors and stairs jammed with students milling about between classes. Save for the absence of shouting monitors and the size of the students, it was, in fact, almost indistinguishable from a typical New York elementary school. Arrived at the third floor, I would be caught—unless I arrived late—in the two-way traffic at the door of my classroom, where students issuing from a class taught there during the previous hour were trying to force their way out against the stream of my students trying to force their way in. The room was invariably strewn with cigarette butts, for though smoking was apparently not forbidden, no ash trays were provided. The room was dingy, the noise from outside—though we were on the "quiet" side of the building—often considerable. Only the students, with their hungry eyes, amazingly varied shapes and sizes, and equally varied styles of dress, were beautiful.

Yes, they were beautiful in their variety, their discontent, their hunger for life and poetry. But I missed the boat with them almost completely that first semester. I made several miscalculations, failed to get through to all but a few of them, and comparing them with my attentive and willing Drew students felt for the latter a love that these difficult and demanding big-city products did not—collectively —elicit in me.

My first miscalculation was in the number of students I accepted for the course. I no longer remember if it was suggested to me by the department that I take as many as possible, or whether I simply decided, since there was no orderly and rational way to choose among them anyway, to let them all come. But in any case, for the kind of course I had in mind to give, there was too large a number—between twenty-five and thirty. In a once-a-week course lasting, in this instance, only one semester, it is impossible for a nonresident teacher to get to know that many students in anything but a very superficial way. In fact, though I announced my availability after class each week for conferences (held in my cubicle-office across the hall), the

158

schedules of many students made it impossible for them to come and see me.

My second miscalculation was in the nature of the course itself. I had been given carte blanche; indeed, my invitation was basically to make myself available weekly as a representative "practicing poet," so that student poets would have the opportunity of association with a professional. Therefore—partly for a change, and because I felt that to teach two workshop courses concurrently would be at the very least confusing to me, and worse, monotonous; partly because it was obvious that the work of each individual in such a large group could not possibly be adequately discussed—I decided to make this a kind of lecture series, though they were to be very informal, interruptible lectures, leading, I hoped, to plenty of free discussion. My plan was to start from myself and work outward: to give a picture of one poet's—my own—early influences—beginning with nursery rhymes and Beatrix Potter—and formative experiences, describing what seemed to me my own beginnings as a poet; and going on to my coming to America, the impact of American poetry on me, and the interplay between me and some of my contemporaries. It was not meant, of course, to be a mere autobiographical excursion; I was to be only the starting point and the connecting thread; the reading would not consist of my own poems (which, again naïvely, I assumed that—once signed up for my course—they would read from simple curiosity, if they had not, indeed, signed up precisely because they *had* read them: both false assumptions), but of, first, fairy tales and English poets, especially the thirties' poets who were my first introduction to contemporary writing; then Williams, Pound, Stevens, and on to Duncan and Creeley and to poets younger than myself about whose work I was excited *that* year—all the way, in fact, from my curiously Victorian childhood reading in England, the tail end of the 1930s caught hold of through my older sister, the British "New Romantic" movement of the forties, then the revelation of Williams, the development of the so-called Black Mountain school, and right on into the advance guard of their own generation. I believed that, peculiar as my own life as a poet was, with my private education, mixed (racial and religious) background, unusually early assumption that I was a poet, and my having come to America only when I was a year or two older than they now were—nevertheless it would provide them, if they examined their own lives, with correspondences, equivalents. I wanted, by dwelling upon my childhood, to recall their own childhoods to them, as Rilke advised the Young Poet to do; and thought that in searching out clues to their own impulses to write, they might find unexpected sources of strength. I wanted, by suggesting how erratic and fortuitous (and nevertheless profitable) a poet's reading might have been, to stimulate in them an exploratory spirit; and by announcing my own lack of formal training, free them a little from the tyranny of grades and course reading. I wanted, instead of anything resembling a survey course on modern poetry, to give them as it were an inside—though necessarily very partial—view of contemporary poetry, as, for example, in what I would have told them of the interchanges of work and news and friendship that come to be called, by critics, a "school."

I still think it was a good idea—for a course given under certain circumstances, almost none of which were present in this case. I have thought in some detail about what these ideal circumstances would be, and shall list them: (1) A full year, not one semester, in which to give the course. (2) A small number of students—not exceeding sixteen, but not less than ten—because there should be (3) as much variety as possible in their personal backgrounds (the C.C.N.Y. class fulfilled this condition, especially in comparison to Drew, as far as ethnic origins were concerned; but their economic and educational backgrounds were almost equally homogeneous). (4) They should all be of the same academic year (preferably juniors and seniors); should all have a fairly good knowledge of poetry up to, say, Yeats and Eliot; and should all have done *some* reading, however random, of contemporary American poetry. (5) They should all be at least as serious about writing poetry as students who enroll in a workshop, since the course would be at least partly an examination of what experiences, what kind of reading (and other art experiences), what kind of living, seems conducive to writing. Or, from hearing about one poet's life at firsthand, what parallels can you draw from your own? (6) The physical circumstances in which the course is taught should be as intimate, comfortable, and generally conducive to relaxed discussion as possible (of course, I think this is a desirable condition for any class). My attempt to teach this course at C.C.N.Y. was a fiasco because none of these conditions was present, with the partial exception of #3, as noted.

On the contrary, there was hardly time to get started; there were too many students (few of whom knew each other before or became acquainted during the semester); and their educational background was in almost all cases New York City public schools, which is to say that they were culturally deprived. C.C.N.Y., with rather high standards and many devoted teachers, cannot with the best will in the world compensate in two, three, or four years for the shortcomings of bad grade- and high-schools. I must emphasize that an astonishingly high proportion of these students in my estimation (and probably according to IQ counts too) were brilliant. But almost all were grossly ignorant.

It is hard to describe this ignorance. There was a lot that they knew, academically, that is, they had taken certain courses and had learned, therefore, the contents of those courses. But—this being a big university—few of them had taken the *same* courses, it seemed, and what they had not yet studied in a course they had no conception existed at all. If all had at least had the *same* lacunae!—but as it was there was no common knowledge, nothing shared, no shared culture, in fact, except the culture of the streets and playgrounds and comic books of their childhoods, which *I* could not penetrate because *I* had not shared it. I don't mean to give the impression that C.C.N.Y. students are illiterate, not in any conventional use of the word. One girl in this class, I remember, gave a most beautiful, deeply felt, and thoroughly prepared talk on a difficult E. E. Cummings poem; a young man, obviously headed for "Grad. School," discussed the prosody of—was it Spenser? Donne?—with devastating erudition (and perhaps a certain spite, because I had shown a disinclination to do anything of that kind); and another gifted and sensitive girl brought in a kind of homage-to-Williams poem that showed she had read Williams deeply and thoroughly—and not for a course, either. But it seemed as if each individual had a specialty and none had a common frame of reference, so that each allusion I made—and such a course as I was attempting, with its personal core and its wide range of citations, must of necessity depend largely on comprehensible, suggestive allusion—was picked up by only one or two students.

What these marvelous, interesting, challenging students had been deprived of was a sense of historical continuity, of context—the very thing a liberal education should provide. (And this was not the fault, most definitely, of C.C.N.Y.'s English Department, but of a much larger situation—of all that is wrong with our society and especially with our cities.) It angers me when I think of it—and I also feel unhappy with myself for not having realized it sooner, so that I could have done more to redeem what for most of them must have been a wasted semester, as far as that class was concerned. What in fact happened was that I did not pursue my original plan very far, since while I did so they sat restless and—or so it seemed to me—either bored or angry. But I did not come up with a satisfactory substitute; instead I tried one thing and then another: one week a discussion of some contemporary poems (chosen usually by a student)—Creeley, Corso, E. E. Cummings—a great favorite among them, incidentally, and not, in general,

162

with me—Ginsberg, are those I remember, and the next, of some student's poems—discussions which failed, usually, to come to grips with anything, but slid off into purely subjective "likes" and "dislikes," because we had not established any evaluative standards; or conversations on life in general which almost said something but, again, fell short of their potential because we did not know each other well enough or because the bell would ring at the crucial moment —and which anyway did not involve enough of the people present.

Some time after the semester began, there was some improvement brought about by the simple fact of our suddenly—myself and several other students—deciding to move the two long tables so that, instead of being end to end, with great distance between the people sitting at the two extremes, they were side by side so as to form a large square. This necessitated sudden physical activity for everyone in the room, as all the chairs had to be moved. A wonderful moment!—everyone in motion, talking, laughing, swearing, and a tremendous noise not just floating in irritatingly from somewhere else but made by us . . . With the exception of—alas—the last class of the semester, when too late a parallel sense of involvement and interchange seemed to occur, but on a less physical, more intellectual level, which might have led to good things if there had been a second semester to follow it up, this stands out for me as the most interesting experience of that fall, as far as the class as a group was concerned. There were, of course, some individual good things that happened too, things said or written by one or another student that I found exciting, or things I said or did that a single student or a few found valuable; but little else that I think was shared by everyone.

Perhaps a group experience is less important in a class small enough for each individual member of it to receive—whether from teacher or fellow student—an

163

epiphany at some time or other; but when a class is held once a week for only one semester and there are more than fifteen people enrolled in it, there is a mathematical likelihood that this kind of individual epiphany will occur only for a minority. Somehow, instead, I think the teacher must generate, and ferment among the students, enough passion and drama to produce a *collective* epiphany; and this not for its own sake (for it is hard to evaluate the depth or lasting value of such collective experiences) so much as for the sake of its function as gateway, portal, to new levels of feeling, to a greater openness after passing through it, and the sense of comradeship that can develop even among quite a large number of people who have been together in a time of crisis or revelation.

When I ask myself how I might have done better with those students in those three months, I come up with no satisfying answers. I could have put it up to them, right at the outset: what kind of class did they hope this would be? Let everyone make suggestions, and vote on them. But I was a total stranger to them, and they, with—as I've said —a kind of typical big-city cageyness (the result of having had to develop strong defenses in the streets and schools just to survive), were distrustful of strangers and therefore unlikely to have made many really sincere suggestions. When the course ended we had just come to the point, I believe, where they *could* have thrashed out among themselves and with me a plan for how to use a *second* semester.

Alternatively, I could have conducted a conventional lecture course on a selection of contemporary poets, with time for questions and discussion, and with writing assignments each week. This would have been familiar to them, and they would probably not have felt they were wasting their time. But, again, many might, not unjustly, have felt disappointment at getting from a "visiting poet" merely *more of the same*, something a professional academic might have given them just as well or better.

C.C.N.Y. II, 1966

Though I considered the fall a fiasco, I was asked to teach at C.C.N.Y. for the spring term also, and accepted dubiously but in the hope of redeeming my failure, even though with a new set of students. (I continued to see three or four members of the "fiasco" class occasionally, either in conference or—later—at meetings of this second group.) I limited enrollment, and devoted the first, and half of the second, session to getting acquainted, for I intended this to be more of a workshop, and believed that freedom and honesty of discussion in a poetry workshop depended heavily on each member having some sense of the value of every other member.

This time I was blessed with students who were, I feel, even more responsive to this kind of situation than even the best of the first group might have been if the fall enrollment had been similarly limited. Though they shared the New York City public school background I have described, their defenses were not up even at the very beginning. I don't think this was due to my establishing, as far as I could, an ideal circumstance, but to some fortunate "psychological chemistry."

I began by asking them, each in turn, to tell their names and something about family background, and when and how they had first begun to write poetry (several had first done so through the encouragement or example of a single memorable and inspiring eighth- or ninth-grade teacher); expecting to have to coax this information from them. But on the contrary: launched into autobiography, it was hard to stop them—and they listened eagerly, as if hungry for just such information about each other. Indeed, as I came to realize, in the hurried, scattered life of a big non-residential university, it is quite possible for a student to go from class to class all year without knowing much more of his fellow students than he knows of the people whom he sees each day in the subway. (And such is the routine of many lives that the same people do actually sit —or stand—in the same car of the same train day after day on their way to job or school. But only an emergency, such as the blackout that struck the East in 1965, breaks down their mutual reserve.)

We found that our group included a Puerto Rican boy who was a painter as well as a poet; a Chinese girl born in Hong Kong; a black girl who was a blues and folk singer and had been to Africa the year before in connection with some intercultural project; a Polish boy who had come to the U.S. when he was about seven years old and could still remember his farm home in Poland; a Jewish boy from the Bronx who was a twin—his twin brother and an older brother both wrote poetry also, it turned out; and so on, round the table—an extraordinarily interesting and varied ten or twelve kids (I am unsure, now, about the number, because a few members of the fall class joined this one on an informal basis). This was almost an ideal group for anyone to work with. Their talent and level of achievement varied, but all had a genuine and keen interest in poetry and were not just taking the course for an easy credit. We had from the beginning a genuinely friendly and even excited relationship. There was no one who really held back —even though, of course, some were more reserved or shy than others—and they actually did begin to do what I hoped for at Drew but which, even though it would have seemed easier to do at Drew, seemed rarely to happen there: they met after or between classes, in the cafeteria or elsewhere, and went on talking about each other's poems and about poetry and life in general.

As often as possible I invited them all to my apartment in downtown New York instead of holding an ordinary session in the noisy, ugly classroom; and though—because these living-room sessions had to be held in the evening, since in the daytime they had full schedules and, in some cases, part-time jobs as well—it was not possible to do this

166

often, yet the intimacy and social familiarity these few occasions gave were a definite help in increasing the cohesiveness and interaction that came to exist among them. I don't imply that all of them met together out of class; but a few had known one another before, and certain others became close friends during the semester; so that most of them gathered in groups of from two or three to five or six. At the end of the year I suggested that they try to remain in touch during the summer, so that in the fall we could continue to meet at my house whenever I could manage it; and a number of them did this. The next winter, though circumstances prevented my doing this on a regular once-a-month basis, we did gather perhaps five times at my apartment, and what was even better, they met a number of times at each other's homes. The learning from each other which took place then—and for a few of them still continues today—as seen in the work several continue to send me from time to time, is one of the greatest pleasures I have known in my teaching experience so far.

Until almost the end of the year, I was quite cautious about letting occasional auditors into the classroom for fear of disturbing our sense of privacy. (I consulted the group about this and they agreed.) But toward the end I did let a few congenial extra students in occasionally; and to the meetings we held in my apartment the following fall and winter I sometimes invited other young—and sometimes older—poets, especially my former Poetry Center students, two or three of whom were by then editing a magazine to which, eventually, some of the C.C.N.Y. students contributed (one, in fact, has since become one of the editors), and a few from Drew, and now and again (it would have been oftener but for the distance) some of my Vassar students—for by then I was teaching at Vassar. On these occasions what occurred was not so much a class as an open poetry reading; the room was crowded to bursting, thick with smoke, and littered cheerfully with wineglasses and coffee cups. The value of so gathering—aside from the fact

that it was fun—was that it gave young writers an opportunity to be heard by, and to hear, a larger group of their
peers than the small class afforded, and—bound as we were
by a shared passion for poetry—to feel some sense of there
being (as I believe there is, despite all that people will
say about professional backbiting and intrigue) a community
of poets, a sense of belonging to a Mystery, a guild. Criticism
would be offered from fresh sources; the way a poem
sounded in a larger context, a context of listeners not all
of whom knew what development had taken place in the
writer's work in the past six months, was often a revelation;
and sometimes a particularly warm response—applause
even—would give pleasure and new confidence to a kid
that needed it. My function became more and more that
of a hostess and occasional point of reference; they were
not dependent on me.

But I have run ahead of myself. What actually went on
during the spring semester classes at City College? And
what of the cultural deprivation of which I spoke in describing my initial impressions there? Well, that existed in this
group too; but somehow, among such a small number, it
didn't seem to get in the way. Because they got to know
each other so much better than the average class, and were
so varied in background and knowledge, each contributed
something which all the others seemed to pick up on, and
so individual deficiencies were to a large extent compensated for: I think that is the explanation. As to what we
did: basically the course was not very different from those
at the Poetry Center and at Drew—an attempt to supply,
by discussion of technical elements and of "stance" (i.e.,
the emotional, moral, and aesthetic attitudes of the artist),
some underpinnings for judgment or—a better word—
evaluation of their own work; an emphasis on *listening
to the sounds* of poetry, not reading merely with the eye,
and upon experiencing the poem as a sonic entity before
embarking on any analysis of its parts; and concomitantly

upon learning—as a part of one's responsibility to the art one serves—to read aloud slowly and clearly.

Here too, as at Drew and later at Vassar, I tried to get them to develop a sense of the concrete and particular, instead of writing about their "feelings" in vague abstract terms. This emphasis had been less necessary at the Poetry Center, where the class members were mostly older and more developed as poets. It is, however, almost always essential with younger students, as I have found not only with those I have taught on a regular basis but also from the many occasional seminars I have conducted when visiting colleges for a few days at a time and from the poems and letters often sent to me by unknown student readers (many of whom seem, in innocent egotism, to look on any published poet as an on-tap Free University-by-Mail!). I shall return to this question of the concrete and sensuous in more detail when I come to speak of my Vassar class.

Notebooks were again emphasized as important tools for their development (but not, in this case, examined by me unless at the request of an individual), and assignments were very few and consisted, I think, exclusively of reading and of translation. I read aloud to them a good deal, and it was, I think, with this class that I first tried out Muriel Rukeyser's wonderful idea of having a whole class read a poem one after another, without previous discussion—something which perhaps sounds boring but in fact turns out to be a sort of alchemical process, a process of filtering, refining, and intensification of understanding that is far more effective and moving than any mere analytical method can be. Usually the first one or two readers stumble and hesitate; the next two read with some confidence and facility; then a period of boredom and irritation may set in—probably most participants feeling they can't bear to hear those same words one more time; and then—subtly—that point is passed, and one finds oneself at a different level of response, finds oneself emerging into an intimate, sensuous com-

169

prehension of the poem that activates both intellect and imagination. I have never known it to fail (though I have not discovered what the optimum number of participants is for this technique—too few, obviously, would in this case probably be worse than too many).

It was not innovations or inventiveness on my part, then, that made this class in most ways the best I have yet experienced, but the fact that I, as well as the students, was relaxed, encouraged, and confident. For the first time I found myself sitting back and letting them do the talking. At the Poetry Center I had sometimes turned the class over to one of the members for some special topic—syllabics, or new methods of measuring quantity (in reference to Williams's "variable foot")—of which their knowledge was obviously greater than mine; and at Drew I asked students, on occasion, to prepare and deliver a talk on some writer in whom they were especially interested. But with this group I was able to let discussion ramble without tensely feeling I was no longer in charge and that if I were not in charge they would feel cheated, ultimately, and not give me their attention when I wanted it. On the contrary, I was now able to rejoice in their being in charge of themselves; and of course, concomitantly, their trust in me and respect for me were much greater, I believe, than that of students with whom I was more authoritarian. With them, incidentally, I became in the most natural way Denise, instead of Miss Levertov. Even with the Poetry Center class, though as I have said they were mainly quite accomplished poets, and older than average too, I remained Miss Levertov in the classroom till the end of the course, and at Drew there seemed no inclination to address me less formally, and indeed I think I would have embarrassed those students by indicating that I didn't care what they called me. Yet *I* always addressed everyone by their first name without even thinking about it— even at Vassar where there was an old-fashioned habit of calling the girls Miss This and Miss That, upheld I suppose by male teachers who wanted to maintain a convenient sense of distance from an all-girl class.

I don't mean to suggest that all was perfect and everybody satisfied. We did have only one semester to work in, and so much to say and do—and at the end of the year I was left with a sad feeling of how much had been left out, how much confusion they still felt among all the possibilities of the craft, how little they still knew of their own possibilities. And the free meetings of the following school year were not as frequent by any means as I had wished. Nevertheless it was an experience that remains for me a model of how a poetry workshop can be at least the beginning of a kind of community; and proof of how, for the "teaching" of poetry at least—I have of course no knowledge of whether this would be true for other studies—a community, an atmosphere of sharing which extends beyond the "subject" in hand, is the most conducive to real learning, a learning in which the teacher shares.

Vassar I (Workshop), 1967–68

At Vassar, the physical environment was all one could ask for. At the beginning and end of the year, at least, we held some classes outdoors in the parklike campus; and the classroom allotted to me was clean, quiet, and quite comfortable—though, since it had a long table it was not possible to move, and because smoking was not allowed, we eventually moved out to a social room in one of the dormitories where there were soft chairs, a rug, and people could sprawl or smoke if they wished. And the girls—thirteen to start with, then eleven, one leaving college for medical reasons and one leaving the class because she had decided she did not want to write poetry after all (she came back at the end of the year, informally)—had the kind of educational background C.C.N.Y. students generally lack. A surprising number of them were very definitely talented—to the degree that one could reasonably expect they might con-

171

tinue writing, and well, after they had left college. (There is of course, a certain amount of creativity that seems a part of being young—not that it is to be despised. Or perhaps it is rather that the creative impulse in some individuals turns toward poetry at a certain period of their lives, though they are not definitively and inescapably poets and will later find their destiny elsewhere. But among these girls were several who perhaps would remain engaged with the art and find in it the focus of their lives, or so it seemed to me—and I shall only find out if I was right ten or twenty years from now.)

On the other hand, the fact that they were all girls and all sophomores and juniors was a disadvantage. The value of such a class being coed seems to lie not in the fact that more different points of view will be voiced (for ten girls are surely liable to have ten points of view as different from each other, taking into account similarity of age and social background, as five boys and five girls), but in the tendency of boys to be more outspoken, less dominated by the desire to please or fear of committing themselves which, consciously or unconsciously, seems to affect a group of girls unleavened by a masculine element. (I arrived at this supposition from talking to the girls themselves about the problem. A number of them said that in coed high-school classes, they had been less afraid to venture opinions.) It is not that boys talk more than girls, but when they do talk they are more apt to blurt out their true feelings. So for a good part of the first term we moved cagily —I trying to get them to talk more freely, and especially to talk *to each other* and not address all their remarks to me; and they resisting and mistrustful of each other, almost as my first C.C.N.Y. students had been mistrustful of *me*.[1]

By the Christmas vacation I was depressed and so were they; it seemed as if, despite talent and excellent conditions

[1]This is curiously different from what I've since learned in Women's Liberation groups.

172

and despite all I felt I had learned at C.C.N.Y. the previous spring, this class was not going to be a success. But somehow after the vacation and the exam period were over (there were no exams in this course, but they had naturally been affected by the tension and anxiety of those in their other subjects) a change seemed to occur for no discernible reason —unless it was the departure of the two girls who dropped the course, though neither had been a disruptive element. Those who remained seemed to draw closer together; something had crystallized, settled. They were now less eager for tête-a-têtes with me, more willing to share ideas and responses with each other. And by the end of the year the level of constructive, appreciative, and intelligent response they were exchanging was in gratifying contrast to the "Like-Don't like" style in which they had begun their association.

My principal efforts with this group were to shake them loose a bit from their timid perfectionism—probably an endemic trouble in the more conservative women's colleges, with high entrance requirements and consequently a high proportion of nervously ambitious girls, the former academic stars of their secondary schools—and to awaken their powers of sensuous observation (often neglected since early childhood in favor of a one-sided intellectuality), as the only foundation for technical development in the art of poetry. So few of them, gifted though they were, seemed ever to have really looked at anything. They walked through that beautiful park with their heads down and their thoughts anywhere but on the natural world. It was not that I wanted them to write "about" Nature—but in fact they were living among, for instance, some of the finest trees I have ever seen, and I thought it as essential for them to notice the fact as I would for a city dweller to notice, say, the movement of people on the streets or the reflection of traffic lights on wet pavement at night.

To demonstrate the principle of what I would call *unsought* objective correlative, I brought in some fallen leaves, one for each student, and asked them to write objec-

173

tively on what they saw. As some sort of model, I had first read them some of Francis Ponge's prose poems, which are phenomenological descriptions of the utmost freshness; as well as some quotations from Rilke's letters, about *looking*, about the kind of humble yet passionate looking that woos a Thing to reveal itself, and which proves to reveal also far more about individual feeling and "voice" than any introspective abstraction. This first in-class assignment produced a general level of writing much higher than most of what they had been doing on their own, and they did not fail to recognize it. The reason was similar to that I have suggested earlier as the reason students write better when they are translating than when dealing directly with their own content; but in this case it was not so much that they were not "starting from scratch" as that they were discovering how the filters of the senses (in this instance, sight, and to a lesser extent, touch) don't subvert but intensify the action on language of underlying mood or preoccupation. Or to put it another way, that there is no purely objective and no purely subjective art—the objective is necessary to genuine "expression," and subjective "feeling" to genuine objectivity. Translating, again—with all its varied technical possibilities—is a marvelous exercise, but I emphasized that it would only be really fruitful if they chose originals for which they felt some affinity.

Other assignments included taking a poem of their own and turning it into plain prose: which revealed the weakness of bad poems and the strengths of good ones; and free-associating (this was a limbering-up exercise) on themes I gave them. The words allotted—which included Fear, Anger, Discovery, Birth, Entrance, among others—had been carefully chosen for each individual as highly emotive for her, my choice being based on what I had by then learned of her both in class and in conference and from her work. I had not, on principle, asked them to write poems—just to write; but as it turned out, many of them did write poems in the course of this and other in-class assignments, or later

174

developed notes written in class-time into poems; and in some cases—for reasons I don't understand—these were some of the best work they did all year.

This fact caused me to relax somewhat, as the year went on, my stringency in regard to assigning any poem writing. I was still—and I am sure will remain—cautious about the value of external pressure on the creative impulse, for I detest the clever verse disguised as poetry that emanates so frequently from the academic poetry factories and makes its way so efficiently in the world, acclaimed by reviewers who, like the verse writers, suppose poetry to be a way of *manipulating* language. But I did begin to suggest that, if they were brewing a poem anyway, they should consider whether this particular material—or some notebook material they had not yet developed—might not lend itself to a narrative form, for instance, or to the form of a dialogue, instead of taking for granted that, because they had done "lyrics" before, it would have the form of a short lyric. One of our most frequent topics of discussion all along was the relation of form to content, not only in the basic word-to-word and line-to-line sense in which one must discuss any poem under close scrutiny, but in the larger sense of what, in the intrinsic nature of content, makes one poem-seed grow into a dramatic monologue and another into a ballad, or a sonnet, or a song.

Since it was too far for these students conveniently to come down to New York to participate in those poetry parties I used to enjoy with the C.C.N.Y. group and other young poets, I decided to start Open Readings at Vassar when, in the spring, I moved up there to live ten weeks while my husband was teaching at Stanford. We made posters and invited anyone to come who was writing poetry, to read or just to listen. There were many girls who were not in my class, or in any class where poems were read, but who were writing poetry; and though not all my own students came to the Open Readings regularly or at all, those who did found these new associates stimulating; while the

175

unknown poets themselves, appearing out of the woodwork, rejoiced in discovering a kind of noncredit class and—again—some sense, I think, of community. A few faculty came to these sessions also; one of whom disturbed me by trying, I felt, to overformalize them by his too-dogmatic comments and by not waiting to be *asked* to comment. His intentions were kind; but my idea was that Open Readings should have a very free atmosphere and not merely be extra classes, though criticism would be available for those who desired it; and that critical comment should not come exclusively from me or from any other faculty member, but should be a matter of peer response. I tried to emphasize this by reading work-in-progress of my own and getting other faculty to do so—in fact, I tried as far as possible to ensure that no one who was not prepared to throw his or her own work into the arena with everyone else's should offer criticism (though, of course, anyone could come as a listener)—and to reduce my own function to seeing that all who wished got a chance to read and were not swamped by the more aggressive.

Some boy friends and students from a nearby men's college came to one or two of the Open Readings, which was a pleasure after our segregated classes. And some foreign students read in their own languages, which gave us an interesting chance to listen to sounds we did not understand (Israeli and, as I recall, Pakistani) which yet we could hear were the sounds of poetry. It was interesting too to note that, while some of the poetry being written "on their own" by girls who had never been in a "workshop" was every bit as good as some of that being written under a poet's guidance, the quality of evaluative, constructive criticism my students were by the late spring able to offer was much higher. They could see why and how a poem was or was not an achieved work, where even accomplished writers who had not done the kind of thinking about craft that they had done were unable to express distinctions or put their finger on what was wrong. This gave me great pleasure, for I felt I had in some substantial measure achieved one of my principal goals: to put underpinnings of understanding beneath "talent." It has been said that talent is of no use without character. I don't know if I agree—it depends on what is meant by character. But I do know talent is effervescent and easily corrupted without a sense of responsibility to craft, of art as a power to which talent may be dedicated *and which demands of its votaries something more than to be used by them for the relief of moods.*

The other principal success in this class was the way the students came during the year to have more tolerance and even respect for each other—even for the less talented among their number. This was partly due to the fact that even the two or three who perhaps should not have been in the class in the first place, because they were neither as capable nor as concerned as the rest, did make some progress in either their writing or their insights as readers, or both; and partly because, since I made a point of taking everybody seriously, assuming they were doing the best they could, the more arrogant members gradually began to do so too.

I think what *I* learned from *them* that year was also more tolerance: I came to see more clearly how precarious the confidence of the seemingly confident young really is, how a piece of writing that to me might seem—seen objectively—weak and banal may mean much to them as a step along their own road; so that though one does not want to let them think they have done something marvelous when they haven't, though one wants to make them learn to make demands on their own capacities and not be self-satisfied, yet it is even more important not to discourage them, by an unfeeling excess of candor, from taking the *next* step. The situation is different with older writers in a student relationship: the middle-aged who have only just begun to write, or who have been writing for years and still write badly, are, I think, extremely unlikely to develop further, and it is kinder to let them know it, in most cases.

177

Vassar II, 1967-68

This was a concurrent class of another kind: a senior semi-
nar in modern poetry, the first and, so far, the only non-
workshop class I had taught.[1] We read Yeats, Pound, Eliot,
Williams, Stevens, H. D., Lawrence, Creeley, and Duncan.
If it differed from other such seminars in being taught by
a poet, not a scholar, it was perhaps chiefly in that, with
the exception of Eliot, all the poets studied were of great
importance to me as a *writer*, not only as a reader. Talking
about a poet who has been or continues to be a personal
influence is inevitably, even if subtly, different from talking
about a writer to whom one stands, however admiringly
or pleasurably, only in the relation of reader.

It was an exciting class to teach, not only because I enjoyed
the close reading and thinking it made necessary, but
because, through the many excellent papers the students
wrote, and in the course of sometimes quite heated discus-
sions, I made so many discoveries and rediscoveries. Not
all were English majors—four or five out of the ten—but
all had had exactly that kind of civilizing, connective educa-
tion I had missed in my first C.C.N.Y. class: one could—with
occasional exceptions—make allusions without drawing
blanks, and if an individual did not know about something
one assumed she did know, the tendency was for her to
go off and look it up without being urged to do so.

Vassar's English Department in general discourages the
use of secondary sources, so my emphasis on reading not
what critics had said but rather the respective poets' own
prose writings—essays, autobiographies, letters, and so
on—as adjuncts to the reading of the poems themselves,
was not an innovation. Having the students keep, for a period
of some weeks, poetry reading journals, was, however, some-
thing new, and proved enjoyable to them and important
to me for the insights they gave me both into the readers'

[1]Except for the amorphous C.C.N.Y. I.

individual approaches and often, through them, into the poems read. These notebooks took the place of regular papers for a while, and were intended to be regular annotations upon their current reading in poetry, not necessarily confined to the poets we were studying in class. They could be as informal as anyone wanted; I hoped they would reveal some interplay between our studies and their free reading, and between their daily lives and other studies and their awareness of poetry. And this did in fact happen. Some girls, indeed, continued to keep the journals going after the assignment was over and we had returned to more formal papers. However, even such papers were not required to be as formal as in most of their courses (or so they seemed to feel); that is to say, while I expected them to do the required reading conscientiously (which was no problem, as they were really interested), I did not have the scholar's horror of the impressionistic paper, if it was well written, and I encouraged them to forget the boring impersonality many had learned was the proper approach (in preparation, alas, for Grad. School!) and try to get hold of their genuine reactions instead of trying to feel what they thought they ought to feel. I find nothing more tiresome than reading papers written in the tone of patronizing omniscience common to many academic critics. What is wrong with saying flatly "I think," "My reaction was"? But even in high school so many good students are browbeaten into thinking it is insolent or in bad taste to use the personal pronoun in an assigned paper.

My great hope in this course was to confirm those who were already readers of poetry in their love for it, and to awaken that love in those who were in the course because it was their last chance, before graduation, to find out a bit about the subject. I was not out to prepare anyone for graduate school or help make scholars. Those who were going to be scholars were already excellently prepared by their four years at a college which gives the best academic training I have yet encountered. What I wanted was to make

179

good readers of them, so that their reading would be an enduring resource to them no matter what they were going to do after graduation. As in poetry-writing courses, I emphasized the sonic, and to this end—as well as reading aloud to them and getting them to read—made frequent use of tapes and records. More often than in workshop classes our discussion led to consideration of ideas and attitudes. They didn't talk as much as I would have wanted, but their enthusiasm can be judged from their having attended voluntarily an extra class I gave in Study Week and from the fact that several wrote on their final exam that the exam itself had been a pleasure. As for myself, I felt privileged to have spent a reading year with such agreeable and enlivening companions.

Influences

I began to teach with nothing but an anxious desire to share as much as I could of what I had learned in a life spent since childhood in engagement with poetry. Though skeptical of the need for anyone who was really likely to be a poet to attend such a class at all, I wanted to make it as useful as possible, since these people had in fact elected to do so. I wanted to give them ground rules, and pack enough into one course to cause them to desist from shopping around for further courses of the same type: there is something sad in the veteran of many workshops who is still not a poet and never will be. I wanted to teach the kind of course that would reveal to the *non*poet that he was on the wrong track, and define more clearly for the *possible* poet what his own voice was. But I had done little if any thinking about how much the possibility of imparting anything might depend on the degree of authoritarianism or permissiveness of the teacher. In occasional seminars and in giving free criticism to various young poets, I had not had to face this problem. My attitude tends naturally to be rather friendly, informal, and respectful of the individual's effort (unless I take a capricious dislike to him, which is not frequent), and it was not until I taught a regular course that I discovered how authoritarian I could be under pressure of my uncertainty of my own ability to satisfy expectations in a new role, and at the same time the conviction that I knew things they didn't know—knowledge which I was eager to give them. However, at about the same time that I became conscious of how tightly I was keeping the reins in my hands, I was fortunately exposed, at the series of conferences of teachers and writers held in several locations in the New York area in 1965–66, to the ideas and educational hopes of people more experienced than myself, and whose concern was more directly with *how* to teach and *how* to learn than mine (whose deepest allegiance was to poetry itself, not to teaching).

Chief, I think, among these influences was Sam Moon, of Knox College, Illinois, brought to the writers and teachers conferences through my husband, who had spent a week at Knox and been much impressed with his journal of a teaching experiment, "Teaching the Self" (subsequently published in *Improving College & University Teaching,* Autumn, 1966, Vol. XIV, #4). I had long since read some of A. S. Neill, also Caroline Pratt's *I Learn from Children;* both deal with childhood education that provides tools, information, and the freedom to use them, and trusts children will have the curiosity and care to utilize what is so provided, when the teacher is guide, philosopher, and friend, but not a dogmatic authority; and I believed them. But I had not thought much about how to put the same principles into action with college students, nor how to adapt nonauthoritarian practice to my own temperament, or my temperament to it. Sam Moon's experiment, the account Florence Howe and Paul Lauter gave of their work with a summer institute of high-school teachers and students (who lived for several weeks on an absolutely equal basis, both in and out of classes), and the temperamental ability, as a teacher, of my husband, Mitch Goodman, to refrain

181

from dominating his students—the confidence in himself and in them that made it possible for him to endure silences in his classes, at times, of a kind I had always nervously filled up—these were among the factors that began to have an effect on my attitude to my responsibilities and opportunities as a teacher: though whatever change took place in me was not radical or dramatic and probably was not even noticeable to my students as a change.

I did not, and still do not, feel ready to attempt anything quite as decentralized as Sam Moon undertook—and indeed I share the doubts he himself expresses, in his concluding remarks on "Teaching the Self," concerning the degree of self-effacement desirable: the teacher's rights should surely be neither greater nor lesser than those of his students, but equal to theirs. One should control one's vivacity and loquacity only so far as is necessary to give the students a fair chance to bring forth theirs, but not so much as to deny one's own spontaneity and passion, nor to deny them its stimulus. But the philosophic basis of Moon's work, his modesty and honesty, and the evidence given in his students' comments on his experiment of their appreciation of his stance and of its value in their development will, I believe, continue to act for me as guides for my own future practice.

The student revolution, from Berkeley on, was not really an influence on me during the teaching experiences I have recounted, because at none of these colleges was it, during that period, an active force. There was at Vassar a small SDS group which was trying to promote curriculum reforms, but I felt so strongly that they were making a storm in a teapot and that their energies should, instead, have been directed to creating a strong antiwar movement in the college (something which did, that year, begin to form, but entirely without their help), that I took no interest in their activities—especially since, compared at any rate with what they would have had to put up with in the huge universities, it seemed to me that they had a minimum of justifiable academic grievances. It has been through my work with the growth of a Peace Council at Vassar and, in this past year,[2] when I have not been teaching but have toured the country visiting many campuses not only to read and talk about poetry but to speak about draft resistance and meet with Resistance groups, that I have come into direct and stimulating contact with student power in action and learned to see how curriculum changes will and must arise naturally out of the greater maturity and self-dependence of a generation that has, in its best representatives, found the will to buck the Power Elite and to refuse to regard obedience as a virtue in itself: and in so doing has begun to discover hitherto unrealized possibilities of inner change and community.

Some Conclusions, 1968

1. I have been extremely fortunate in having been given, at each place I have taught, without exception, a completely free hand both as to what I taught and how I taught it and in the selection of students. This good fortune has, it is true, deprived me of the chance to contrast such conditions with more conventional ones; however, my husband, during the same period, had more varied conditions of teaching, ranging from large classes and a prescribed curriculum at Hofstra College and the C.C.N.Y. evening division to circumstances at Drew (where he taught the year after I did) identical with those I have described there, and to the Voice Project at Stanford where, to an even greater degree, every condition of freedom and autonomy was met. And his very strong sense of being able best to give and to receive in a small, seminar-type class, where the materials used were chosen by himself and the students and not prescribed impersonally, confirms my conviction that intimacy and flexibility are prerequisites to a good teaching-learning

[2]1968.

183

relationship. Lectures, surely, can only be adjuncts to the seminar—not vice versa.

2. Physically, a pleasant room in which smokers can smoke and lollers can loll seems quite important. If one is going to sit at a table, a round table would be preferable to the usual long rectangle. A noisy room, where one is continually interrupted by sounds of traffic or by talk from the corridor, is obviously distracting—but how little thought architects and planners seem to give to this rudimentary problem! Worst of all, in this connection, is the bell—the nerve-shattering, primitive device that plays Person from Porlock in so many moments of revelation. If possible, poetry classes should be open-ended—i.e., scheduled at a time of day when no one has other classes immediately afterward.

3. The better students get to know each other out of class, the better they will use their time in class, and the better—thereby—the teacher will learn to listen to them and curb his tendency to boss them.

4. If the writer as teacher has a special contribution to make, it can only be, surely, his passion for his art and the story of his personal experience in his craft. Therefore he must put these unequivocally at the service of his students and not try to compete with the scholars or to protect himself by withholding his peculiarities. If he feels a need for such self-protection, he shouldn't be teaching at all. On the other hand there is no denial, it seems to me, that teaching, even at its most rewarding, uses up some of the same kind of energies that go into his own work; therefore I think it is extremely risky for any artist to teach full-time—perhaps especially if he enjoys teaching. That very enjoyment can be a form of seduction, away from his own work—and so, ultimately, a bitterness. He is also more valuable to his students as a part-time or occasional teacher, because he is then ensured against staleness and the development of professional pedagogic tricks, and he brings to the class some of the excitement of having come freshly from the making of literature, rather than from the study

184

of what others have made. At the same time I think it important not to *impose* on others the particularities of one's own point of view and one's own style. I bent over backward not to do this, and have taken pride in the fact that my writing students were not turning out imitations of my own poems. But in retrospect I think it might have been better to take more of a risk in that respect for the sake of sharing with them more of my current working experience, if I could have found a way to do so without violating my necessary solitude. This is a problem to be worked out, perhaps, in the future.

5. As to papers, other assignments, and grades: when, in Vassar II, I assigned papers, I proposed a subject, but at the same time I made it clear that if an individual found it more appropriate to write about some other aspect of the poet we were studying, she was free to do so. I wanted relevance, but I wanted independence also, and not to hear my own words parroted back to me. And I tried, in correcting papers, to stress the importance of good writing, both for its own sake and because the effort to write well promotes clearer thinking and more sensitive reading. Three of the last and best papers in this course were, respectively, a poem, a letter addressed to one of the poets we had read, and an account of the phases of response undergone by the writer in studying Robert Duncan's work and then hearing him read.

I have noted already that I came to modify my resistance to giving "creative" writing assignments to the extent of asking students to undertake the verbal equivalent of still-life drawings, or of attempting to free-associate as an equivalent of a dancer's stretching exercises. But I would still never demand a poem by a certain date or that it be written in a prescribed form.

I was obliged to give half-term and final grades in most of these courses, but made it clear at the start that no one would fail unless he had a grossly inadequate attendance record or had made no contribution at all. I gave (in the workshop courses) A's to those who had been writing exceptionally good poems and had also participated generously and usefully in discussion; B's to those who had written a few good poems, showed definite signs of development, and participated well in discussion, and a few C's to those who were neither productive nor spoke much in class. It so happened that at Vassar at any rate—I no longer remember for sure whether this was so elsewhere—no one who was very active in discussion was notably unproductive of good poems. One girl rarely said a word in class but did write some good poems and was obviously serious about her work. She got a B. I would prefer a no-grading or pass-fail system, but as long as the whole spirit of a course ensures that people are not just working for grades but out of interest in the subject, I don't think it matters very much. In the Vassar senior seminar I tried to get them to adopt Sam Moon's plan, asking each student to suggest what she felt her final grade ought to be, but it didn't work out: some of the best students were too modest—and all of them hated the idea. Indeed it seems feasible to me only in entirely student-run courses. I am not sure how such courses have been arranged in the Free Universities, but my idea of such a course would be that all the planning assignments and grading would be done by a student committee, or if possible by a whole-class voting system, with the "expert"—whether scholar or writer—called in to "do his stuff," but not to pass judgment on the students' achievement at all. Several such experts might be utilized in the semester. This might be a very fruitful way of study in a reading course, and would be a good way for the teaching writer, at any rate, to avoid both developing an autocratic mentality and the expenditure of time and energy in correcting papers and so on, except in response to occasional requests. I don't think, however, that it would be suited to a workshop course, where students, especially beginners, need above all to gain some sense of initiation into the service and practice of an art, and some standards of evaluation, which they are not equipped to give each other but must be handed down by an older practitioner.

A Berkeley Postscript, 1969

I taught at Berkeley from January till early June of 1969—two quarters. Groovy Berkeley! My experiences there, brief though they were, make much of what I have written up to this point seem to me quaint and old-fashioned. My Berkeley students (in the classes called 143 and 108—the freshmen were another matter) demanded and gave more than any others I had known, and by their attitudes made me much more deeply and genuinely nonauthoritarian. I grew younger there, and more open to suggestion; and at the same time more confident. There was no need of establishing and maintaining authority since I had their trust and they had mine. I could see that they respected me more for making and admitting mistakes than if I had carefully avoided any but "successful" sessions.

To be accurate, I met with two distinct adventures at the University of California. One was my first attempt to wrestle with an ordinary, nonelite freshman class in Reading and Expository Writing. The other was a brief but intense taste of the possibility of true human community. I shall treat of them accordingly in two sections, describing first the less satisfying, but nonetheless valuable, segment of my Berkeley experience:

1. In English 1A, section something, I had the privilege of choosing my own texts, but no choice of students. There were thirty of them, preponderantly square, rather timid, and in a few cases semi-illiterate kids; several were athletes, several (including one of the most imaginative and sensitive) belonged to fraternities; quite a large proportion of them were commuters (living with their parents), and just about all of them were desperately worried about grades. Why they were so different from the other two groups I taught

187

I was never sure. Did they represent a changing admissions policy? Apparently not, since, supposedly, University of California admissions are administered by computer (though this fact—the standard answer to questions about possible changes in admissions standards to favor "obedient," nonradical entrants—does not seem to me to preclude the possibility of attitudes being fed into the computer which, based on the applicants' social and "behavior" records in high school, would tend to exclude the brilliant but dissident). Had the remarkable, highly differentiated, third- and fourth-year students in my other classes been as unawakened and timid in their freshman year? Or was it simply that the kind of student who applies for electives in poetry—writing and reading—is such a special type of student that I had in fact never before encountered anything but an elite? At all events I found this class pretty hard going, even though I had an excellent TA (the poet David Bromige).

However, the principal event of the quarter was the Third World Strike, which, while it made things more difficult for me in some ways, probably brought the class further, if raising of consciousness were the measure, than it could have gone in such a limited time without it. I was in agreement with the principles of the strike, even though I had many questions about its timing and tactics; so, when it was declared, I immediately announced my support of it to my class, and told them all my classes would be conducted off campus as long as it continued. There was no question in my mind about continuing to teach: in the three weeks or so that had passed before the strike began I had learned enough about these students to feel confident that I would serve the interests of the Movement and of the Third World infinitely better by staying with these kids and providing a forum for discussion of what was happening than by, as it were, abandoning them. Almost none of them were striking, and almost none of their other classes were taken off campus—the few that were, were not conducted off campus in support of the strike but merely because some teachers feared violence and disruption. As far as I could gather, very little discussion of the issues took place either in these classes or in those that continued to be taught in the classrooms. Yet these students daily had to pass picket lines whose purpose they barely understood, and were witnesses to scenes of police brutality and to the reaction to it, without, I felt, receiving any help in interpreting these events unless I gave it.[3]

For the first few classes after we abandoned the classroom I could not find a suitable location: we met in a student's apartment in Oakland, which meant extra carfares and other inconveniences. There was some resentment, and a good deal of anxiety about the effect of this disruption on their (damned!) grades. One student (who later made his peace with me) complained to the department chairman. Many students were absent—not because they were striking, but because of the journey to and from Oakland. I began to feel the group, so tenuously established *as* a group in any real sense, was breaking hopelessly apart. But I then secured the hospitality of an excellent room in the Newman Center (Catholic Campus Ministry) near the campus, and things picked up again. Anxiety lessened, and they began—albeit grudgingly at first—to acknowledge the actual advantages of a more attractive and relaxed setting, with comfortable chairs and a seminar atmosphere, which freshmen in a huge university so rarely experience.

Since the books I had chosen (providentially) for the course—*The Harmless People,* by Elizabeth Marshall Thomas, *Etruscan Places,* by D. H. Lawrence, *Division Street: America,* by Studs Terkel, and *Night Flight to Hanoi,* by Father Daniel Berrigan—all dealt with kinds of human community (or, in the case of *Division Street,* with its absence

[3]There were, of course, some other faculty members whose position was similar to mine; but I am speaking of the other classes in which these particular thirty students happened to be enrolled.

189

too), it was not difficult to co-ordinate discussion of strike issues, and the broader ones of war, violence, and institutionalized injustice, with the reading material. When they experienced their first tear-gassing and, though they were not strikers but just happened to be in the Plaza at the time, found themselves running from billy-club charges, I felt that my class at least provided them—however reactionary they were, and some of them were indeed!—with a place to express their shock and confusion. The majority were increasingly in sympathy with the aims of the strike (I obliged them to read the Third World manifestoes and do some research on the history of the demands and the Administration's response to them), but many had racist attitudes they were scarcely conscious of, and had had no experience of making any personal sacrifice for anything they believed in. Ethically they were savages (as so-called savages are not). The concept of solidarity for an ideal was strange to them. This says a great deal about our nonculture and our educational system. Individually they were nice kids. Within the grave limits of the quarter system (which means that just as one is getting somewhere the course ends) I believe they learned something, morally and socially: at least they were prevented from following their tendency to try to ignore the whole situation as much as they could; they were forced to think about it a bit. A few eventually joined the picket line (I myself picketed every day after the thrice weekly classes, and on most of the Tuesdays and Thursdays in between), and the next quarter I ran into some of them in the People's Park demonstrations. What of the reading and writing skills freshman English is supposed to be all about? Well, a quarter was not long enough to ensure radical improvements, in most cases, under any circumstances; but I don't think their development in this respect suffered. By the last couple of classes, when, the strike over (but the class still held in the Newman Center, for by then I don't think anyone would have preferred to go back to the drab classroom and its desks), they did in-class writing about a show of photographs on view in the gallery room where we met, I felt that the informality, the tensions we had lived through, and my encouragement of personal, original observation and expression of feeling in their papers, had begun to pay off and that they had a better idea of what constituted good writing than when we started.

2. Meanwhile I had also been teaching a poetry workshop class (fourteen students), which I shall not describe in detail since it did not differ greatly from earlier ones I have already written about, and to which (since it was held off campus anyway, and its members were all far more aware and liberated people than the English 1A students) the strike did not pose any problems. What did distinguish it (along with the high quality of those fourteen as people and as talented poets) was that it met in rotation in each student's apartment; and this fact added to the already discussed advantages of meeting in any thoroughly humanized setting that of an increased sense, for all of us, of each one's personal life, of who each one was as expressed by the way he lived, the pictures he chose to hang or tack on his walls, the books on his shelves. This increased intimacy deepened our relationships and gave the class a cohesive quality even greater than that of the City College class I have described. In the second quarter most of the fourteen reregistered, and the places vacated by those who were unable to do so were filled by new students without that cohesiveness being broken.

In place of the freshman English my second course in the second quarter was an elective seminar, in which we read poetry and prose by Rilke, Supervielle, Guillevic, William Carlos Williams, Wallace Stevens, Margaret Avison— with more time spent on Rilke than on any other. There were thirty students (ten more than I was obliged to take), chosen by pulling names out of a hat, since there were seventy-nine or eighty applicants and it was impossible to interview them all. They were mostly third- and fourth-year students and—despite the random choice—an astonishingly sensitive, intelligent, responsive bunch; though the group was, alas, too large and the quarter too short to allow for each one to contribute and receive to anywhere near the maximum degree. We met—having been given a ridiculous classroom, the kind in which the desk chairs are clamped to the floor—in the cavernous, red-check-tableclothed coffeehouse of the off-campus Lutheran Center (for whose hospitality, as for that of the Newman Center, I am most grateful).

And now I come to the experience from which I learned most at Berkeley, for which much of what I have just been telling is only the background, though necessary, I feel, to understanding its impact.

The People's Park[4] had, during the first part of the second quarter, been coming steadily into more and more manifest existence—created by students and "street people"—two blocks away from our coffeehouse classroom. Many of us had spent some pleasant time there; a few were actively involved in its construction. I suggested that those from the class who wished to (plus some from the poetry workshop) meet in the park one afternoon to work at digging or planting or whatever was going on. In fact we ended up taking a truckload of garbage out to the city dump. In my poem, "From a Notebook," I have written about this:

May 14th, 1969—Berkeley
Went with some of my students to work in the People's Park. There seemed to be plenty of digging and gardening help so we decided, as Jeff had his truck available, to

[4]For documentation of the People's Park events, see *New York Review of Books* for June 17, 1969.

shovel up the garbage that had been thrown into the west
part of the lot and take it out to the city dump.
        Oh happiness
        in the sun! Is it
        that simple, then,
        to live?
        —crazy rhythm of
        scooping up barehanded
        (all the shovels already in use)
        careless of filth and broken glass
        —scooping up garbage together
        poets and dreamers studying
        joy together, clearing
        refuse off the neglected, newly recognized,
humbly waiting ground, place, locus, of what could be our
New World even now, our revolution, one and one and
one and one together, black children swinging, green
guitars, that energy, that music, no one
                telling anyone what to do,
                everyone doing,
      each leaf of
      the new grass near us
      a new testament . . .

Out to the dump:
acres of garbage glitter and stink in wild sunlight, gulls
float and scream in the brilliant sky,
polluted waters bob and dazzle, we laugh, our arms ache,
                    we work together
shoving and kicking and scraping to empty our truckload
                    over the bank
even though we know
the irony of adding to the Bay fill, the System has us there—
but we love each other and return to the Park.

Thursday, May 15th
At 6 a.m. the ominous zooming, war-sound, of helicopters
breaks into our sleep.

To the Park:
ringed with police.
Bulldozers have moved in.
Barely awake, the people—
those who have made for each other
a green place—
begin to gather at the corners.

Their tears fall on sidewalk cement.
The fence goes up, twice a man's height.
Everyone knows (yet no one yet
believes it) what all shall know
this day, and the days that follow:
now, the clubs, the gas,
bayonets, bullets. The War
comes home to us . . .

   For almost three weeks thereafter there were daily rallies
and protest marches, with attempts (some at least temporar-
ily successful) to start new parks on other empty lots; there
were many tear-gassings, police billy-club charges, the
naked bayonets of the National Guard. And always the threat
of a repetition of the first day's buckshot fire when the police
killed one young man, blinded another (an artist), and
wounded three hundred more . . . Under these circum-
stances, what happened to my classes?
   Miraculously, beautifully, even though we found it impos-
sible to continue our planned reading and discussion of
the books on my list and of students' resulting papers (which
sometimes were poems), yet the larger class (as well as
the poetry workshop) continued to meet every Monday,
Wednesday, and Friday at 11 A.M., usually with full
attendance, and often with the addition of some members

of the workshop also. We rapped about the preceding day's events and life in general—sometimes with reference made to what we had been reading before the crisis began, or to some poem or other book that suddenly occurred as relevant—and then at 12, instead of continuing till 12:30 or 1 P.M., we walked together over to Sproul Plaza for the noon rally and the afternoon's demonstration. No one put any pressure on anyone else to come along; but just about everyone did come. And out of these, a smaller group soon formed that stayed together each day throughout the terror, and most truly—and with a love and mutual care that made that terror into a time of joy and wonder—practiced the injunction with which a list of points of conduct and tactics for the demonstrators, published in the "Instant News" (a sheet distributed daily at this period from the Free Church), concluded: *"Be your brothers' and sisters' keeper."*

What is it that made the experience so important to me, even aside from its immediate qualities of drama and emotion? What made it a learning experience for me *as a teacher?* Something like this: Even though, in the brief portion of the quarter that was left after the crisis had abated, the soldiers and sheriffs gone from the streets, and (though the issue had not, and still has not at the time of writing, been settled) things had returned to "normal"—even though, since everyone was deeply shaken, we found it hard to go into our studies again with a certain calm and orderliness that had seemed present when we began, yet I am convinced that if only we had had more time—even if only another month—that class, *which had lived through something important together outside of class meetings—* could have gone further than any I have witnessed. It was only a gleam—a glimpse—but things were said in those last meetings, perceptions were exchanged, not only verbally, but by tone and look and gesture, that attained, or at the least gave promise of, levels of shared learning far beyond the average.

I am not suggesting that we can only teach and learn on the barricades. Indeed there was very real disruption and distraction of the attention from material we would have liked to explore; no doubt of that. But if some degree of the commonest social intimacy—the exchange of some biographical information, meeting in settings less formal than the classroom, getting to see one another's bookshelves—if even this can make mutual criticism and appreciation and the exchange of insights at once more candid and more sensitive, then the sharing not only of—as in this case—danger, trauma, and the experience of community under provocation—but of all kinds of other realities would surely make shared learning in any field—of the humanities especially—more profound. To have lived through the Berkeley siege means to me, then, not only a new vision of what life might be like in a world of gentle and life-loving people. It means not only the knowledge that there is no such thing as a generation gap when people are engaged in a common task in which they believe. It means not these things alone, though they are much, very much; but also the conviction that a meaningful education in the future—if there is a future worth the name—will be broken down into the smallest viable units (classes averaging between ten and fifteen) and that these units will do many more things together than study specific subjects: they will cook together (something that would restore meaning to eating together), and grow vegetables and flowers together, and mend each other's clothes—and study not only one subject as a group, but several related and unrelated ones, while each individual would also be sharing some study and other activities with other semiautonomous groups. In such educational interweavings each teacher would also be, part of the time, a student along with the rest; and all teachers would share, at least to the extent consonant with his or her age and family situation, in the life of the commune—for such educational units would certainly be communes, to a far greater degree even than

196

such forerunners as Black Mountain College seem to have been. A pipe dream? I don't believe it is merely that, remote and hard to effectuate as such a scheme may sound at a time when colleges everywhere are *expanding*. I can't see it as a mere pipe dream because I believe it is a necessity. (If Paul Goodman's proposal for store-front elementary and high schools had been taken seriously several years ago, it would have been one of the greatest advances ever made in the history of education.)

The idea of a new kind of college that began to emerge for me, and for my husband and for two or three young teachers in the history and political science departments, and which met with great enthusiasm and useful additional suggestions from the students with whom I discussed it, involved a minimum capital outlay. Since classes would all be small, they could be held in people's apartments, a few store-fronts, and—for an occasional lecture or assembly—church halls. All students would work part time and support themselves as far as possible, so that problems of parental approval and disapproval would be minimized. Each would pay according to his ability. Teachers would pool their resources (i.e., inherited income if any, royalties, income from advisory or other jobs undertaken, etc.) and receive pay according to their need. Need would have to be evaluated by the community as a whole. Staple foods, and certain other necessities, could be bought in common. A day-care center would be established for the children of the community. And a piece of land outside the city would be used to produce food and flowers, and as a place for people to go to camp out and rest and breathe fresh air. Administrative staff would be minimal, and, indeed, secretarial work, running Xerox machines, doing janitorial tasks, and so on would provide work for students within the co-operative framework. Obviously plenty of problems would arise (of which the most serious seems to me to be how to provide for the sciences, those which necessitate all sorts of expensive and large laboratory equipment; and perhaps that is an insoluble problem for any very small college—we were envisaging a maximum of say, two hundred students). But with that exception, are any of them worse problems than the monster institutions we have now are faced with? And would not the existing small colleges be more lively and satisfying places for all concerned if they became teacher-student communes, no longer afflicted with boards of directors, parental anxieties and ambitions, real-estate management headaches, etc., etc., and people were free to teach and learn in an atmosphere of mutual aid?

"And the degrees?" someone asks. "Accreditation?" All I can answer to that is that the most intelligent students I have known care less and less for the degree (here again I am necessarily speaking only of the humanities, I admit) and many quit school before getting it. The basic—perhaps the only—criterion for admission to such a commune/school would have to be that the applicants were interested in sharing their living and learning and that they did not care about ending up with a stamp of approval. Knowing, as they do, these bright, aware, growing individuals of whom every year there seem to be more (if we live . . .), that education as it now exists is as much a part of the Channelling System as the Draft (and I assume most readers of this book will be familiar with the now no longer circulated paper on that topic put out a very few years ago by the Selective Service Department in Washington)—knowing that, there would quite certainly be a more than adequate potential enrollment for my pipe-dream college.

I flew from Berkeley early in June to give the commencement address at Bennington College in Vermont. I concluded my speech by suggesting that Bennington turn itself into just such a commune—that faculty, administration, and students pool their (quite considerable) resources, lower their *material* standard of living, and raise their *spiritual* standard of living by sharing, through an "open admissions" policy, the many indisputably good things a Bennington

198

education has to offer. The speech was loudly applauded—but it was not subsequently published, as previous commencement addresses had been, in the alumnae magazine. Despite assurances to the contrary, I am unable to believe that this had nothing to do with the proposals I had made. It seems clear that if teachers and students want (and I know there are many, many who do) the kind of new college I have sketched, there is little hope of persuading existing institutions to change radically in that direction. People are going to have to get together and do it themselves—without big preliminary (and exhausting) fund-raising campaigns, without expectations of each experiment enduring for years and becoming institutionalized (better they should not!), and without wasting time and energy in setting up a lot of rules and regulations and boards of trustees. Let a thousand "hedge schools" bloom.

SECTION IV:
PERHAPS FICTION

A Note on the Work of the Imagination

The *work* of the imagination, its far-reaching and faithful permeation of those details that, in a work of art, illuminate the whole, was recently illustrated for me in a dream with particular clarity.

I had been dreaming of a large house, set in a flat landscape, and of its history, which is not relevant here. At a certain point I half awoke; and when I returned to the dream I was conscious that I was dreaming. Still close to the threshold of waking, I knew very well that I was lying down for an afternoon nap, in my son's room, because there the street noises would hardly reach me; that though I had a blanket over me I was cold; and that he would soon be home from school and I must get up. But all this was unimportant: what gripped me was the knowledge that I was dreaming, and vividly. A black, white, and gray tiled pavement I crossed—how "real" it felt under my feet! To see, as I saw the poplar avenue and the bluish misty fields around the large buildings, was good, but at no time is it hard to call up scenes to the mind's eye; it was the sensations of touch—the pavement felt through the ball of the foot, the handle of a door in my hand—and of space—the outdoors sensation first, then the spaces of rooms and of the confinement of corridors and of turns in the corridors when I re-entered the house—that interested me, in being so complete even though I knew I was dreaming.

At length I came into a small bedroom fitted with a washbasin and mirror, and the idea came to me of looking in the mirror as a test of how far in fidelity the dream would go; but I was afraid. I was afraid the mirror would show me a blank, or a strange face. I was afraid of the fright that this would give me. However, I dared: and approached the mirror. It was rather high on the wall, and not tilted;

Published in *New Directions in Prose and Poetry 17* (New York, New Directions, 1961).

so what first appeared, as I slowly drew near, was the top of my head. But yes, surely something was wrong—a misty whiteness glimmered there.

I crept nearer still, and standing straight, almost on tiptoe, now saw my whole face, my usual face-in-the-glass—pale, the dark eyes somewhat anxious, but in no way changed or lacking, or causing me fear. What then was the radiant glimmer that had startled me just before?

Why!—in the dark, somewhat fluffy hair was a network of little dew or mist diamonds, like spider's webs on a fall morning! The creative unconscious—the imagination—had *provided*, instead of a fright, this exquisitely realistic detail. For hadn't I been walking in the misty fields in the dewfall hour? Just so, then, would my damp hair look. I awoke in delight, reminded forcibly of just what it is we love in the greatest writers—what quality, above all others, surely, makes us open ourselves freely to Homer, Shakespeare, Tolstoy, Hardy—that *following through*, that *permeation* of detail—relevant, illuminating detail—which marks the total imagination, distinct from intellect, at work. *"The mind's tongue, working and tasting into the very rock heart"* as Ruskin wrote of Turner. The feared Hoffman-esque blank—the possible monster or stranger—would have illustrated the work of Fancy, that *"by invisible wires puts marionettes in motion, and pins butterflies to blotting-paper, and plays Little-Go among the Fairies"* (Landor, in *Imaginary Conversations*). And mere Reason can place two eyes and a nose where we suppose them to be. But it was Imagination put seed pearls of summer fog in Tess Durbeyfield's hair (and *"an intenser little fog amid the prevailing one,"* as a friendly cow breathed in recognition of her approach)—and it was the same holy, independent faculty that sprinkled my hair with winter-evening diamonds.

We sigh—or I do—for the days when whole cultures were infused with noble simplicity; when though there were cruelty and grief, there was no ugliness; when King Alcinoüs himself stowed the bronze pots for Odysseus under the rowers' benches; when from shepherd's pipe and warrior's sandal to palace door and bard's song, all was *well made*. Any culture worth the name, in fact, though "noble simplicity" may be partially an illusion, has the quality of harmony; the bloodstream flows right to the fingertips and the toes; no matter how complex the structure, the parts accord with the whole. Our age appears to me a chaos and our environment lacks the qualities for which one could call it a culture. But by way of consolation we have this knowledge of power that perhaps no one in such a supposed harmonious time had; what in the greatest poets is recognizable as Imagination, that breathing of life into the dust, is present in us all embryonically—manifests itself in the life of dream—and in that manifestation shows us the possibility: to permeate, to quicken, all of our life and the works we make. What joy to be reminded by truth in dream that the Imagination does not arise from the environment but has the power to create it!

Homunculus. Monkey was his name, but in no way his nature. He had been in my environs, that is, domiciled with my family, seven years before I was born. In my infancy I was told that: (1) his appearance had radically changed at some time during those years (I don't understand the significance of this); (2) he had been lost one day, and the peasants left their work in the fields (in Saxony) to help search for him, but he was found at last on the threshold of the house where my family then lived (this I took as proof of his magic powers and as reassurance—seemingly proved once or twice in later years, once on Codden Hill in Devonshire—that he would never be lost); and (3) his personality was cheerful and even cheeky (this last may once have been true, but in the years he was with me he was characterized increasingly by a kindly melancholy).

In my earliest years, busy with other presences, I scarcely realized his. Perhaps my unawareness stemmed partly from the knowledge that he was my sister's, not mine. Property, he was considered. But at some moment of revelation I saw him as it were for the first time, a unique being; and when I asked her, unhoping, if he could from then on be accounted mine, she agreed without hesitation. If she had seen in him what I came to see this could not have been; no amount of loving-kindness could have given him up without a shadow of pain, at a moment's notice. Therefore I believed I had a natural right to his company. (But was this the beginning of her downfall? Or did that begin at my birth when she was nine? Did her mana pass to me as she let him go?)

Of his appearance what can I say that will not mislead you? If I tell you he was barely a foot high you may laugh; yet I wouldn't have you fancy him still smaller. His skin

Written *c.* 1955.

was of glove-leather, and in color partly black and partly the warm brown of a chestnut shell; his hair short, black, and silky; his eyes black also. He smelt faintly and deliciously of old leather.

There was a little song of nonsense words my mother told me he had sung to my sister when she was very young. She repeated it to me as she remembered it, and I understood what she did not understand, that it was a song about a well, and about the wet stones around the wellhead.

Each year that passed I felt more and more aware of his presence as something inexhaustibly wise and consoling. It is the nature of his presence I want to describe, not the grief and shock of his loss when I was almost thirty. Since he had not the power of speech—or since I had very early lost the power to hear him, if I ever had it—he could not be said to be my adviser. But he received my most silent questions and confidences in full understanding. Witness to every misdeed and mistake, unable to warn me, he never emanated reproaches but always forgiveness. (I have since known a human being with this quality, which I did not recognize until she was dying.)

Had I myself breathed life into him? But he appears to have had life before I lived; was it my sister, or my mother, animated him? Was it I who changed him from a light to a serious character, then? How? Out of need?

Certainly such forgiveness, such wholeness of understanding, was an active love. And though he could not—perhaps would not if he could—warn, yet the foreknowledge of his continuing love prevented some meanness in me. There never was a doubt of him, a fear he would turn against me. If I disappointed him, his love overcame his disappointment before the disappointment reached me. The only fear was the fear of his loss or destruction.

Oh, I understand you when you say he was only a projection of my self-love. I understand you, it makes sense, but I cannot be sure. You see, I cannot ever be sure he did not suffer. If he fell into strange hands—and the exact location of his loss, and whether he was lost or destroyed, was never established—he would not have been able to speak. They would not have known that he was wise. And he would have known how I was suffering. Would he not have suffered then, dumb and helpless to return to me? After the first weeks of hoping against hope that he would reappear on my threshold, as I had been told he once in another time and place had reappeared, I began to believe, or at least to wish to believe, that death had befallen him—for I had always known physical pain could not affect him, so that crushing, tearing, dismemberment might kill but not hurt him. (That terrible moment some years before—terrible it seemed then, though so much less so than the time of his loss—when I returned home at evening to find a change had been effected in his appearance, I wept not because of any idea of physical hurt to him where the needle and thread had mended his torn skin, but because so much of what he told me was conveyed in his gaze, and I feared I would be cut off from his spirit when his look was altered by one millimeter. I wept in fright, a fright soothed as I realized there had been no essential change.)

Was it of his own volition he disappeared? Because I needed to know *that* desolation? To learn to do without the security of his friendship? Have I? Is he watching me from afar? Who was he, Monkey, my homunculus? You may tell me he was an illusion—I would be glad to believe you (for since no remains were ever discovered, I am left with the question always, is he somewhere suffering and unrecognized at this moment?)—but I can imagine no way in which you could convince me.

Meanwhile, you know, don't you, that I am not preoccupied with his memory. So much pain and joy of a nature indisputably real has been lived in the seven years since I saw him for the last time. But when I do think of him—my pardoner—it is the *questions* bring the tears again, not his not being with me any more—yes, I did learn that, to live in the suspense of unpardonedness, simply to live.

208

But the questions: was it for me he died? Or did he not die, but lives and suffers?

Or again, and without tears: was he a god? And will he return? Or was he a god who will not return? Or a god who never in fact left—his loss the illusion?—his presence at last to be rediscovered at some threshold—a threshold I am to cross and enter, he being within?

In the Night

The woman who had gone early to bed and was lying a long time almost asleep, but only almost, lies still as her husband very quietly pushes open the bedroom door. She lies still because she is heavy and slow with the nearness of sleep. He is so sorry she was tired, and sometimes she has reproached him with taking no care not to wake her on such occasions, and described to him her own efforts not to disturb him when it is he who has gone to bed early. Now he is stealthy in his planned quietness. He steps so carefully that not a board creaks. There is no rustling of clothes dropping to the floor in the dark, for he has undressed in the bathroom, as she does when he is sleeping. Naked, he climbs carefully into the bed. His body is not touching hers yet, but she feels its nearness. She wants to put her arms around him. She is wide awake now. But she is ashamed to turn to him and reveal that she is not asleep; ashamed to disappoint the sense of success he must have in having managed not to wake her. It has gone too far. She must lie quiet and pretend to sleep until she hears by his breathing that he is asleep. The position of her limbs, which had been comfortable, begins to make them ache. The itching of insomnia, which begins anywhere and moves anywhere or at instants seems to be everywhere on the body's surface, starts now on her left ankle. She feels her breathing become uneven and wonders if he will notice it and find out that she is awake. Cautiously she moves her legs, as if in sleep, and shifts her whole body near enough to his to touch it at knee and thigh and shoulder. He remains perfectly still, she feels his breathing, but though it is quiet and regular she can tell he is not asleep. Now that her back and side are curved in the curve of his body she is a little less tense, the aches do not increase,

Originally published in *Chicago Review*, Vol. 18, Nos. 3 & 4, 1966.

but the itching wanders—cheek, toe, side. She calls on her fortitude and remains quiet. He too remains quietly breathing, unmoving. Her heart had seemed to pound, but as time passes she forgets it. Her thoughts begin to move away from the one thought, the two thoughts in one: "I mustn't let on I'm not asleep" and "But I wish I could put my arms around him." As her body relaxes, slowly, her mind ranges away into many distances. At last, almost unaware, almost as if she were really asleep, she changes position so that she is even closer to him, half turned toward him, an arm across him, her hand on his soft flat belly. But evidently she has succeeded in convincing him—if her rapid breathing had for a moment made him doubt it—that she was really asleep; for with the greatest care he gently disengages himself and turns from his back to his side, away from her. She opens her eyes. It is very dark. Certain mechanical hummings, whirrings, that they are used to, and sometimes do not even hear, rise from the surrounding city and seep angularly into the room. He should be asleep by now, if he is going to fall asleep. She tries, without moving, to see her luminous wrist watch, for now she is lying on her left side, her right arm around his waist and her left arm bent on the pillow beyond her head. The watch is old and dim, but it seems to say 1:30. She knows, she thinks she knows, he is not lying awake in a pleasant drifting way, the way that leads to sleep, but in an intense unhappy clarity, or not clarity, a confusion of anxiety that seems clear because each separate element of confusion is so intensely felt. The bafflement, the trying to understand, to act, to get out of the impasse; the anguish. She knows about them, she loves him, she feels them herself. She must tell him now that she is awake, loves him, is with him. She must make him speak, make him say what he is thinking. She thinks she knows what he is thinking, but only if she can drag the words out of him will the weight of it leave him for a while. But just then the man who believes his wife is asleep, deep asleep like a child, and that he is alone and free to vent

211

his anguish, gives a profound sigh. So private that sigh is, she loses courage: can she speak to him now without intruding?

The sound of a machine in a nearby factory ceases with modest suddenness as it does every twenty minutes or so. His body feels cool as it so often does when he is unhappy, even though the electric blanket is on and she is sweating slightly. She squeezes up to him and holds him tighter. He is silent. He will not acknowledge she is awake. She cannot quite bring herself to break into his solitude. If his flesh were warm she would; but his cool body makes her lose confidence, makes the idea of revealing her awareness seem *will*, not impulse. Their many years of marriage seem annulled by this anguish, shared and yet not shared, their bodies so close but as if lifeless to one another. Husband and wife lie there in an abyss of silence.

At last the machine in the world outside starts up again with a heave. And without forethought she whispers, "Are you awake?" "I guess so," he answers. And then out loud, in a voice that reveals nothing, she says she has to get up and get a drink of milk, she has woken up hungry after going to bed so early. Would he like some too? She is out of bed, she turns on a lamp on the dressing table, they both squint in the light, he gets up to look for some aspirin, she puts her dressing-gown on and goes down the corridor to the kitchen, buttoning it as she goes. In the kitchen the cats uncurl and approach the icebox expectantly, in case it is breakfast time. She talks to them cheerfully. The relief at being up, at the tension being broken, makes her forget all her dark thoughts. She remembers getting up in the night like this when their daughter was a baby, to heat the bottle. She remembers the grim fatigue of those nights of broken sleep, the panic of waking to the baby's sharp cry, the daze in which she used to stumble out to the kitchen of those days, in another place. She heats the milk, pours it into mugs, holds both mugs in one hand as she turns out the light and shuts the door on the cats, goes back down

212

the corridor past their daughter's room, empty now except during vacations, into the bedroom. He has turned on the light over the bed and is reading. She hands him the mug of warm milk, he takes it and thanks her, they look at each other freely and calmly, he even smiles. She smiles back, they drink their milk, she sitting at the foot of the bed. Before getting back into bed, she decides to go to the bathroom. While she's there she rinses the milky taste out of her mouth with a glass of water. By the time she gets back he is out of bed again brushing his teeth at the bedroom washbasin. All this coming and going takes time and continues to break up the tension of the darkness and silence. Taking off her dressing gown she glances at herself in the long mirror. Her image glimmers white and youthful there. He is already back in bed; he looks at her without smiling but without intensity. She gets in. They agree to read for a while. She feels interested in her book. He appears to be interested in his. All the anguish that was there before the putting on of the light seems now what is annulled. But it is there. They have not spoken to one another of anything except trivialities. It is there, it has not gone away, the questions are there, and the wan hope and the dull fear are subtly, quietly pulsing. Just before they put out the light their eyes meet for an instant. He raises his hand to put out the light, in the new dark they settle closer to each other, in a few minutes they have both fallen asleep.

People talk sometimes of the sufferings of the artist, his convulsive sturggles, the blood and sweat of birth. And of course it is true that the artist, having a high degree of awareness, not only suffers the common agonies of mankind but at times doubles them by *knowing* he has them. But this knowing he shares with many other conscious people. Also, having the imagination of how things might be, he suffers at witnessing how they are—but this too is a suffering shared by all people with imagination, not all of whom, God knows, are artists. The people who talk with awe about this suffering of artists are usually not artists themselves. Their insistence on the pains of creativity sometimes sounds like a kind of envy; is it that they feel numb, and believe the artist enviably *feels* more? Or is it (and if so it is evidently resisted) that they get a sadistic pleasure from believing that artists suffer and that they *ought* to suffer? Just recently I read what a critic had to say about a play others had acclaimed but which he felt had not *earned* its success because its author claimed she had written it painlessly. There were other things in the play to which he raised objections; but not convincingly, it seemed to me; what really was bugging him was (yes, the Protestant ethic) the playwright's avowed ease in bringing forth her work.

Well, a secret artists share—but it's so secret they don't talk about it even to each other—is the strange ease and pleasure there is in their work. The suffering is all—or almost all—about other things. They may have lousy lives. They often make bad marriages, ruin their children's lives, look back with remorse on the memory of their parents or of friends and lovers lost or betrayed. Or else they may have rather good, rather tender, but difficult lives, struggling for money, space, time to do their work. And they see with

Written 1966? Published in *Stony Brook*, No. 2/3, 1970.

such an acute vividness the pain and destruction going on around them, next door or ten thousand miles away. All that. But the work itself—the way it just *pops into your head*, or your hand. . . ? Well, as far as the work's concerned, the greatest suffering seems to be the lack of control one has over it. The panic that it may not come again. Of course there's the control of the craftsman, yes. But there again the critics, the same ones who are so keen on the artist taking his punishment, don't really have a clue. For craftsmanship means only that you know what to do with your material, your *concept,* ridiculous word—your miraculous bird when it has alighted on your shoulder. It doesn't mean you can whistle and it will come. The most you can do is haunt the places where it came to you before, and the hours, like dreams; there's very little indeed you can deliberately do to induce them. But though we may pine for our dreams (and physically need them) one can't call that pining a profound suffering—unless there's a dangerous, prolonged deprivation. Imagine having complete control over our dreams! They wouldn't be worth having. Then there's that period of irritable *brewing,* sometimes— knowing there's something pending, getting clues, flashes, losing it again—the suffering involved in that's nothing more, when you come right down to it, than the anxiety you have that someone or something—including yourself —may interrupt, may distract you, and drive off whatever it is that is about to appear. Persons from Porlock *are* The Devil.

But to be a person to whom miraculous birds, or caverns measureless to man, *do* appear!—isn't that the most astounding good fortune? I feel ashamed, often, hearing that stuff about suffering—or people letting artists off from some moral tax or other because they are supposedly "so sensitive." And all the time we have, we lucky ones, this amazing secret, the way vision slides on, like a well-talcumed kid glove, to enclose one in its words, or in, like an erect cock into a completely ready cunt!

215

I'm a person of a certain clumsiness in "daily life," often a clumsy violence of response that leaves me baffled, frustrated. I say too much, or not enough, to the people I love. Perhaps I don't know myself very well, for at times I see myself as having boundless energy and a savage will, and at other times as someone easily tired and so impressionable as to be, like Keats, weighed on almost unbearably by the identities around me—people or sparrows. But, willful or impressionable, that knowledge of my human clumsiness is pretty constant. Yet I can turn from that sober consciousness to the things I've *made*, that have made themselves through me, and it's like having a third hand—as if you were physically clumsy and were just about to drop a plate you were washing, when lo!—out shoots your strong and graceful third hand and plucks it from the air. Yes, I know what Picasso meant—"To draw is to close the eyes and sing." The pursuit of the right shade of color, the exact chord, the precise word—oh yes, that's part of it. But for those who have the luck to be so engaged—by nature, by their natures, their destinies—is there any *pleasure* deeper, more seductive, than that painful search? And only a rare critic who happens also to be, if not an artist himself, then a good dreamer by night, will ever believe it. Working at art is so much like dreaming, sometimes I don't know which is which. Take this story I dreamed:

A Japanese lady, wife of a General who was part of the Japanese forces occupying Paris during the world war, walks out alone on an impulse—out of the courtyard gate of the handsome eighteenth-century *hôtel particulier* in which she and her husband are living, and which is also the Japanese military headquarters, into the soft gray Parisian morning. The streets, in which she had never walked alone before—indeed she had scarcely walked in them at all—are almost deserted. Her impulse to go out alone, announcing her intention to no one, springs from an obscure awareness of impending crisis in her life. She is patient, she is disciplined, but there is a pressure in her existence that has

216

slowly built up almost to the limits of tolerance. And there is already crisis around her, in the world she, as the General's wife, is a passive part of: the victorious Japanese military, who had been boasting about their permanent takeover of *la ville lumière* only a few months before, were now threatened. The Free French and their Italian allies were advancing rapidly, and many people had already left the city, apprehensive of a battle in the streets. Those who remained were preoccupied with departure—here and there, as she walks, people emerge from buildings or appear from alleyways burdened with suitcases and bundles. An old woman passes by pushing a handcart piled high with household goods, a little barefoot boy running at her heels.

No one gave more than an absent glance at the slender, black-haired woman in her dark kimono. And she turned a corner into another street that was absolutely empty of human life. She was thinking about her husband, the desert their life had become, the way, over the ten childless years of their marriage, he had changed from the rather gay, rather appealing man, still young, she had been caused to marry, into a sullenly ambitious, thick-necked officer who scarcely spoke to her. Somehow to communicate with him—perhaps the defeat he was about to suffer, though he had not spoken of it to her, would open a way? At that moment she catches sight of some objects lying half on the sidewalk, half in the gutter, seemingly abandoned by someone fleeing the city: a black purse, and a bird cage with a bird in it.

The bird was alive and she recognized it as a young sea gull. It looked past her in mute terror and beat its wings against the wire bars. She looked around to see if someone was still nearby to claim it. But in the soft pearly mid-morning light, there was no one to be seen and only a distant sound of traffic to be heard, blocks away. She stooped in her tight skirt and examined the purse. There were a ten-dollar bill in the wallet section and a few coins in the change compartment. "There—there—don't be afraid," she murmured to the bird. It seemed to hear her, and ceased to flutter painfully in its cage. She picks up the cage and with a strong sense that these things, the purse and the caged bird, were not found by accident, begins slowly to return the way she had come, afraid to lose her way if she took other streets.

It was strange for her, hemmed in as her life had been by rules of etiquette, never going out alone, never carrying any burdens, to be trudging the sidewalks thus, both hands full. In these months—almost a year now—they had been in Paris, she had walked sometimes on the most elegant streets or in the Tuileries gardens, but always with a chauffeured car waiting nearby, and if she went shopping she was expected to take her maid to carry the parcels. This hour of solitude now was very precious to her. She had solitude indoors in abundance—a loneliness, in the great dark formal rooms of the little palace, made bitter by the sense she had of her uselessness, of the waste of her intelligence and her sensibility, which she knew to be fine instruments. I am a lute going out of tune for lack of use, she would think to herself at times. Now she found the feel of the purse, thick and awkward for her small delicate hand to grasp, an unaccustomed pleasure—and the ache in her other arm as she held the cage stiffly, not to let the poor bird swing more than she could help. It was as if this small physical use of herself were an emblem of some use to which her nature might yet be put.

When she came to the gate of the *hôtel* she was resolved to speak to her husband, openly, calmly. She was thirty-one, he forty. Wasn't there time to live humanly? But entering the courtyard she is bitterly disappointed to find him not alone, as she had imagined, but sitting drinking with the officers of his staff at a great trestle table that had been dragged out there. The servants are running back and forth with bottles of liquor. There is an air of squalor, of disarray, about the courtyard. Her husband caught sight of her hesitating in the archway and called her to him peremptorily. She took heart and walked swiftly over to where he sat at the

218

head of the table. "Where have you been?" he said loudly, angrily; but not waiting for an answer he glances scornfully at the bird in its cage, snatches the purse from her, looks into it, sees only the small change, and tosses it back to her. She saw the rings of wet from the glasses on the bare table; the maps spread out for study were stained with spilt liquor. Without a word said, she bows in customary courtesy and turns away, into the main house entrance and up the great stairs.

In the vast reception room at the head of the stairs the wives of the other officers were gathered, frightened, whispering together. When they catch sight of her some of them hurry forward to greet her obsequiously, to exclaim over the bird cage and the bird, huddled now in a corner of it, a dull, unpreened, pitiful heap of gray feathers, its beak sharp and cruel-looking, its eyes staring blindly. She dismissed the women by her look of reserve, her deep need to pass them and be alone, which they mistook for hauteur. They retreated, twittering, and she continued up another flight of stairs to her own suite. The house servants—mercifully—were nowhere to be seen, aside from those who were waiting upon the drinkers in the courtyard.

In her bedroom she sets down the cage, fetches some water, and fills the little water-container fixed into the cage. Then she sits down, folds her hands, and waits for the bird to drink. The half-darkened room is striped with light from between the slats of the jalousies.

Sooner than she had hoped, the bird cocked its head, shook its wings, and drank. It was weak, perhaps wounded; but it had not decided to die. She opened the cage door, put in her hand—the gull pecked at her wildly but she managed to feel the feathers and the warmth under them. At that moment she hears her name being called. A junior officer's wife puts a scared face around the door—"We're all to go down."

The General's wife withdrew her hand from the bird cage, locked the cage door firmly, glanced at the black purse lying

219

on her dressing table, and left the room, closing that door also with precision.

She follows the young woman down the stairs and joins the little cluster of other women already descending the lower flight into the courtyard. None of them was dressed in Western style; that was forbidden to officers' wives. They chattered in hushed tones as they went down the broad shallow staircase with little steps, their pretty kimonos fluttering. When they came down into the courtyard they fell silent. It was evident that the men, in a short time, had become very drunk. The General gives an order to one of his staff, and he in turn raps out, like a drill sergeant, an order to the women. They have at first—all save the General's wife, who knew at once, grimly, what they were to do—some difficulty in understanding what is meant. Incredulous, but without protest, they let themselves be placed in a neat line. Then they have to march—left, right, left, right—up and down the courtyard, on parade. The captain-drill sergeant bawls out reprimands concerning their style, their failure to goosestep smartly and keep in line. The men roar. Tears run down the General's face, his wife sees, as he laughs and yells. And she marched with the rest of them, a daughter of the samurai. Some of them blushed, some of them giggled, some wept tears of fright and humiliation. All were obedient; and she too, in all her pride, was obedient—but pale, and deeply preoccupied, as she marched, with the knowledge that this was the crest of a wave that was about to curl over and break.

At perhaps the eighth movement to the left of the line of women, just as they wheel to move right again, a courier arrives breathlessly at the street gate, looks around the courtyard blankly, catches sight of the General, and runs straight up to him. The General, stopped in the middle of a laugh, stiffens, suddenly sober. It is the news of defeat. The laughter, the raucous shouting, peter out. The women stood still, uncertainly; they then began to clutch one another, to huddle together. The whispered message rippled from person to person. Enemy motorcyclists were already in the suburbs. The great army followed close behind.

And now another kind of shouting begins. Common soldiers appear from somewhere, the officers are calling out contradictory orders, the women run indoors and out again, servants hurry out the gate with great bundles, not stopping to pick up anything they drop. The General has vanished.

The General's wife went swiftly up to her room, and sat there quite still; the sounds of retreat died down, and after a little while there was silence. The bird in its cage was quite still, but it looked at her with its fierce eyes. She could see it was weak, not ready to be let free yet. It needed a great space of water, a river, the sea.

She took up the black purse and the cage, and went down the stairs, through the great empty reception room that lay all disordered, down the other stairs, across the littered courtyard where smashed bottles and glasses glittered in the afternoon light, and out the gateway into the silent gray street. Walking fast, her tokens of new life in each hand, she came sooner than she had hoped to the place where she had found them in the morning, and passed it without pausing. She knew that all the people she had known had gone in the opposite direction. Every step took her further from them. She stopped only to put down her purse and bird cage for a moment and rip her skirt further up the side seam so she could lengthen her stride. The bird, dry and starving though it was, was beginning to flutter restlessly now, growing stronger on air, as she swung along.

That's where the story ends—the dream, I mean. Unsummoned by defined conscious preoccupations, it glided through my mind. I wrote it down in brief form, a two-page note. Years later I returned to the note, recalled the dream vividly (by which I mean I was in no doubt of whether, for instance, stepping into the street, the Japanese lady

221

turned right or left,[1] and began to write it out whole, step by step. The words glided as the dream had, so that as I wrote I was almost dreaming again—I had only to look, to observe, and say what I knew. I know very well that I happen to be a person better at writing poems than prose, on the whole. But in this case I was not impelled toward a poem but toward straight narrative prose. Perhaps the smooth glide of it, broken only by the changes of tense one experiences in dreaming, is a weakness; I can say only that it is germane to the dream, the drama of which was not violent, though there was violence in the situation. The solitude of the protagonist remained unbroken throughout the scenes she passed through, and it was this unbroken solitude that gave to the flow of words whatever degree of smoothness, or quietness, it has.

What relevance has this dream-story to my proposition, that the sufferings of the creative artist are a false concept due to misunderstanding of process by critics and other nonartists? I am not saying that dreams are the only, or the only valid, sources of art, obviously. I am suggesting that dreams, an experience common to artist and nonartist, provide for the nonartist a clue to the understanding of artistic process more accurate than the usual assumption by critics that that process—say the writing of a poem—is paralleled by the labor of analysis, the arduous patience of scholarship.

If the artist as a human being is clumsy, alternately strenuous and lackadaisical; if he is spouse, parent, wage-earner, citizen—then he, like the scholar, knows what labor is; and all the more does he laugh up his sleeve at the idea of his *art* being a painful struggle. He laughs, he blushes, and perhaps too he swears and weeps. For it is this fiction, piously upheld, that accounts for his own hypocrisy and shame when he finds himself unable and unwilling to admit the brutal ease and shameless joy of his best moments. In

[1] She turned right, then right again, i.e., N., then E. At the end she is moving SE.

222

an authoritarian and competitive society, work as such, effort, is overvalued, and the fact that work, when it is of a kind natural to the worker, is pleasure, and not grimly laborious, is (deliberately?) overlooked.

The motif of a poem or story can arise from preliminary conscious thought or emerge like a dream from the unconscious, but once it begins to so emerge it glides or leaps past the watching mind's eye at its own uncontrollable pace. How clear it is, and how much clearer it *becomes*, under scrutiny, depends on the writer's attention, and on the degree to which he is able to translate into words, that which he experiences; or rather, on how well he can listen for the words that are its incarnation, its *taking on the flesh*. The closer his initial attention, the more easily he will be able to recall his vision and repeat and intensify his scrutiny. The dream, or the initial inspiration, grows, develops, gives forth more of its own substance upon each recall, if he is lucky.

Yes, there *is* something of labor in the creative process: but it consists in that *focusing of attention upon what is given,* and not in the "struggle for expression." That is where the basic misunderstanding lies.

If I return my attention for a few moments to my dream, I see something I had not earlier been aware of: the Japanese lady walked at first with smallish steps and with her arms close to her sides. By the end of the story, even though her arm movements were still constricted by the fact that she held the bird cage, she stepped out in a different, freer rhythm. But though I have only just noticed it, I am aware now that I had already dreamed it—first passively, in the dream as seen, then actively, in the telling. I did not struggle to express what I saw; but given the sight, I focused my attention; and being what I am—not a painter, not a sculptor, not a musician, but a writer—my attention emerged, or *realized itself,* as *words:* she has ripped her skirt so she could lengthen her stride and now, as the bird "grew stronger on air . . . *she swung along.*"

223

If the dream had gone further, or the imaginative attention, verbalizing while it looks, could pursue it further —(and perhaps it could—perhaps indeed it could)—the rhythms of the prose would inevitably begin to change too, as the rhythm of her walk and all that happened next—and next—changed. She is swept into a new life, inexorably. And if the artist sweats and suffers, it is not because he must toil to discover the words to tell that new story, but because his attention faltered, he looked away, and she has vanished—most likely forever—around one of the several corners, without a trace. The streets out toward the edge of town are growing dark. Only a single gray feather, perhaps from a young sea gull, lies at his feet.

SECTION V:
OTHER WRITERS

John Wieners's poems are abundant in that quality—call
it "magic" or "grace" or "the poetry beyond the poem (but
inseparable from it)"—which is not in all poems, rarely
informs all of any poem, is shared by the other arts and
by natural phenomena, but which when we discover it in
a poem seems wholly germane to it and to be its very savor.

He is not a "natural poet" in the sense of being one who
sang from the start and to whom the poem comes easy:
in his earlier book, *The Hotel Wentley Poems*, moving and
individual though it was—a remarkable first book—one
heard only occasionally anything of the music that has
been granted him in *Ace of Pentacles*. I say *granted* because
I think a certain kind of *believing abandon* to poetry can
bring about what seems a miracle (and perhaps it is): the
tapping of a buried fountain in the poet from which the
music flows. Mediocrity is perhaps due not so much to lack
of imagination as to lack of faith in the imagination, lack
of the capacity for this abandon. Wieners has trusted poetry
as children in George MacDonald's fairy tales trust the
ancient/youthful woman at her spinning wheel, and she has
given him access to the mysteries.

He reveals a life unusually defenseless against grief and
disaster. The things various confessional poets describe
have happened to him too—drug addiction, the pain and
loneliness of homosexual love, the mental breakdown—
everything except marriage problems and divorce; but in
his case they are not autobiographically written *about*, they
are conditions out of which it happens that the songs arise.
There is never any sense that he capitalizes on dramatic
events or is dependent upon them for his poetry; he doesn't
see them as dramatic. What moves us is not the darkness

A review of *Ace of Pentacles*, by John Wieners; originally published
in *Poetry*, Vol. 105, No. 5, 1965.

of the world in which the poems were written, but the pity and terror and joy that is beauty in the poems themselves. When there is no song, no honey on the lips, only the presentation of drama, it can happen that the subject matter itself is invested with a false glamor. In Wieners the glamor is the word-music itself. I am brought to remember Orpheus, who did not sing *about* hell: he was *in* hell, and sang there, leading the way out. Not by coincidence, perhaps—though undoubtedly unconsciously—"The Love that Moves the World, the Sun and Stars" is surely a version of part of the story of Orpheus:

> I look for the woman as I would
> a lucky charm to place over the mantelpiece.
> Jewels of the night I would hang in
> her hair. And the stars of space
> to light her eyes.
>
> I hope the dawn catch her by surprise
> the melody of her voice the music
> of the spheres and the rushing of a
> brook in summer country.
>
> It is time I tried the knowledge of
> her flesh, her legs straight as
> sticks under a gray skirt, our lips
> meet on Sixtieth Street.
>
>   It is her hair,
> like a web of spun thread from
> purple India; and leaning over a
> bridge I would like to say, you are
> like a white duck below us on
> the rocks
>
>   But despair enters as a drug, to
> deaden the sense, so that I give up
> the effort of making love to you

in words and turn again to the flesh
where your whiteness gleams and tiny
lines around your eyes show as threads
in a fine cloak to wrap around us
in the night as we hurry off to different
cities.

"To draw is to shut your eyes and sing," Picasso has said.
For Wieners—although he revises—writing poems is surely
an analogous process: "To write is to listen," perhaps. His
working of poems is toward accuracy of notation for that
experience, not in support of the superficial clarity that is
only a compulsive neatness and takes insufficient care of
the complexities of the live material. That is why there
are many lines of odd grammatical structure, syntactical
loose ends. I am usually irritated by such things, for there
is another clarity I am deeply committed to and which struc-
tural looseness can obstruct; but the peculiarities of lan-
guage in these poems are, I have come to see, often the
very crises of poignant truth, the pivots of the poem. They
are not carelessnesses, just the contrary; change them and
you change a note of a chord. It is the same with his occa-
sional inversions of word order or with his innocent invoca-
tion of tradition in a poem like the early "Ode on a Common
Fountain" (antedating, I think, *The Hotel Wentley Poems*).
Whatever happens is there because that is how the song
goes, as a wind blowing in certain branches, a wave breaking
on certain stones. It may seem "anachronistic," as one bewil-
dered reader complained to me; but it is purely functional
in its own context (a present context)—and therefore
ultimately in a historical context too. As well accuse John
Clare of "literariness." *Ace of Pentacles* will disturb anyone
looking for preconceived benefits, whether "cooked" or
"raw"; it attempts to fulfill no such expectations, only to
testify to inner voices. There are few books today so utterly
clear of some sense that the author is sneaking a glance
at the reader to see how he's taking it.

One must listen to the sounds. It is essentially a melopoeic language. The components include many irregular and interior rhymes, an instinctive right placing of vowels, and—most characteristically—a pace, or rather a gait, that is almost ceremonial, the serious saunter of dream-walking, in dreams that take one a stage on a pilgrimage. (This would be the quality a translator into another language would most essentially have to parallel.)

There are poems I like less than others; but since I care so much for the book as a whole it is hard to choose which poem to quote in closing. I want to mention "Poem for Trapped Things," already known to many readers from its inclusion in the Grove Press anthology *The New American Poetry;* and "The Suicide" and "Address to the Woman," which are concerned with the figure of Sylvia Plath and which speak of the communion of poets. Perhaps these stanzas from "The Acts of Youth" will illustrate as well as any the sensuous substance of Wieners's work and the tender, passionate, and solemn spirit that informs it:

> Pain and suffering. Give me strength
> to bear it, to enter those places where the
> great animals are caged. And we can live
> at peace by their side. A bride to the burden
> that no god imposes but knows we have the means
> to sustain its force unto the end of our days.
> For that it is what we are made for; for that
> we are created. Until the dark hours are done.
>
> And we rise again in the dawn.
> Infinite particles of the divine sun, now
> worshiped in the pitches of the night.

What is the message?—

> an artist is lucky who is busy
> with what is necessary! . . .

writes Paul Goodman in a poem to his brother the architect.
And he himself has that luck. His keen sense of human
needs, of our failure to meet our own needs, of ways in
which we *could* meet them, informs his poetry as it does
his fiction and other prose. It's an unusually direct poetry
—direct not in the sense of "highly concrete," "sensuous,"
but as contrasted with obliquity: an explicit poetry. Wallace
Stevens wrote a poem, "How to Live, What to Do," but
it does not tell. Some of the time Paul Goodman is actually
telling us:

> If a life must be lost, let it be the rescuer's
> for that has a meaning, it is our Emblem.
> Therefore since all must be lost, be a rescuer.
>
> . . .
>
> Warriors as they drown in death shout "Victory!"
> but a life guard when he rescues someone, curses.

Or;

> I dream my country
> has quit her desperate course
> and is now at peace.
>
> My people now take
> a lively satisfaction
> in one another.

A review of *The Lordly Hudson: Collected Poems* by Paul Goodman;
published originally in *The Nation*, April 13, 1963.

231

. . .
Imagine, only
useful machines are now seen
that all can repair. . . .

As in his prose, he is saying in his poems: Make a com-
munity! Discover "the creative animal, man," in yourself
and in those with whom you live—for we *must* live *together,*
if we are to live! Then let us learn to live with *ourselves,*
live with ourselves, *live* together.

If I do not associate with people,
with whom shall I associate?

Exhortation can be exasperating; Paul Goodman is often
exasperating, but in a tonic way, and his insistences are
always tempered by an anguish in the face of the mess
we make of the world, an anguish that is a sort of humility,
for it recognizes his own involvement in the mess. That
is, he sees himself as a man who can point to alternatives,
but he doesn't talk *de haut en bas,* as if he himself had
successfully taken them. Because no man can take them
alone: one alone can only *make a beginning,* or try to. He
speaks of Vulcan, the lame smith, as one of the lucky, busy
with what is necessary; and his own anguish, his recurring
sense of defeat, of not being put to full use, is like Vulcan's
lameness: it makes him real to us, and it has some
unmeasured effect on the forging of the bright shield.

"Resign! Resign!" the word rings in my soul
—is it for me? or shall I make a sign
and picket the White House blindly in the rain,
or hold it up on Madison Avenue
until I vomit, or trudge to and fro
gloomily in front of the public school?

This is not rhetoric: Paul Goodman *does* trudge to and fro

with signs, was one of the instigators of the General Strike for Peace, works on the West Side School Board, and in other such ways strives to implement what he believes in. His actions would not be of interest in considering his poetry if he didn't write well; but since he does, it is important to know them, to know that such lines are simple truth.

What is the special texture of his poetry, the music by virtue of which, and only by that virtue, we come to know the ideas? As in a fabric woven of contrasting threads, harsh thick ones crisscrossing with soft fine ones, the idomatic crisscrosses in Paul Goodman's language with the highly formal. And the rhythmic structure likewise alternates formalized stress-patterns with lines that give us that felicity, the truly expressive variant—whether extra syllable, muted or occasional rhyme, or whatever is unpredictable and inevitable in the context.

> Three-personed Fate, who draw my thread
> and measure out and cut its length,
> passing along from hand to hand
> I rest assured in their strength.
>
> I know you as Persephone
> the queen of Hell and Flowers
> who idly guide my course
> to where is only guessed by me.
>
> My limbs are shuddering
> but I am not afraid
> for I the requiem made
> of one who died in the Dead of Spring.

I don't accept his every use of the inversion as functional; but there are many instances—as above—where it does seem absolutely right.

"Public" themes do not dominate the book; essentially, all of Paul Goodman's poems are about himself, and social

233

or political concepts are present not programmatically, but because they are interwoven with his private concerns—that is to say, they *are* private concerns. Thus the erotic is just as likely to be present in a political context as the political in an erotic context, and we gain some beginnings of insight into their still obscure interaction. The relationship between sexual fear and the politics of murder and suicide; and the alternative relationship of an architecture of community and the use of human energy for peace and pleasure: these concepts are as integral to his poetry as Pound's insistence on the reciprocity of monetary reform and vitality of language is to *The Cantos*.

The seven sections of this volume comprise "Short Poems," "Longer Poems," "Stories," "Sonnets," "Ballades," "Love Poems," and finally "Sentences and Prayers." Rhythmically, most of the story poems tend to go flat, and inventive though Paul Goodman is, he cannot put life, for me, into the long-since dead ballade. But the sonnets are among the few readable sonnets of the century (others are the little-known ones of Edwin Denby). The remaining sections each contain marvels of true, peculiar, irreducible poetry. On the back of the book is quoted a perspicacious piece of self-evaluation in which Mr. Goodman speaks of the "attitude" of the poems, "the proof that a man can still experience his life in this way. I have not tried for individual beautiful poems—though I think I have occasionally hit one by luck—but I am more satisfied with the whole than with the parts." And this total effect—the *voice* that sounds even in those few poems that are strikingly bad, close to doggerel, or startling overextensions of a sort of *faux-naif* sententiousness—makes the quoting of this poem or that particularly inadequate as a way of suggesting something of his quality. At least half of the poems in the book seem to me to be of the highest order. Since I obviously cannot name so many, I will mention only one—"Red Jacket (Lake Seneca)"—not necessarily the "best" poem of them all, but one for which I have an especial love.

234

Paul Goodman has written, besides his better-known novels, short stories that I believe stand with the greatest American short stories. Many of his poems are not inferior to these fictions.

I pitched a tent in the twilight
By morning who knows where it had flown off

My house is built of heaped-up poems
Here is where I married and had children

Chairil Anwar lived only twenty-seven years and left only about seventy-five poems behind him. Yet he has been a major force in Indonesian poetry. Open this selection almost anywhere and one knows at once that this was a pure poet; that is, not one who chose to be a poet and earnestly and with more or less ambition cultivated a talent—a way of life that accounts for about ninety-five per cent of contemporary poetry—but one who could not help himself, who did not choose but (even though he wrote little and not easily) was chosen; a poet as García Lorca was a poet, or Hart Crane.

This by itself might not have made his work influential in the development of other young poets; but it seems that Anwar's brief years of literary activity coincided not only with the social and political ferment preceding and immediately following the end of Japanese rule in Indonesia, but also with a period of flux and development in the Indonesian language, so that in his stripping away of flounces, his brilliant use of what he found in foreign poets, his searching candor and technical courage, Anwar was "purifying the language of the tribe" with special pertinence.

Anwar was born in Sumatra in 1922, moved to Java as a boy, and for financial reasons was unable to continue his formal education beyond the second year of high school.

A review of *Selected Poems* by Chairil Anwar (trans. by Burton Raffel and Nurdin Salam); originally published in *The Nation*, December 21, 1963.

He fought as a guerrilla against the Dutch, consorted with sailors and prostitutes, and died in 1949 from the combined attack of typhus and tuberculosis upon a system already weakened by syphilis. Certain Dutch writers—"Multatule" ("an eccentric breaker-of-images" and "the one exciting writer in the doldrums of the Dutch nineteenth century," says James Holmes in his introduction) and Henrik Marsman, whose poetry of the early twenties perhaps gave Anwar his first example of the possibilities of organic form; and after the war the contemporary English and American poets whose books he found in the libraries of the British and United States information services in Djakarta—these seem to have been nourishing influences, as was the folk poetry of the archipelago. But even in translation one can feel that Anwar was continually absorbing anything and everything into his *own* life, his *own* poetry. "I'll dig down," he had written to a friend during the war, "and root out every word until I've gone deep enough to find the germinal word, the germinal image."

Burton Raffel, whose work as a translator is always notably intelligent and artistic, has collaborated here with the Indonesian writer and scholar Nurdin Salam to make us feel the fascination of Anwar's poetic presence. In a prefatory note Mr. Raffel points out that he has adhered to Anwar's "seemingly erratic" punctuation, omission of initial capitals, etc.; he has understood that Anwar knew these things as integral parts of the poem. "A line," writes Raffel, "that begins with a capital letter has for him a different weight than one beginning with a lower-case letter; a line ending with a period or a comma has a different speed and flow than one ending of its own motion alone." This is still something generally unrealized or misunderstood, and every intelligent restatement of it is important. In the process of translation these nuances can rarely be reproduced with validity, but I surmise that Raffel has written his English versions in the spirit of the original and created equivalent effects, so that the best ones stand on

237

their own feet in the new language, and even those that fall short of that autonomy give one a keen sense of what the tone of the original must be.

AT THE MOSQUE

I shouted at Him
Until He came

We met face to face.

Afterwards He burned in my breast.
All my strength struggles to extinguish Him

My body, which won't be driven, is soaked with sweat

This room
Is the arena where we fight

Destroying each other
One hurling insults, the other gone mad.

Inevitably, one is left with many questions. How long did Anwar spend as a guerrilla fighter? How did he live the rest of the time? Which American poets, besides those mentioned (Emily Dickinson, Eliot, Auden) is he known to have read? (Williams? Cummings? Pound?) Had he made a beginning on the Lorca translations he mentioned in a letter shortly before his death? We don't know. But we have encountered briefly a representative of "the real thing." Fierce, casual, bitter, tender, these are the poems of a man vividly present, careless of order in his living, uncompromisingly engaged in the order and life of the poem.

Creeley's early poems were concerned with mental pro-
cesses, the intellect if you will, evidences of the intelligence.
Then they became concerned increasingly with feeling as
distinct from intellection, but still feeling handled by the
intellectual intelligence. *Kore,* supremely beautiful, was an
exception, and of course there were other exceptions, but
that's my retrospective sense of the general tendency. "The
Door" seemed to open up a new direction, because, even
aside from its autonomous strength, the deep authentic
dream experience of it (all of his poems are authentic but
not all go that deep) was, more than any other poem of
his up to that time, not an examination of what happens
but an immersion in what happens—and this affected the
form of the poem, so that though from stanza to stanza it
was not atypical, its totality—in length, the *staying with
it* rather than *whittling down*–was. The reflections upon
the event are completely a part of the event; and at the same
time "The Door" has a very clear narrative line. But for
a while the kind of exploration adumbrated by this poem
didn't seem to be pursued. Creeley went on writing mostly
more *conclusive* poems: many of them are of a ravishing
perfection, but sometimes it has seemed as if that perfection
were a limitation, a sealing off when one wanted him to
go on, to go further, not to be obsessed with refining what
he had already done impeccably.

In *Pieces* something different happens—or *is happening,*
for it is anything but a static work. Somebody glancing
through it who did not know Creeley's earlier books might
get an impression of sloppiness and ask, "What's this guy
think he's doing, publishing unfinished drafts?" Someone
who knew and dug his work, its elegance and concision

A review of *Pieces,* by Robert Creeley; originally published in *Cater-
pillar,* No. 10, 1970.

and (most of the time) its clarity—dug it just for those attributes—might similarly think *Pieces* weak, self-indulgent, a falling off. But it's not. Its very sprawl and openness, its notebook quality, its absence of perfectionism, Creeley letting his hair down, is in fact a movement of energy in his work, to my ear: not a breaking down but a breaking open.

Titled poems (including "The Fingers," a poem that does relate pretty closely to "The Door," and "Numbers," which goes deep into a long-present obsessive interest) alternate with untitled poems and fragments, and bits of prose; often it's hard to tell where one poem ends and another begins, even if you refer to the table of contents it doesn't matter, it's good, they are all related, it's a complete book, the way a notebook or diary has its own completeness and co-herence, a relatedness of part to part that is not identical with the coherence of the deliberately arranged. One poem says,

> Such strangeness of mind I know
> I cannot find there more
> than what I know.
>
> I am tired of purposes,
> intent that leads itself
> back to its own belief. I want
>
> nothing more of such brilliance
> but what makes the shadows darker
> and that fire grow dimmer.

It is in keeping with the spirit of *Pieces* that there is no intro-duction. Creeley's prefatory notes in the past have seemed to me unnecessary, defensive. Here, in place of such a note, is an epigraph—these lines from Allen Ginsberg:

```
                yes, yes,
                        that's what
                I wanted,
                        I always wanted,
                I always wanted,
                        to return
                to the body
                        where I was born.
```

I don't think (whatever Allen meant by it) that means a
desire to return to the womb; it's one's own body, the primal,
the instinctive, and intuitive basics one started with, that
is being spoken of. His own body that he was born in, and
that the mind, the way we live, keeps wandering from. The
freedom in *Pieces* is also a kind of wandering, but back
to sources—even literally (as in the poem "I" in *Words*–"is
the grandson of"):

```
                Falling-in windows—
                the greenhouse back of
                Curley's house. The
                Curleys were so good
                to me, their mother
                held me in her lap.
```

A piece like "Mazatlan: Sea" begins with highly wrought,
finely written stanzas, and drifts off into scattered notes;
peters out, almost: but I can't see it as sloppy or arrogant
to publish such irresolutions, as it would be for someone
without Creeley's body of accomplishment behind him.
Having that work in back of it, a book like this is, on the
contrary, an act of trust and humility.

"Gists and piths"—Pound quotes the Japanese student
defining poetry. Inadequate, like all definitions of the com-
plex; but a damn good try. Well, some poetry is stronger
in one element than in the other; in fact, "classic" could

be equated with piths, and "romantic" with gists. In that sense *Pieces* is a romantic book, by a poet whose previous work has often been (impressively) "classic." Because of its energy, candor, mystery, and try-anything courage, I find it exciting. It moves me, not only poem by poem (and there are some that don't say anything to me, taken by themselves) but as an organic event. If Creeley has seemed to be building himself, year by year, an elaborate box, he has now revealed its door; the process is shown to have resembled the way an Eskimo builds an igloo, from inside out, the exit last.

(Postscript: Physically, the book's clear, rather large type, though a bit black and heavy, seems more right for the contents than anything lighter would; though even better, perhaps, would have been the typewriter look of David Antin's *"definitions."* Or would that have seemed too obvious? Maybe.)

For Robert Duncan's Early Poems

What is a master? Not one whom one imitates, emulates even; but rather, a powerful presence acknowledged, looked up to in all weathers. A mountain. A great upheaval of rock and earth. Contours, declivities, the tufted ridge that defines the horizon, curly bloom of foggy woods, a rock face far up implying "the sounding cataract" ("haunted me like a passion"). A Mount Blue, say, whose massive flanks lie in Temple but cannot be reached directly from there unless by the most intrepid woodsman, the road going a long way round into another township; a mountain whose majestic identity can be recognized from any point of the compass, orienting the traveler, and yet cannot, in its three-dimensional complexity, be drawn from memory or recalled accurately except perhaps in dream. . . . Enter the first slopes of it, feet of the lion at rest by a little brook, and find under the shadows that from afar were blue but among bark and branches are not a color but a scent, the smell of leafmold and mushrooms, find a hage of midges dancing, find fern and rue and corpsecandle; and on the ancient gold wrappings of great-grandfather yellow birch, delicate lively tree frogs the size of a thimble.

The mountain is master of the landscape in which it is a presence. One does not emulate such a master, except by being more oneself. The early work of a master poet is like the entwined, scratchy, capillary undergrowth at the mountain's base. Here are bitter fungi full of worms, sweet wild raspberries dropping from the stem at a touch, blackberries shining but not yet darkened to ripeness. All is fragrant, all is of the enticing substance of the forest, first threads of the tapestry, outgrowing from the mountain itself, into whose life we enter as we begin to climb.

Statement from a 1966 flyer advertising *The Years as Catches*, by Robert Duncan.

Like so many others, I was for years familiar only with a handful of H. D.'s early poems, "Peartree," "Orchard," "Heat," "Oread." Beautiful though they were, they did not lead me to look further, at the time. Perhaps it was that being such absolutes of their kind they seemed final, the end of some road not mine; and I was looking for doors, ways in, tunnels through.

When I came, late, to her later work, not searching but by inevitable chance, what I found was precisely doors, ways in, tunnels through. One of these later poems, "The Moon in Your Hands," says:

> If you take the moon in your hands
> and turn it round
> (heavy slightly tarnished platter)
> you're there;

This was to find not a finality but a beginning. The poem ends with that sense of beginning:

> when my soul turned round,
> perceiving the other-side of everything,
> mullein-leaf, dogwood-leaf, moth-wing
> and dandelion-seed under the ground.

It was not until after the publication, in *Evergreen Review* #5, of her poem "Sagesse" that I read the great War Trilogy.[1] In "Sagesse" the photograph of an owl—a White Faced Scops Owl from Sierra Leone, which is reproduced along with the poem—starts a train of thought and feeling which

---

First published in *Poetry*, Vol. 100, No. 3, 1962.

[1] "Sagesse" is included in *Hermetic Definition* (1972), and the entire War Trilogy is now available in one volume, entitled, simply, *Trilogy* (1973). Both these books are available from New Directions.

leads poet and reader far back into childhood, by way of word origins and word-sound associations, and back again to a present more resonant, more full of possibilities and subtle awareness, because of that journey. The interpenetration of past and present, of mundane reality and intangible reality, is typical of H. D. For me this poem (written in 1957) was an introduction to the world of the Trilogy—*The Walls Do Not Fall* (1944), *Tribute to the Angels* (1945), *The Flowering of the Rod* (1946). These were an experience life had been storing for me until I was ready to begin to receive it. (For I had been in London myself throughout the period when these books were being written and published, and had, as I came to recall, even "seen"—without seeing—those parts of them that appeared, before book publication, in *Life and Letters Today*. But I had been too young to know them; just as I was too young—younger than my years—to *experience*, as a poet, the bombing of London: I lived in the midst of it but in a sense it did not *happen* to me, and though my own first book, in 1946, was written during that time, the war appeared in it only off-stage or as the dark background of adolescent anxiety.)

What was it I discovered, face to face at last with the great poetry of H. D.'s maturity? What was—is—the core of the experience? I think this is it: that the icily passionate precision of the earlier work, the "Greek" vision, had not been an *end*, a closed achievement, but a preparation: so that all the strength built up, poem by poem, as if in the bones, in the remorseless clear light of that world—

> Great, bright portal,
> shelf of rock,
> rocks fitted in long ledges,
> rocks fitted to dark, to silver granite,
> to lighter rock—
> clean cut, white against white—

was *there,* there to carry darkness and mystery and the questions behind questions when she came to that darkness and those questions. She showed a way to penetrate mystery; which means, not to flood darkness with light so that darkness is destroyed, but to *enter into* darkness, mystery, so that it is experienced. And by *darkness* I don't mean *evil;* not evil but the Other Side, the Hiddenness before which man must shed his arrogance; Sea out of which the first creeping thing and Aphrodite emerge; Cosmos in which the little speck of the earth whirls, and in the earth "the dandelion seed."

> *Sirius:*
> *what mystery is this?*
>
> you are seed,
> corn near the sand,
> enclosed in black-lead,
> ploughed land.
>
> *Sirius:*
> *what mystery is this?*
>
> you are drowned
> in the river;
> the spring freshets
> push open the water-gates.
>
> *Sirius:*
> *what mystery is this?*
>
> where heat breaks, and cracks
> the sand-waste,
> you are a mist
> of snow: white, little flowers.

The "style"—or since style too often means *manner*, I would rather say the *mode*, the means—is invisible: or no, not invisible but transparent, something one both sees and sees through, like hand-blown glass of the palest smoke-color or the palest water-green. And in this transparent mode H. D. spoke of essentials. It is a simplicity not of reduction but of having gone further, further out of the circle of known light, further in toward an unknown center. Whoever wishes a particular example, let him read part VI of *The Walls Do Not Fall*–the part beginning:

> In me (the worm) clearly
> is no righteousness, but this—

I would like to quote the whole; but it is too long; and it is such a marvelous musical whole that I cannot bear to quote fragments.

After I had begun to know the later poems I returned to the *Collected Poems* of 1925 and saw them anew. "The great, bright portal . . . clean cut, white against white" was not the dominant I had thought it. The poems I had thought of as shadowless were full of shadows, planes, movement: correspondences with what was to come. But I, and perhaps others of my generation, could come to realize this only through a knowledge of the after-work.

About a year and a half before her death I had the privilege of meeting H. D. (and thereafter exchanging some letters with her until the stroke which began her last illness broke off communication). The woman of whom Horace Gregory has written that he could distinguish her from far off in a crowd by her tall grace was old and badly crippled; but full of eager life. Yet even though her novel, *Bid Me to Live*, was newly published, and she had just received the Gold Medal for Poetry of the Academy of Arts and Letters, there were at that time many, alas, who believed her dead, and who dismissed her as "one of the Imagistes—a poet of that period." So little was her most important poetry read and recognized for the great work it is, that my homage and Robert Duncan's seemed to be a surprise to her, and to move her in a way deeply moving to us. She herself had, at the time of my second meeting with her, been reading some of the youngest young poets; and how quick she was to respond to what she found there of life, of energy.

There is no poet from whom one can learn more about precision; about the music, the play of sound, that arises miraculously out of fidelity to the truth of experience; about the possibility of the disappearance, in the crucible, of *manner*.

She wrote much that has not been published. Her last book, *Helen in Egypt,* the publication of which almost coincided with her death, is (like *Bid Me to Live* in its different form) a world which one may enter if one will; a life-experience that gives rise to changes in the reader, small at first, but who knows how far-reaching. The alternations, in *Helen,* of prose and poetry are not alternations of flatness and intensity but of contrasted tone, as in a Bach cantata the vocal parts are varied by the sinfonias, and each illumines and complements the other. *Bid Me to Live* and *Helen in Egypt* are neither of them works to be idly dipped into: one must go inside and live in them, live them through.

Indeed this is true of all her work: the more one reads it, the more it yields. It is poetry both "pure" and "engaged"; attaining its purity—that is, its unassailable identity as word-music, the music of word-sounds and the rhythmic structure built of them—through its very engagement, its concern with matters of the greatest importance to everyone: the life of the soul, the interplay of psychic and material life.

Grass Seed and Cherry Stones

("respect for the kind of intelligence that enables grass seed to grow grass; the cherry-stone to make cherries":)

I do not feel competent to make general statements about Ezra Pound; therefore I shall confine my remarks to my own relations with his work.

The body of his work (both prose and poetry) and the spirit that—albeit with lapses—chiefly informs it, mean to me above all *just measure, awareness, disdain of fakery.* Whatever departures from justice, whatever failures of awareness, exist here and there in his writings, they do not seriously detract, I have come to feel, from the clarity and urgency of the Confucian message embodied in the greater part of it. And fakery there is none.

The Confucian justice is merciful:

> And they said: If a man commit murder
> > Should his father protect him, and hide him?
> And Kung said:
> > He should hide him.
>
> > > *(Canto XIII)*

Racist and rightist views are abhorrent to me—but I look on these when they occur in Pound as an aberration; and who among us does not have some kind of aberration? And all the evidence points to Ezra Pound's personal dealings with whoever came in contact with him as being marked by kindness and probity. Moreover, his Fascist affiliations seem to me to have been made originally not in support of brute authoritarianism and cynical contempt of the individual, but because he mistakenly supposed the

---

Written originally for a symposium on Ezra Pound in *L'Herne*, Paris. Later reprinted in *The Antigonish Review*, No. 8, 1972.

economic changes he correctly saw as necessary for a more decent human life would be made under Fascism.

An active force in my life as a poet is frequent reference to *The ABC of Reading.* If, in the midst of a poem, I turn to this book, what actually happens? "The way to learn the music of verse is to listen to it," I read. And I am reminded thereby to read aloud what I have so far written; I discover here a line and here another where the vibrant pace and tone consonant with the content have given way to the dull pace and tone of essaylike thinking. "Poetry atrophies when it gets too far from music," I read. "Incompetence will show in the use of too many words . . . look for words that do not function." And I am brought once more to an examination of my poetic conscience. "Good writing is coterminous with the writer's thought, it has the form of thought, the form of the way the man feels his thought." What stimulus and assurance those words give to the intention or hope of discovering the innate form of an experience, what Gerard Manley Hopkins called the *inscape* of it! These are a few typical instances of the direct aid to craft and probity with which I am accustomed to fortify myself. I speak especially of *The ABC of Reading* because it happens to be the volume I have used most; but *Guide to Kulchur,* the *Literary Essays,* etc., are full too of such reminders or fresheners, for a writer, of his obligations to himself and his art.

It used to seem to me that there was a discrepancy between Pound's emphasis on knowledge, accuracy, clarity ("Dante's precision . . . comes from the attempt to reproduce exactly the thing which has been clearly seen" [*The Spirit of Romance*] or, "Put down exactly what you feel and mean; say it as briefly as possible . . ." etc. [*Patria Mia*] or the well-known anecdotes of Pisanello and the Duke of Milan's horses, and of Agassiz and the student with the fish [*ABC*], for instance) and my own experience of words or whole lines or whole poems appearing out of that unconscious he seems to ignore. But if such words,

250

lines, poems, *function*, i.e., if one does (as I believe) come to "know what one thinks after one sees what one says" (and then can review or remeasure the sound and structure of what one has said, testing it against one's perceptions for accuracy), then one is not in fact twisting the standards of decent honesty and intelligence which Pound provides for one to work with: one is only *extending their application*. Besides, perhaps the apparent discrepancy rests on a misunderstanding: it is too easy to suppose that Pound, in such passages as those just mentioned, necessarily assumes a rigid sequence in which perception precedes record of perception by an appreciable interval. In the actual process of writing a poem, unfaked perception and accurate record thereof are often coincident, or only fractionally separated; I have not found a statement of Pound's that denies this.

Pound pays no attention to so many great artists; for instance, Rilke (I found one scornful allusion), Dostoevsky, Kafka, Thomas Mann, Antonio Machado. It doesn't matter. He gives the practicing poet not a rigid syllabus, despite his several overlapping lists of essential reading, but examples of various virtues and possibilities against which we may learn to test our own predilections (in reading), our own powers (in writing). A man has a right to set up his own pantheon in the expectation that an intelligent reader will not simply take it over. Both in his prose and in his poetry—by precept and example—Pound teaches me not to accept received ideas without question, but to derive my own from concrete detail observed and felt, from my individual experience. "The serious artist," Pound says, "will want to present as much of life as he knows" *(Patria Mia)*. And, "KRINO, to pick out for oneself, to choose. That's what the word ['criticism'] means" *(ABC)*. He stirs me into a sharper realization of my own sensibility. I learn to desire not *to know what he knows* but *to know what I know;* to emulate, not to imitate.

Reading *The Cantos* was for me until quite recently an experience which seemed to have little direct connection

251

with the experience of studying the *ABC* and other prose. Though there was much that I responded to in *The Cantos*, all that appeared unclear and even chaotic in them seemed to me disturbingly at variance with Pound the critic's emphasis on clarity, on communication, and at the same time on music. Of course that to which I *was* responding was the magic ingredient (missing from so many poems!) —poetry itself; but I was interpreting its nature too exclusively as *lyricism*. The lyric element in *The Cantos* comes and goes—sometimes imbuing a whole canto at a time, sometimes scattered groups of lines—and if one's view of poetry is confined to that element, then all that surrounds these passages will seem only connective, or even dross. This is, in effect, to make of one's reading a mere collection of "Gems from Pound," the most abusive act it is possible to perform upon the body of a poem. Once I really grasped the idea that lyric poetry ("meant to be sung to the harp or the lyre; expressing the individual emotions of the poet," says the dictionary) is not the only kind there is, I began to be better able to respond to the other kinds. This is rudimentary, certainly; but are not our sensibilities, for historical reasons, more attuned to the lyric than to other kinds of poetry? After I had recognized this, it began to seem to me that it is not the mosaic of documentary material but the "beautiful" passages—the images of light, the ripple of wind in olive trees, small lamps drifting in the bay, or the clouds over Taishan—that are the *connectives:* but integral, not merely applied, connectives.

> The ideographic method consists of presenting one facet and then another until at some point one gets off the dead and desensitized surface of the reader's mind, onto a new part that will register.
>
> *(Kulchur)*

In the same way the chaotic aspects of the mosaic method

began to be comprehensible when I realized that I had all along been standing too close, as it were, so that all I could see was chips of stone, sometimes beautiful, sometimes dull; but not the larger design. Of course I had known this *theoretically* before; that is, I had been told that it was so; but I have only quite recently begun to experience it.

> I am not being merely incoherent. I haven't "lost my thread" in the sense that I haven't just dropped one thread to pick up another of a different shade. I need more than one string for a fabric.
>
> *(Kulchur)*

I begin to apprehend the poetry of history, that flickers both in the olive leaves and in the voices speaking of trade; in the ant and the lynx, the sensuous imagination and the dry implications of document, in legislation and song and all the fabric of "news that stays news."

William Carlos Williams, 1883–1963

William Carlos Williams has left more for us than we realize. Even those—an increasing number in recent years—who love his work are often curiously unfamiliar with it; not because they have not troubled to read it well, but because of its inner abundance and intrinsic freshness. One is forever coming across something new on pages one thought one had known long since. It is as if his poems were plants, changing with the seasons, budding and blossoming over and over.

> Of asphodel, that greeny flower. . . .

And this is timelessness.

But he has given us also a great gift within time: that is to say, his historical importance is, above all, that more than anyone else he made available to us the whole range of the language, he showed us the rhythms of speech *as poetry*–the rhythms and idioms not only of what we say aloud but of what we say in our thoughts. It is a mistake to suppose that Williams's insistence on "the American idiom" ever implied a reduction; on the contrary, it means the recognition of wide resources. Williams's poems, God knows, are not written in "the speech of Polish mothers": but he demonstrated that the poem could (and in some sense must) encompass that speech. Only a poetry with its roots in the language *as it is used* can be free to explore and reclaim all those levels that otherwise become "only literature." Only a poetry freed from rhythmic patterns that had become habitual and inapt can discover the rhythms of our experience. He cleared ground, he gave us tools.

When I first met Dr. Williams about twelve years ago he had already had a serious stroke. Over the years I used

---

An obituary written for *The Nation*, March 16, 1963.

to say to myself each time I went to Rutherford, "He's old and frail; this may be the last time you will see him." And each time he would astonish me again with his vitality, his shrewd humor, his undeviating, illuminating attention to what concerned him—the poem, the poem. This passionate concern flamed up out of his frailness and made one forget it. Always I left his house in a state of exhilaration. Except for the last time of all, a few weeks ago, when his tongue could no longer find the words he needed for the ideas one could see in his eyes, and he kept giving up in mid-sentence, sad and baffled. Yet even then, vague as he had become about many things, there remained that eagerness to hear a new poem, that acute, *distinguishing* listening. Concerning dates and events he was more confused that day than I had ever seen him, but poetry remained in pristine focus.

I have always felt that all of his works—the tremendous output of poems, plays, essays, stories, letters, novels—were to an unusual degree parts of a whole, complete though each was in itself. This is perhaps one of the marks of a great writer. The shorter poems in particular partake, in their multiplicity, of this unity that is meant by Arnold's term, "criticism of life": when we see them in relation to one another, each separate poem, though it had given us of itself before, begins to release more levels of meaning than we realized when we read it in isolation.

Working always toward an order, a measure consonant with his time, it was in old age, with a body of work already done that would have appeased the demon of a lesser man, that he arrived at his greatest poems—those in *The Desert Music* (1954) and *Journey to Love* (1955). Is there a human joy deeper than the joy of being made aware that another human being has *gone on* developing?

It's a strange courage
you give me, ancient star:

255

Shine alone in the sunrise
toward which you lend no part!

The name of the poem is "El Hombre"; a poem that speaks across many decades, brief as it is, to "The Ivy Crown" and the long majestic "Asphodel, That Greeny Flower" with which *Journey to Love* culminates.

It was a culmination, but what followed was not a deterioration; rather, in the last book of *Paterson,* the movement of a wave withdrawing, a part of the same rhythm.

And at the very last—in the poems collected last year as *Pictures from Brueghel*—he gave us, when he could hardly speak, could no longer read to himself, typed with one hand with great difficulty—a sheaf of flowers, fresh flowers of a new, ancient spring. This one, which itself speaks of a flower, was among them:

> The rose fades
> and is renewed again
> by its seed, naturally
> but where
>
> save in the poem
> shall it go
> to suffer no diminution
> of its splendor

Though in William Carlos Williams there is what I have thought of sometimes as a Franciscan sense of wonder that illumines what is accounted ordinary—

> I never tire of the mystery
> of these streets: the three baskets
> of dried fruit in the high
>
> bar-room window, the gulls wheeling
> above the factory, the dirty
> snow—the humility of the snow that
> silvers everything and is
>
> trampled and lined with use. . . .
> ("Approach to a City," *The Collected Later Poems*, p. 177)

—an illumination reminiscent of Chardin's still-lifes and his paintings of servants among their kitchen utensils (indeed parts of Proust's beautiful essay on Chardin read like a description of this aspect of Williams); and though this quiet and tender celebration deepened for me, as I first read him, as a great writer always does for his readers, some latent capacity in myself to see the world more freshly: yet my strongest sense of his vision, as I grow older, is of the way it encompasses the dark, the painful, the fierce.

> This is the time of year
> when boys fifteen and seventeen
> wear two horned lilac blossoms
> in their caps—or over one ear

Written in 1972 and delivered as an Elliston Lecture at the University of Cincinnati in the spring of 1973.

. . .
They have stolen them
broken the bushes apart
with a curse for the owner—

Lilacs—

They stand in the doorways
on the business streets with a sneer
on their faces

adorned with blossoms

Out of their sweet heads
dark kisses— . . .
("Horned Purple," *Collected Earlier Poems*, pp. 273–74)

Williams's fierce delight in the contradictions of life is
not a passive acceptance, a kind of fatalism. He is anguished,
he rails against stupidity and gracelessness and man's inhu-
manity to man. "The Mind's Games" is one of his little-
known political poems; he writes in it that to a human being
at a moment of ecstasy and completion, the world

. . . is radiant and even the fact
of poverty is wholly without despair.

So it seems until there rouse
to him pictures of the systematically
starved—for a purpose, at the mind's
proposal. . . .

. . .
Beauty should make us paupers,
should blind us, rob us—for it
does not feed the sufferer but makes
his suffering a fly-blown putrescence

and ourselves decay—unless
the ecstasy be general.
(Collected Later Poems, pp. 109–10)

There are many other poems of his which, in differing
degrees of overtness, are of political import; so pervasive
was the historical sense in him that there is virtually nothing
he wrote that does not—especially within the context of
his work as a whole—have social implications. "In Chains"
(from *The Wedge,* 1944) seems to me one of the most interes-
ting, and least known, of twentieth-century political poems:

When blackguards and murderers
under cover of their offices
accuse the world of those villainies
which they themselves invent to
torture it—we have no choice
but to bend to their designs,
buck them or be trampled while
our thoughts gnaw, snap and bite
within us helplessly—unless
we learn from that to avoid
being as they are, how love
will rise out of its ashes if
we water it, tie up the slender
stem and keep the image of its
lively flower chiseled upon our minds.
(Collected Later Poems, p. 19)

It has, however, a flaw of logic: he poses as choices, (1)
to bend to their designs, to go along with the system and
be a party to its crimes; (2) to buck them; (3) to neither
buck them, that is, struggle in rebellion against their designs,
nor become complicit, but to suffer ourselves to be trampled
while inwardly—helpless—our thoughts gnaw at us; or
(4) to learn "from that"—i.e., apparently from the equal
negativity of the first three alternatives—to "avoid being

as they are." The lapse in logic occurs when Williams fails
to develop a definition of what "bucking them"—resistance
—might be and why he is treating it as a negative. It
cannot be because he sees it has small chance of succeeding;
Williams consistently manifested a love of "pure grit," put-
ting a high value on boldness, daring, a refusal to resigned-
ly anticipate defeat. He loved generosity, and was moved not
by the ingenious prudence of Ben Franklin but by the rash
and adventurous Aaron Burr. The shad making their way
"unrelenting" upstream, the two starlings landing back-
ward, facing "into the wind's teeth," are images central
to Williams; and one finds throughout his work variations
on that theme of defiance—as, for example, in the little
poem that forms part one of the three-part "A History of
Love"—

> And would you gather turds
> for your grandmother's garden?
> Out with you then, dustpan and broom;
> she has seen the horse passing!
>
> Out you go, bold again
> as you promise always to be.
> Stick your tongue out at the neighbors
> that her flowers may grow.
>
> *(Collected Later Poems,* p. 77)

Is it then, as choice (4) implies, that resistance *without*
keeping the image of love's "lively flower chiseled on our
minds" is self-defeating, because a struggle uninformed by
love and compassion makes of the rebel a mirror image
of the executioner—the ultimate irony of co-option? This
is what it means to me—and I like to think Williams, though
he was never a political revolutionary (except in the *implica-
tions* of much of his work) and was rather repelled than en-
thused by the left-wing politics of his day, meant it to con-
vey to the reader that meaning I attribute to it. But the way

in which he lets the syntax slide him past "buck them" without defining qualification deflects some of the impact. It is a flaw of form, of form considered as *revelation* of content, not as something imposed upon it, and which should therefore not stop short of all possible lucidity consonant with not oversimplifying. Not seldom Williams, in the prose as well as the poetry—or perhaps oftener, indeed, in prose—gives inadequate attention to detail, fails to follow all the way through, as if he were in too much haste to get on to the next matter. This may have been the price paid for his amazing productivity as an artist even while leading to the full the busy life of a doctor. Given the wealth and vigor of his artistic output, I have always found petty and unresponsive to the point of absurdity the caviling of those critics who have loftily characterized him as "lacking in intellectual force" and so on. He had in fact a sweep and depth of original intellectual insight. If one takes a close look, what gave a handle to even his sympathetic, "favorable" critics when they dismissed him as

> even less logical than the average good poet . . . an "intellectual" in neither the good nor the bad sense of the word,
>
> (Randall Jarrell)

or as a man whose

> pronouncements on poetry and poetics are almost never of such a quality as would force us to take them seriously.
>
> (Hyatt Waggoner)

was not the invalidity of his concepts (and certainly not the *absence* of concepts, as some anthologists who try to reduce him to a sort of witless imagist miniaturist would have one suppose), but simply the occasional impulsive abandonment of a piece of writing before checking out all

261

of its nuts and bolts. In its positive aspect this can be regarded as a manifestation of his largeness, his boldness, in contrast to the compulsive perfectionism of many a smaller, less fertile imagination, though it results in a good deal of frustration for his greatest admirers.

But in speaking of his vision as encompassing the darkness, wildness, fierceness of life as well as celebrating the common, the ordinary, I'm thinking not only of his political/historical/social understanding, his grappling with America, his constantly taking up the challenge to deal with his time and place, but also of the deep and equally pervasive sense of loneliness and strangeness I find in his poetry. The fairly early "Lighthearted William" "twirls his November moustaches" and sighs "gaily" (this delightful poem has a certain kinship with some of Stevens's short poems), but the world on which he looks out is the same "fearful" one of the even earlier "Winter Sunset," where

> Then I raised my head
> and stared out over
> the blue February waste
> to the blue bank of hill
> with stars on it
> in strings and festoons—
> but above that:
> one opaque
> stone of a cloud
> just on the hill
> left and right
> as far as I could see;
> and above that
> a red streak, then
> icy blue sky!
>
> It was a fearful thing
> to come into a man's heart
> at that time; that stone

over the little blinking stars
they'd set there.

(Collected Earlier Poems, p. 127)

Nowadays Williams is "taught" in the colleges and pre-
sumably widely read—but what does this teaching and read-
ing amount to? I am constantly meeting people who have
been taken, bewildered, on a tour of *Paterson* without any
reference to *The Wanderer,* the early poem in which so
many clues to the understanding of *Paterson* are embedded
(which is in fact one of those early works in which the
whole subsequent development of an artist is shadowed
forth prophetically), and equally without reference to the
rest of his work except for the tiresomely familiar and basi-
cally unrevealing anthology "specimens," such as "The Red
Wheelbarrow" and "The Yachts." Or else they have read
some of the really late poems—"Asphodel, That Greeny
Flower," perhaps—again with no sense of what led up to
them during a whole lifetime. I don't mean to imply that
"Asphodel," for example, does not very firmly stand as a
work of art on its own supreme merits; nor that a student
eighteen or nineteen years old has not the ability to respond
to it; but surely few readers of any age are likely to receive
Williams most rewardingly by beginning with a poem whose
content is a summing up, a testament prepared for by a
whole lifetime of other work, and whose formal structure
has likewise grown slowly out of a long development, a
long history of experimentation and exploration. A strictly
chronological approach is not necessary; it is often fascinat-
ing and revealing to read concurrently works from different
periods of any writer's life; but a recent tendency (due partly,
I suppose, to the availability of the last poems, *Pictures
from Brueghel,* in paperback, while the *Collected Earlier*
and *Collected Later Poems* are more expensive) in the formal
study of Williams—and even among individuals reading him
of their own free choice—has been a *reverse* chronology
that does not even lead all the way back to the beginnings

but leaves readers ignorant of all the earlier work except for the small selection Randall Jarrell edited. Few students are brought to recognize, and rarely discover for themselves, the high degree of his relevance to contemporary concerns, to the daily questions of "how to live, what to do" that they have such a hungry need to ask and answer and for which they are given (in the childhood and student years) so poor a provision for doing so. Young writers of fiction might learn something from "A Morning Imagination of Russia"[1] (1923)—not a "narrative poem" yet one that seems to suggest, not only in its Chekhovian content but in its condensed interpretation of situation and ideas, something of fictional life-essence. How different Williams, re-explored, is from the stereotype in which he has been cursorily presented to many minds (despite the spate of books about him in the last few years—few of which, for better or worse, are read anyway except by other professional critics). Assuming him to be essentially prosaic, a putter-together of scraps of reportage merely, the best of his potential ongoing audience—the young poets in their early twenties, the fervent and intense readers who, consciously or not, are looking for magic, illumination, the Dionysian, the incantatory word, the numinous song—turn aside from him to look elsewhere. Yet a whole course of study in poetics, leading precisely to the *going-beyond*—beyond the end, beyond the brilliantly conceived and perfectly executed, as García Lorca in his famous essay describes so memorably—which is the Duende, might be built around a single difficult but rewarding poem of Williams, "The Sound of Waves" (*Collected Later Poems*, p. 171). Perhaps "soul" is the closest approximation to the meaning of Duende. A standard Spanish dictionary translates the term merely as "elf, hobgoblin, ghost," but it is *soul* in the sense in which Black Americans have contributed that word to our language that was lacking in

[1] Part of "The Descent of Winter," p. 305 in the *Collected Early Poems*.

the famous Flamenco singer as she sang so well, and which came into her singing only later as, hoarse and strident she flung herself forward into the song beyond song. In "The Sound of Waves," a poem about poetry, in which the poet-voyager asks himself the eternal human/ artistic question, How to proceed . . .? Williams moves by a process of elimination toward an image in which the mist, rain, sea-spume of language is blown against jutting rock, and takes its hard shape. But then a pause (a line of dots on the page) and:

> Past that, past the image:
> . . .
> above the waves and
>
> the sound of waves, a
> voice   speaking!

The poem requires a study and analysis I should like to try and give it elsewhere; but perhaps even this brief allusion may give some hint of one way—maybe not the only one—to undersand it: a way which to me suggests a twentieth-century poetics; not an "applied metrics," but a poetics inseparable from the rest of human experience and—*not* because of its content but by its very nature, its forms, its sensuous forms that are its very essence—expresses and defines the nature of humanness; and in so doing arrives at the edge of the world, where all is unknown, undefined, the abyss of the gods. From there at last, beyond the human,

> a voice   speaks.

Like most artists of large scope and complex substance, Williams cannot be narrowly categorized as Apollonian or Dionysian, classic or romantic. His lifelong concern with structure and technique, his insistence on the need for

265

"measure," a certain aristocratic elegance of gesture in the turn of phrases, the impeccable completeness and brevity of countless "little" poems, the tone of controlled passion, austere, sober, solemn, we hear tolling in the very late long poems—these could be called Apollonian. But if the Apollonian form-sense is the bones of an art, the intuitive, that which is pliant, receptive—but not docile!—rather abandoning itself fiercely, recklessly, to experience—is the flesh and blood of it, and this is Dionysian. As a young man he committed himself to the Muse; She had cried to him,

> . . . "Haia! Here I am, son!
> See how strong my little finger is!
> Can I not swim well?
> I can fly too!" And with that a great sea-gull
> Went to the left, vanishing with a wild cry—
> But in my mind all the persons of godhead
> Followed after . . .

and he responded with the realization that,

> I know all my time is forespent!
> For me one face is all the world!
> ("The Wanderer," *Collected Earlier Poems*, pp. 3, 4)

—the face of a Muse who is both wild gull and godhead, "marvelous old woman" and "horrible old woman; mighty, crafty, feared and beloved." The reader who would know Williams must know his diversity and experience the plunge of the understanding into his frightening depths.

266

INDEX

Index

270

271

273